SUPERVISORY TRAINING

UNIT 8

Managing the Project— The Supervisor's Role

Participant's Manual

Associated General Contractors of America

Seventh Edition

Managing the Project: The Supervisor's Role
Participant's Manual
Seventh Edition
©2006 AGC of America

Managing the Project: The Supervisor's Role **was written by**
Kelly C. Strong
Kevin R. Behling
Department of Civil, Construction and Environmental Engineering
Iowa State University
Ames, IA 50010

The Supervisory Training Program is developed, published and distributed by:

Associated General Contractors of America
2300 Wilson Boulevard, Suite 400
Arlington, VA 22201

Phone: (800) 242-1767

FAX: (703) 837-5405

www.agc.org/stp

Printed in the United States of America

Table of Contents

Introduction to the Course — vii

Unit 8 Themes — vii

Session Descriptions — ix

Unit 8 Special Feature (Sponsor's Guide) — x

STP Courses — xii

Design of this Unit — xiii

How this Course is Organized — xv

Sponsor's Guide Pages — xvii

Session 1: Understanding Project Delivery Systems — 1-1

Goal and Performance Objectives — 1-1

Construction Delivery Systems — 1-1

Interdependence of Project Team Roles — 1-6

How Delivery Systems Change the Role of the Supervisor — 1-7

To Implement What You Have Learned — 1-7

Session 2: Managing Information — 2-1

Goal and Performance Objectives — 2-1

Project Life Cycles — 2-1

Documentation — 2-2

Conducting Effective Meetings — 2-7

Types of Meetings — 2-8

Purpose of the Meetings — 2-10

Use of Technology for Managing Information — 2-10

Protocols and Chains of Command — 2-11

To Implement What You Have Learned — 2-12

Session 3: Understanding and Managing Risk — 3-1

Goal and Performance Objectives — 3-1

The Project Team's Role in Risk Control — 3-1

General Sources of Risk — 3-2

Project-Specific Sources of Risk — 3-4

Risks Primarily Assigned to the Field — 3-7

An Overview of Risk Management — 3-9

To Implement What You Have Learned — 3-16

Session 4: Planning the Work   4-1

Goal and Performance Objectives   4-1

Preconstruction Phase Planning and Management   4-1

Preconstruction Project Planning   4-2

Preconstruction Site Planning   4-3

Preconstruction Information Planning   4-4

Preconstruction Project Scheduling   4-4

To Implement What You Have Learned   4-6

Session 5: Working the Plan   5-1

Goal and Performance Objectives   5-1

Construction Phase Tasks   5-1

Mobilization   5-2

Purchasing   5-2

Expediting   5-3

Approvals   5-4

Updating   5-5

Closeout   5-6

To Implement What You Have Learned   5-7

Session 6: Managing Methods and Materials   6-1

Goal and Performance Objectives   6-1

Site Layout   6-1

Equipment Selection   6-4

Material Handling, Storage and Protection   6-5

Onsite Fabrication vs. Modular Units/Panelization   6-6

To Implement What You Have Learned   6-7

Session 7: Understanding Finances   7-1

Goal and Performance Objectives   7-1

Cost Information Cycle   7-1

Information Flows   7-2

Cost Coding Accuracy   7-3

Project Cash Flow   7-4

Retainage   7-5

To Implement What You Have Learned   7-6

Session 8: Working with Project Partners — 8-1

Goal and Performance Objectives — 8-1
Working with Owners (The Supervisor as the Salesperson) — 8-1
Working with Subcontractors in the Field — 8-3
Working with Designers — 8-4
Working with Inspectors/Government Agencies — 8-4
Working with Unions — 8-5
Working with Internal Stakeholders (Co-workers) — 8-6
To Implement What You Have Learned — 8-7

Session 9: Understanding People — 9-1

Goal and Performance Objectives — 9-1
The Project Team — 9-1
Motivation and Rewards — 9-2
Leadership Skills — 9-5
Personality Styles — 9-8
To Implement What You Have Learned — 9-9

Session 10: Understanding Corporate Policies/Procedures — 10-1

Goal and Performance Objectives — 10-1
Compliance Issues — 10-1
Project Portfolio/Risk Diversification — 10-3
Project Staffing Decisions — 10-4
Sales Prospecting — 10-4
Corporate Overhead — 10-5
Corporate Culture/Personality — 10-6
To Implement What You Have Learned — 10-8
Unit Summary — 10-9

Appendix of Worksheets — A-1

Glossary — R-1

Reference Worksheets — R-5

AGC Standard Contract Document
AGC200

Application for STP Completion Certificate — End of Book

Introduction to the Course

Welcome to *Managing the Project: The Supervisor's Role.*

Supervisory Training Program (STP) Unit 8, *Managing the Project: The Supervisor's Role,* is intended to assist project supervisors in understanding the relationship between the roles and responsibilities of project managers and project supervisors. Arguably, the capabilities of the project manager and the project supervisor and their ability to work together effectively are the most critical aspects of project success. The material presented in the 10 sessions of Unit 8, along with the activities and the shared experiences of other participants, will help you to understand the roles of the project manager and project supervisor. You'll discuss how the roles and responsibilities change depending on project parameters such as delivery system, project team characteristics, and organizational policies. The main point to keep in mind is that project managers and project supervisors must work together effectively for projects to be successful. There is no one best way to run a project, either as a project manager or as a project supervisor. The determinants of project success, however, are usually consistent across all projects:

- satisfied client
- safety of the workers and visitors on the site
- fair profit for the risk taken
- a rewarding experience for all members of the project team, in which their contributions are recognized and appreciated

The following section outlines the major themes to be examined in this unit.

> Your instructor may start the class with some "icebreakers" and class activities to help you get to know the other participants in your class. The instructor may ask you to complete Worksheet 1 (WS 1) as part of the icebreaker activity. WS 1 can be found in the Appendix.

Unit 8 Themes

- **The role of the contractor in delivering construction services is evolving.** Modern construction methods rely more on professional construction practices, integrated knowledge, and teamwork than ever before. The role of a general contractor as a separate and independent contracting party who need not act in the best interests of the owner is rapidly becoming a thing of the past.

- **Type of delivery system affects how you manage the project.** The Associated General Contractors of America generally recognizes three separate forms of delivering construction projects:

    1. Design-bid-build, or the hard-bid method
    2. Construction management at-risk
    3. Design-build

The role of the project management team will change depending on the type of delivery system used. For instance, in a Design-Build or design-assist negotiated project, the project supervisor may have a great deal of input in the design phase on issues such as constructability, design-for-safety, and equipment limits. On a competitively bid job using Design-Bid-Build delivery, the focus will be much more on scope control and documentation of claims, but if the same job is negotiated (still using Design-Bid-Build), the focus may shift to accommodating owner needs to improve the chances of securing repeat business.

- **Job descriptions and responsibilities of project managers and superintendents vary by project.** As the construction industry moves toward integrated services and team-based delivery methods, the project manager and the project field supervisor will increasingly share the work of managing the construction means and methods. Decisions about crew sizes, equipment usage, and sequencing of the tasks will be made as part of a team. From this trend, it naturally follows that the project supervisor will need to focus on different issues depending on project complexity, experience of the project team members, and the relationship with owners and designers.

- **The role of the jobsite supervisor is evolving.** From the three themes described above, it becomes obvious that the jobsite supervisor will need more management skills in the future, as projects are delivered with integrated, team-based delivery. Good business practices and the nature of competition in the industry require contractors to minimize overhead. At the same time, contractors will be asked to take on more risk as part of an integrated services team. In addition, the contractors have to achieve profitability over the long run to remain in business. How can contractors provide more services, take on more risk, and not increase overhead? The answer is by having highly trained and productive employees, including project managers and supervisors—and that is why you are here.

Session Descriptions

Session 1—Understanding Project Delivery Systems/Alternate Contracting Methods

- General Contracting
  - Design-bid-build (Hard bid)
  - Negotiated
- Construction Management
  - At-risk
  - Agent (not at-risk)
- Design-Build (and Assist)

Session 2—Managing Information

- Documentation
- Effective meetings
- Use (and abuse) of technology
- Protocols/chain of command

Session 3—Managing and Understanding Risk

- Bonding and sureties
- Insurance
- Subcontract vs. self-perform
- Site security and traffic
- Quality control
- Safety

Session 4—Planning the Work

- Project planning
- Scheduling
- Record keeping/information systems

Session 5—Working the Plan

- Purchasing
- Expediting
- Approvals

Session 6—Managing Methods and Materials

- Site layout
- Equipment selection
- Material handling, storage, protection
- Onsite fabrication vs. modular units/panelization

Session 7—Understanding Finances

- Cost information cycle
  - Estimate to budget
  - Budget to actual
  - Actual to historical
  - Historical to estimate
- Cost coding accuracy
- Schedule of payments/project cash flow

Session 8—Working with Project Partners

- Working with owners (the supervisor as the salesperson)
- Working with subcontractors in the field
- Working with designers
- Working with inspectors/governments
- Working with internal stakeholders (accounting, PM, corporate, etc.)

Session 9—Understanding People

- Motivation and rewards
- Leadership skills
- Personality styles

Session 10—Understanding Corporate Policies/Procedures

- Compliance
- Project portfolio/Risk diversification
- Sales prospecting
- Project staffing decisions
- Corporate overhead

Unit 8 Special Feature

Your instructor will review how to use the Sponsor's Guide with someone at your place of employment. The Sponsor's Guide is intended to bring the skills and knowledge you have learned in each session back to your company so that others can benefit from what you know. The discussion of the Sponsor's Guide is Activity 2 and is outlined in Worksheet 2 (WS 2) in the Appendix.

Unit 8 includes a **Sponsor's Guide** to be sent to the participant's sponsor (usually the participant's direct supervisor at his or her place of employment). The Sponsor's Guide will list the learning objectives for each session, and what skills or knowledge the participant is expected to gain from attendance at each of the sessions. The sponsor will then be asked to assist the participant in devising methods for implementing what he or she has learned into their regular work routines to improve the overall business environment at the sponsoring organization.

Why Should You Study Supervision?

Contractors often have a difficult time filling supervisory positions with properly trained people. Although some larger companies have an extensive in-house training program, many smaller companies do not, so supervisors learn through experience on the jobsite. Job demands on a supervisor are increasing because of rapid changes in technology and workers' attitudes. Project locations are scattered over large geographical areas. New laws and regulations covering construction have restricted and complicated production, and increased the focus on compliance, quality and cost control. Fewer people are entering the construction workforce.

At the same time, more and more opportunities exist in the construction industry. There is much new work to be done, and many rehab projects. Increased competition brings pressure to do things more efficiently. The companies that meet these challenges by developing and maintaining an effectively supervised workforce of well-trained people will survive and prosper. Those who don't—won't.

Construction supervisors are the critical link in the production process—and the profit-making process—and much is expected of them. They are expected to control costs and meet specs; they are expected to complete projects within tight time schedules and optimistic budgets; they are expected to maintain high morale among their workers; and they are expected to be the contractor's representative on a daily basis, dealing with the traveling public and various inspectors and engineers. This is an extraordinarily difficult job description, and to be successful, every supervisor must learn new skills and sharpen others he or she has already learned.

Because job responsibilities are different on each construction project, no single definition of a construction supervisor fits all situations. However, in this course, a construction supervisor is the person with overall responsibility for all field activities and direct responsibility for subcontractors on a project, as well as crew members who are working to accomplish tasks. In this course, the construction supervisor is the first-line jobsite supervisor and a critical member of the overall project management team.

How This Course Is Designed

The word **supervisor** is the title of the position. **Supervision** is the activity that is performed by supervisors. This unit is designed to train project supervisors and potential supervisors how to improve their ability to supervise the construction process, resolve problems and create win-win situations for all parties involved in a construction project. The sessions are particularly useful as an overview of the construction management process. Therefore, we have provided a suggestion for further study at the end of each session for those participants who want more in-depth knowledge of a particular subject.

Each of the activities throughout Unit 8 will have a corresponding worksheet which is included in the Appendix.

Purpose of This Unit

Unit 8 can be thought of as an introduction to project management for those supervisors who are frequently asked to help with project management functions, or who may be considering a career move into project management. It also will be useful for those whose companies use a team-based management structure, in which job responsibilities are shared, for their projects.

A Supervisor's Role Differs from a Craftworker's Role

There are basic differences between a craftworker's job and a supervisor's job. Craft work is technical work. Using a transit or level, using equipment to place and finish concrete, operating a scraper productively and safely, hanging iron and bolting it up, and reading and understanding slope stakes are all technical skills that are consistent from one project to another. Craft work is personal, "I-centered" or "me-centered," and it is the first set of skills construction workers learn.

Supervision requires the use of human and conceptual skills and is likely to be applied differently to different supervisory problems on the same project. To complicate this process, there are frequently no pat answers to supervisory problems. Often, difficult decisions must be made, and sometimes these decisions are not clearly right or wrong.

STP Courses

AGC has developed a series of units for the Supervisory Training Program. They are designed for supervisors who want to become managers of construction and for other people who want to learn about important ideas and skills that effective construction supervisors need to know. From time to time, there will be reference to various related courses in the Program.

The STP units are:

- Unit 1: *Leadership and Motivation*
- Unit 2: *Oral and Written Communication*
- Unit 3: *Problem Solving and Decision Making*
- Unit 4: *Contract Documents and Construction Law*
- Unit 5: *Planning and Scheduling*
- Unit 6: *Understanding and Managing Project Costs*
- Unit 7: *Accident Prevention and Loss Control*
- Unit 8: *Managing the Project: The Supervisor's Role*

– Unit 9: *Productivity Improvement*
– Unit 10: *General and Specialty Contractor Dynamics*
– *Construction Supervisor: An Overview*
– *Heavy/Highway Construction Supervisor: An Overview*

You will receive a special certificate of recognition and a wallet card from AGC of America when you have completed all 10 of the STP courses.

Design of this Unit

This unit should not be viewed as a set of rules and regulations, or an introduction into specific, detailed practices to use on all construction projects. Instead, Unit 8 is designed to get people thinking and sharing experiences in order to help participants develop flexibility in thought and practice.

The in-class exercises and discussions will require participants to put managerial principles into practice through simulated experiences in the classroom and realistic applications on the jobsite, and in their personal lives. All activities are designed to be highly participatory, to encourage partnering and teamwork, to promote self-directed learning through shared knowledge, and to foster cooperative problem solving. Because of the highly participatory format, the value of the learning process is largely a function of the willingness of the participants to join in the discussions and activities. For this reason, we will emphasize class preparation, quality, professionalism, and effective communication throughout all 10 sessions.

Unit content will answer, "What does a construction supervisor need to know to manage different kinds of projects?" "How can the supervisor better understand corporate policies and procedures?" "How does the supervisor in the field coordinate with the project manager in the office?"

Specific Management competencies you will develop over the 10 sessions include:

- Balancing work and personal time
- Claims recognition
- Communication
- Construction sequencing
- Coordinating office/field
- Costs/budget
- Critical thinking
- Dispute resolution
- Documentation using Lotus, Microsoft Project or Primavera, Excel, etc.

- Estimating change orders
- Ethics
- Evaluation of personnel
- Human resources management, handling of harassment/discrimination
- Typing and estimating
- Negotiation skills
- People skills
- Presentation skills
- Problem solving
- Productivity
- Project coordination
- Project startup
- Quality control
- Regulatory compliance
- Project closeout

Notes about Your Manual

You will notice some blank pages in your Participant's Manual and some pages that are partially filled with text. This manual is yours to keep and use as a reference on future construction projects. It is recommended that you make notes on the blank pages and in the wide margins where appropriate, and use a highlighter to mark or underline key ideas.

Unless told otherwise, you are to complete the registration section and have it signed by your instructor. This, or a registration form completed by the class sponsor, should then be sent to AGC. A registration form is the only way to add your name to the list of persons who have completed this course. Although your instructor will normally collect the Participant's Registration and Course Evaluation forms, it is your responsibility to see that your signed completed form is sent to AGC. The evaluation section asks questions about the subject matter of this course and its value to you. Your comments will help AGC know how to make *Managing the Project: The Supervisor's Role* more effective when it is revised.

Continuous Improvement

AGC needs your feedback to improve this unit and the manuals used to present it. You are encouraged to note your comments about the Participant's Manual on the Participant's Registration and Course Evaluation form in the back of your Participant's Manual. Your instructor will direct you to complete this form at the end of the last class session, or you may complete the appropriate questions after each session.

How This Course Is Organized

This course is designed to be presented in two different ways. You may be attending 10 classes where a session of approximately 2$\frac{1}{2}$ hours is presented each meeting. If so, your instructor will encourage you to read the text in your Participant's Manual before coming to each class session. This will help you become familiar with important concepts and skills and will help you prepare for discussions and other class activities. If you are unable to read a session before class—come to class anyway. You will still be able to learn much by listening to and participating in class activities.

You may be attending a course where all 10 sessions are presented in a concentrated format over three days. If so, you will not have as much time to read ahead except in the evenings or during breaks, although time will be allowed during class for you to review the material presented in the Participant's Manual.

No matter which attendance format is used, as you read, think about actual jobsite situations you have seen or experienced that illustrate the points presented. It's important to talk about your experiences during class discussions so everyone can understand how the ideas, skills and solutions discussed in the course are actually applied in the field.

In this course, you won't be simply sitting and listening; this is not a lecture course or a seminar! You'll become involved in the discussions and activities in an active exchange of ideas, questions and solutions that will be relevant to you and your work. Much of what you and others in the class learn from this course will come from each other, and your active participation is essential. Case studies will present both good examples and bad examples to help you understand each session's concepts and skills.

Refer to the Appendix for Activities 1 (WS 1) and 2 (WS 2).

Notes

The Sponsor's Guide

As the individual within your company who recommended that (participant names) participate in Unit 8 of the AGC of America Supervisory Training Program, you are interested in their success. The ultimate goal of the AGC of America Supervisory Training Program is to have the participants bring back knowledge for use by others in their organizations. We hope that as the sponsor of (participant names) you will be an active member of the learning team and will meet regularly to identify methods for applying what (participant names) has learned into the everyday activities of your company.

This Sponsor's Guide lists the learning objectives for each session, and what skills or knowledge the participant is expected to gain from attendance at each of the sessions. (Participant names) will be contacting you to schedule regular meetings in order to devise methods for implementing what has been learned in the classroom into the regular work routines to improve the overall business environment at the sponsoring organization.

Some of the implementation ideas could be as simple as adding an agenda item to a standing coordination meeting (weekly project manager's meeting, weekly superintendent's meeting, job-site toolbox talks, etc.) or as complex as the development of a training program for new superintendents. Implementation could involve incremental changes to a standing procedure, or development of an entirely new policy. The idea is to leverage attendance of individuals in the STP sessions to produce benefit for the company and the industry. By discussing ideas with their sponsor, participants have the opportunity to share their newfound knowledge with others in their companies and bring about positive change in their organizations.

Please reply to (participant names) when they contact you to set up a meeting. We have included short summaries of each of the sessions/topics for Unit 8 so that you will be aware of the subject of each meeting.

(Instructors: Please see www.agc.org/stp for a download of this document that you can customize and print for the sponsor.)

Thank you for your cooperation and support of the AGC Supervisory Training Program.

Introduction to the Course

Welcome to *Managing the Project: The Supervisor's Role.*

STP Unit 8, *Managing the Project: The Supervisor's Role,* is intended to assist project supervisors in understanding the relationship between the roles and responsibilities of project managers and project supervisors. Arguably, the capabilities of the project manager and the project supervisor and their ability to work together effectively are the most critical aspects of project success. The material presented in the 10 sessions of Unit 8, along with the activities and the shared experiences of other participants, will help your project supervisor to understand the roles of the project manager and project supervisor and how the roles and responsibilities change depending upon project parameters such as delivery system, project team characteristics, and organizational policies.

Unit 8 Themes

- The role of the contractor in delivering construction services is evolving
- The type of delivery system affects how you manage the project
- Job descriptions and responsibilities of project managers and superintendents vary by project
- The role of the jobsite supervisor is evolving

Session Descriptions

Like other STP units, Unit 8 may be delivered in 10 sessions, each about two and one-half hours long. The 10 sessions are as follows:

Session 1—Understanding Project Delivery Systems/Alternate Contracting Methods

- General Contracting: Design-bid-build and Negotiated
- Construction Management: At risk and Agent
- Design/Build (and Assist)

Session 2—Managing Information

- Documentation, meetings, technology and protocols/chain of command

Session 3—Managing and Understanding Risk

- Bonding and insurance
- Subcontract vs. self-perform
- Site security and traffic
- Quality control and safety

Session 4—Planning the Work

- Project planning and scheduling
- Record keeping/information systems

Session 5—Working the Plan

- Purchasing and expediting
- Approvals

Session 6—Managing Methods and Materials

- Site layout, material handling, storage, protection
- Equipment selection
- Onsite fabrication vs. modular units/panelization

Session 7—Understanding Finances

- Cost information cycle
- Cost coding accuracy
- Schedule of payments/project cash flow

Session 8—Working with Project Partners

- Working with owners, designers, subcontractors and inspectors
- Working with internal stakeholders (accounting, PM, corporate, etc.)

Session 9—Understanding People

- Motivation and reward
- Leadership skills
- Personality styles

Session 10—Understanding Corporate Policies/Procedures

- Compliance
- Project portfolio/risk diversification and sales prospecting
- Project staffing decisions and corporate overhead

Session 1 Understanding Delivery Systems

The goals and objectives for participant learning in Session 1 are:

- To create an awareness of how the type of delivery system or contracting method affects the roles and responsibilities of the project management team
- To understand how different strengths and weaknesses of the individual project team members may affect the delegation of project management responsibility
- To develop an appreciation for the interdependence of the project management team and the various roles and responsibilities that must be coordinated to achieve optimum project performance
- To broaden the project supervisor's awareness of his or her roles and responsibilities on the project, and how they might change based on project contracting method, team strengths and weaknesses, and market conditions

Session 1 includes the following topics:

General Contracting
- Design-bid-build (Hard bid)
- Negotiated

Construction Management
- At risk
- Agent (not at risk)

Design/Build (and Assist)

The supervisor's roles and responsibilities change under each delivery system

The supervisor's roles and responsibilities can also change under different team characteristics (experience, staffing level, leadership, etc.)

In a broad sense, the project supervisor has three basic responsibilities on every project:
- Managing tasks
- Managing people
- Managing risk

In Session 1, the participants discussed among themselves the types of projects and project owners that are best suited to the different delivery types, and how the focus of the project supervisor may change based on the delivery system used.

They also participated in a role-playing activity in which they were each assigned a project role (project manager, field engineer, lead foreman, etc.). They were given a profile of their assignment (experience with the job, experience with the type of project, etc.) and some project characteristics (delivery type, market conditions, etc.). They were then asked to plan a meeting with the new project supervisor to explain to him or her what was expected of them on the project.

The participants used the task ❯ people ❯ risk performance profile to structure their discussion.

Sponsor Notes for Session 1

Session 2 Managing Information

The goals and objectives for participant learning in Session 2 are:

- To create an awareness of how information flows throughout the project life cycle
- To understand the types of information the project supervisor is typically responsible for generating, coordinating and/or managing
- To develop an appreciation for how information created and managed by the project supervisor is used by other project team members
- To broaden the project supervisor's awareness of how the scope and nature of information management may vary based on project contracting method, team strengths and weaknesses, and means and methods

Session 2 includes the following topics:

Information Flows
- To the superintendent
- From the superintendent

Project Life Cycle
Effective Control Systems
Documentation
- Requests for information
- Construction changes
- Daily field reports
- Quality Control logs
- Labor production and labor time
- Toolbox safety talk attendance
- Two-week look-ahead plans
- Speed-memos (performance problem notifications)

Types of Meetings
- Preconstruction planning meetings
- Pre-award meeting with each sub
- Kickoff meeting
- Weekly project meetings
- Bimonthly management meetings
- Design review meetings (for design-build delivery)

Purpose of Meetings
- Communication
- Problem solving
- Coordination

Effective Meetings
Use (and Abuse) of Technology
Protocols/Chain of Command
Responsibility Matrix

In Session 2, the participants discussed among themselves how the management of ideas and information varies on a project depending upon project delivery system. They also compared and contrasted change management from the concrete subcontractor (or self-perform foreman) in light of the project delivery system. Lastly, the participants developed a roles and responsibilities matrix for the Sure Fresh project and discussed how the matrix would change if the project delivery system was changed.

Sponsor Notes for Session 2

<u>Session 3 Managing and Understanding Risk</u>

The goals and objectives for participant learning in Session 3 are:

- To create an awareness of how risk changes over the life of a project
- To understand the types and sources of risk in the construction phase of the project life cycle
- To develop knowledge of techniques for managing risk, specifically risks that are the primary responsibility of the project supervisor
- To broaden the project supervisor's awareness of how the scope and nature of risk management may vary based on project contracting method, team strengths and weaknesses, and means and methods

Session 3 includes the following topics:

The Project Team's Role in Risk Control
Risk Management
- Owners "delegate" risk
- Contractors "delegate" risk
- Subcontractors further "delegate" risk

General Sources of Risk
- Budget/cost (money problems)
- Time (schedule problems)
- Design (design flaws)
- Quality (construction defects)
- Safety (loss of life, loss of time, loss of property)

Managing the Risks
- Bonding and sureties (monetary risk/construction defects)
- Insurance (safety)
- Subcontract vs. self-perform (cost risk, schedule risk)
- Site management (safety)
- Budget and cost controls (monetary risk)
- Quality Control plan (construction defects, design flaws)
- Schedule (time)
- Safety plan (loss of life; loss of time)

Project Factors Affecting Risk
- Location of project
- Nature of project
- Construction process
- Project organization

Risks Managed in the Field
- Enforcement of safety requirements
- Quality assurance
- Labor cost control

Costs Associated with Poor Risk Management
The Future of Risk Management

In Session 3, the participants analyzed and discussed the costs and risks associated with schedule acceleration at the request of an owner. The focus was on identifying all the relevant costs so the contractor could request adequate funding in the change order to cover the acceleration costs, overhead and profit. In another activity, the class reviewed a typical supplementary general conditions to the contract to determine how risks had been allocated between the owner and the contractor.

Sponsor Notes for Session 3

Session 4 Planning the Work

The goals and objectives for participant learning in Session 4 are:

- To learn how preconstruction planning is defined and how it should be done
- To learn what planning tasks are required of the project supervisor
- To learn the basics of site planning in preparation for a future session
- To learn how to set up a system to manage information
- To learn basic scheduling techniques

Session 4 includes the following topics:

Preconstruction Phase Planning and Management
Preconstruction Project Planning
- Determining work tasks (what)
- Means and methods selection (how)
- Delegating primary responsibilities (who)
- Allocation and prioritization of resources (why)
- Sequencing of the work on the project (where)
- Scheduling of the work (when)

Preconstruction Site Planning
- Delivery routing
- Lay-down areas
- Parking areas
- Public access control
- Storage trailers
- Office trailers
- Temporary utilities

Preconstruction Information Planning
- Job files
- Design clarification and communication
- Daily logs
- Time sheets
- Job trailer set-up
- Computer set-up

Preconstruction Project Scheduling
- Sequencing of work
- Activity durations
- Predecessor and successor activities
- Resource loading (balanced crew sizing)
- Critical path calculations
- Contract compliance

In Session 4, the participants worked with a hypothetical project called Sure Fresh. First they developed a schedule for the preconstruction activities. Next they worked out a summary schedule for the complete project. Lastly they generated a work breakdown schedule that could be used to fully develop the project schedule and to facilitate cost accounting and productivity tracking.

Sponsor Notes for Session 4

Session 5 Working the Plan

The goals and objectives for participant learning in Session 5 are:

- To learn how to mobilize and to organize a project in the field
- To learn the basics of field purchasing for commodity materials
- To learn how to expedite material and equipment orders
- To learn how to manage the inspection and approval processes
- To understand the importance of keeping plans and schedules up-to-date
- To learn the basics of closing out a project in the field

Session 5 includes the following topics:

Construction Phase Tasks
Mobilization
- Identify team members (foremen, field engineer)
- Temporary utility hook-ups
- Data link and networking
- Move-in trailers
- Project sign
- Install security fence and gates

Purchasing
- Setting up accounts
- Standing purchase orders
- Reviewing POs and subcontracts for scope
- Scheduling deliveries
- Pricing of commodity items
- Make-or-rent decisions (e.g., formwork)
- Own-or-rent decisions (e.g., all-terrain forklift)

Expediting
- Assist project manager in tracking submittals
- Assist project manager in buy-out
- Track subcontractor progress
- Verify deliveries (e.g., PRO numbers)

Approvals
- Building inspections
- Owner/architect inspections
- Testing agency inspections
- EPA/surface water

Closeout
- Operation and maintenance data
- Warranties and guarantees
- Attic stock
- Training
- Punch list
- Final inspections
- Final pay application
- Final lien waivers

In Session 5, the participants worked with a hypothetical project called Sure Fresh. First they developed a field staffing plan for the project. Next they worked out a procurement schedule for it. Then they performed an analysis of the general requirements to determine what the responsibilities of the owner and the contractor would be. Lastly they worked through a rent-or-buy decision process.

Sponsor Notes for Session 5

Session 6 Managing Methods and Materials

The goals and objectives for participant learning in Session 6 are:

- To learn the details of site layout
- To understand factors influencing equipment selection
- To learn material handling, storage and protection techniques
- To be able to analyze prefabrication vs. onsite fabrication options

Session 6 includes the following topics:

Site Layout
- Delivery routing
- Lay-down areas
- Parking areas
- Security fences
- Public-access control
- Storage trailers
- Office trailers
- Temporary utilities

Equipment Selection
- Equipment type
- Equipment size and capacity
- Equipment quantities
- Safety (wind, indoor exhaust, hand signals)
- Minimization of downtime (equipment sharing)
- Maintenance
- Allocating equipment time

Material Handling, Storage, Protection
- Storage trailers
- Offsite storage
- Security
- Other protection (sun, weathering, etc.)
- Coordinating deliveries
- Allocating lay-down space
- Inspecting deliveries
- Minimizing handling

Onsite Fabrication vs. Modular Units/Panelization
- Cost
- Schedule
- Compliance with specifications/design intent
- Compatibility with weather conditions
- Compliance with codes
- Compatibility with local labor climate
- Control of quality

In Session 6, the participants again worked with a hypothetical project called Sure Fresh. First they developed a construction site layout plan for the project. Next they designed a "dream" yard for a construction company, with attention to what it would cost to have such a yard. Lastly they compared and contrasted tilt-up vs. precast walls for the project.

Sponsor Notes for Session 6

Session 7 Understanding Finances

The goals and objectives for participant learning in Session 7 are:

- To create an awareness of how cost information cycles through companies and projects
- To understand project cash flows
- To develop knowledge of the uses and importance of accurate cost coding
- To broaden the project supervisor's awareness of how retainage affects financing costs and cash flows

Session 7 includes the following topics:

Cost Information Cycle
- Measures
  - Estimate to budget
  - Budget to actual
  - Actual to historical
  - Historical to estimate
- Information flows
  - Field to office
  - Subcontractor/supplier to office
  - Office to A/E/owner
  - Office to field (feedback)

Cost Coding Accuracy
- Understanding cost codes
  - Level of detail
  - Direct work vs. indirect work
- Asking for more cost codes when necessary
- Accurate assignment of work to code(s)
- Assessing impact of change
- Garbage in, garbage out (GIGO)
- Bidding accuracy depends highly upon timesheet accuracy

Schedule of Payments/Project Cash Flow
- Contractor self-finances first portion of work
- Monthly progress pay application
  - Project S curve
  - Aggressive billing
  - Cost-loaded schedules
  - Cost-plus/unit-price/lump-sum
- Retainage
- Reduction in retainage
- "Pay when paid" clauses

In Session 7, the participants worked on a cash flow and project funding exercise, designed a (hypothetical) ideal cost-coding system, and worked through the difficulties of using a cost cycle with imperfect information (e.g., tried to put a bid together with inaccurate data from a previous similar job).

Sponsor Notes for Session 7

Session 8 Working with Project Partners

The goals and objectives for participant learning in Session 8 are:

- To learn how your actions on the project may affect future work with the client
- To learn how to work effectively with subcontractors
- To understand how to work with design firms in different types of projects
- To appreciate the importance of working with inspectors and government agencies
- To understand how to work with trade union representatives
- To understand how to work better with other internal stake-holders (co-workers)

Session 8 includes the following topics:

Working with Owners (Supervisor as the Salesperson)
- Effect of delivery system
- Professionalism
- "Can do" attitude
- Customer is almost always right
- Respect the owner's chain of command
- Problem solving ability (managing changes)

Working with Subcontractors in the Field
- Hard bid vs. negotiated subs
- Resolve/firmness
- Resolution of performance issues
- Taking excuses away
- Coordinated planning
- Cleanup
- Monitoring sub progress
- Assessing sub completion percentage

Working with Designers
- Project delivery system effect
- Constructability
- Safety
- Change management
- Punch list management
- Quality and inspections

Working with Inspectors/Governments
- Entities with limited or no stake in project having power to bring project to a halt
- Coordinating inspection schedules
- Allowing lead time for inspections prior to Cert. of Occup./ Cert. of Comp. and move-in
- Involving inspectors in change as necessary
- Acknowledging limited technical knowledge of some code officials

Unions
- Jurisdictional disputes
- Political power
- Dual gates
- Work rules

Working with Internal Stakeholders (accounting, PM, corporate, etc.)
- Timely response to requests for information
- Respect for other parts of organization
- Setting appropriate boundaries
- Respect of higher decision-making authority
- Profit center vs. cost center

In Session 8, the participants worked through a conflict resolution activity dealing with the Sure Fresh project. They also dealt with a jurisdictional dispute regarding the project. Lastly they discussed how to respond as a group to a surprise OSHA inspection at the site.

Sponsor Notes for Session 8

Session 9 Understanding People

The goals and objectives for participant learning in Session 9 are:

- To create an awareness of how relationships affect project performance
- To understand various leadership styles
- To develop knowledge of techniques for motivating and rewarding project team members
- To broaden the project supervisor's awareness of how the appropriate leadership style may vary based on project contracting method and the nature of the team

Session 9 includes the following topics:

Motivation and Rewards
- Compensation
- Benefits
- Threats/coercion (short-term and infrequent)
- Recognition
- Working conditions
- Co-worker relations
- Personal growth
- Career advancement

Leadership Skills
- Charisma and personality/styles
- Tasks vs. people
- Adjusting style to the individual
- Adjusting style to the situation
- Managing vs. leading
- Power
- Competency

Personality styles (MBTI)
- Extrovert vs. Introvert
- Intuition vs. Sensing
- Thinking vs. Feeling
- Judging vs. Perceiving

In Session 9, the participants used an interactive role-playing exercise to learn more about how communication is affected by personality types. They worked on an activity to help them understand how to match leadership styles to situations, and worked in teams to develop low-cost reward and recognition systems for craftworkers on a project.

Sponsor Notes for Session 9

Session 10 Understanding Corporate Policies/ Procedures

The goals and objectives for participant learning in Session 10 are:

- To learn how local governments and state and federal agencies affect the execution of your project and how corporate policies affect your actions as a supervisor
- To understand some of the rationale behind why a company might take a certain project
- To appreciate why you might be assigned to a particular project
- To learn how construction companies approach the sales function
- To understand what corporate overhead is and how it is recovered through projects
- To learn how each construction company is somewhat unique based upon its culture and personality

Session 10 includes the following topics:

Compliance
- Government policies
  - EEO
  - Right-To-Know rules
  - OSHA 4-in-1 notification
  - OSHA 300 logs
- Corporate policies
  - At-will employment and termination
  - The role of the human resources department
  - Promotion and hiring practices
  - Personal use of company resources (e.g., company truck)

Project Portfolio/Risk Diversification
- Why did we take this project?
  - Repeat client
  - Develop new expertise
  - Reinforce existing expertise
  - Low-risk project to balance high-risk contract elsewhere (or vice versa)
  - Keep competitors out of market
  - Retain skilled workers
  - Need for certain level of revenue to recover overhead

Sales/Marketing
- Sales prospecting
  - Networking opportunities
  - Dedicated sales staff vs. "all-sell"
  - Qualifying leads
  - Targeted cold calls and mailings

- Information sources
  - Commercial report services
  - Bid exchanges
  - Public notices

Project Staffing Decisions
- Why am I on this project?
  - Prior experience or existing technical expertise matches project needs
  - Opportunity to develop new expertise
  - You were available (next-in-line selection)
  - Past working relationship with client or partners
  - Physical location of the project
  - Result of client request or project promises
  - Compensate for weaknesses of other team members

Corporate Overhead
- Project profits and investing must cover general corporate overhead
- When in doubt, assign it to a project (not feasible for all types of overhead or projects)
- Categories of corporate overhead
  - Officer salaries and benefits
  - Support staff salaries and benefits
  - Office space (rent, light, heat, phone, etc.)
  - General supplies and expenses
  - Yard warehouse and storage
  - Certain types of insurance
  - General equipment/fleet depreciation

Corporate Culture/Personality
- Employee as a "whole person" vs. a resource
- Employee recognition for achievement
- Balance of employer-focus vs. employee-focus
- Delegation of decision-making authority
- Job descriptions
- Professional development support
- Employee compensation and benefit plans
- Company's professional reputation
- Company's community reputation

In Session 10, the participants discussed how the corporate culture drives project selection. They also designed a system for bouncing up sales leads to the office from the field. Finally they were challenged to summarize their implementation notes from each of the sessions and develop an action plan for personal development within the organization.

Sponsor Notes for Session 10

Session 1

Understanding Project Delivery Systems

Goal and Performance Objectives of Session 1

The goals and objectives for participant learning in Session 1 are:

■ To create an awareness of how the type of delivery system or contracting method affects the roles and responsibilities of the project management team

■ To understand how different strengths and weaknesses of the individual project team members may affect how project management responsibility is delegated

■ To develop an appreciation for the interdependence of the project management team and the various roles and responsibilities that must be coordinated to achieve optimum project performance

■ To broaden the project supervisor's awareness of his or her role and responsibilities on the project, and how they might change based on project contracting method, team strengths and weaknesses, and market conditions

To Get Ready for Session 1

Read Session 1 and complete any preparatory assignments given by your instructor. Spend some time thinking about projects you have been involved with, those that went well and those that did not go as well as you would have liked. Try to create a list of reasons why the "good" projects went so well, and the "bad" projects did not turn out as well.

Construction Delivery Systems

Design-Bid-Build

This method involves three roles in the project delivery process— owner, designer, and contractor—in traditionally separate contracts. "Traditional" is frequently used to describe the Design-Bid-Build method, which typically involves competitively bid, lump-sum unit prices construction contracts that are based on complete and prescriptive contract documents prepared by architects and engineers. These documents generally include drawings, specifications, and supporting information. The phases of work are usually conducted in linear sequence. The owner contracts with an architect for design; uses the design documents produced by the architect to secure competitive bids from contractors; and, based on an accepted bid, contracts with a contractor for construction of the building. Sometimes (though rarely) the owner may also be the designer; examples would be a developer with in-house Design-Build capability, or the Department of Transportation designing new transportation systems.

For most of the 20th century, public work was routinely built using the Design-Bid-Build/lump-sum (or stipulated sum) delivery method. This has included competitive bidding among general contractors, performance bonds, and employment of various other statutory requirements to protect taxpayers' investments. Much private work has also been performed for a lump-sum figure, in the belief that the marketplace ensures economic discipline and yields the lowest cost. (In particular, private organizations with large constituencies, such as churches and schools, are often required to use project delivery methods with sealed bids and formal procedures, similar to procedures for public projects.)

Design-Bid-Build is identified by the following *defining characteristics*:

■ Three prime players—owner, designer, contractor

■ Two separate contracts—owner-designer, owner-builder

■ Final contractor selection based on lowest responsible bid or total contract price

Typical characteristics of the Design-Bid-Build approach include the following:

■ Three linear phases—design, bid, build

■ Well-established and broadly documented roles

■ Carefully crafted legal and procedural guidelines

■ A lowest responsible bid that provides a reliable market price for the project

■ Contract documents that are typically completed in a single package before construction begins, requiring construction-related decisions in advance of actual execution

■ An opportunity for construction planning based on completed documents

■ Complete specifications that produce clear quality standards

■ Configuration and details of finished product agreed to by all parties before construction begins

Currently, approximately 45% of all non-residential construction in the United States is delivered using Design-Bid-Build methodology.

Construction Management at-Risk

Construction management at-risk (CM at-Risk) approaches involve a construction manager who takes on the risk of building a project. The architect is hired under a separate contract. The construction manager, working with the designer, oversees project management and building technology issues, in which a construction manager typically has particular background and expertise. Such management services may include advice on the time and cost consequences of design and construction decisions, scheduling, cost control, coordination of construction contract negotiations and awards, timely purchasing of critical materials and long-lead-time items, and coordination of construction activities.

In CM at-Risk, the construction entity, after providing preconstruction services during the design phase, takes on the financial obligation for construction under a specified cost agreement. The construction manager frequently provides a guaranteed maximum price (GMP). CM at-Risk is sometimes referred to as CM/GC, because the construction entity becomes a general contractor (GC) through the at-risk agreement.

The term "at-risk" is often a source of confusion. Sometimes it refers to the fact that the contractor holds the trade contracts and takes the performance risk for construction. In other contexts, the term is tied to the existence of a cost guarantee or GMP. Because "at-risk" has two distinct meanings, it is important to understand how it is being used in a particular situation. The definition used for CM at-Risk in this manual is based primarily on the concept that the construction manager holds the trade contracts and takes the performance risk. The eventual establishment of a guaranteed maximum price is typical of CM at-Risk project delivery, but it is not a defining characteristic of the delivery method in this case.

When a GMP is used, the CM at-Risk approach is flexible as to when the construction price becomes fixed. As a result, the timing for agreeing to a GMP varies by project. Considerations of risk should include an evaluation of the amount of design information available, the amount of contingency included, and the owner's willingness to share in the risk of cost overruns.

As with Design-Bid-Build, the CM at-Risk contracts with trade contractors who perform the construction. These entities are contractually bound only to the CM at-Risk. It should be noted that there is no contractual relationship between the designer and the CM at-Risk.

The following *defining characteristics* identify CM at-Risk:

- Three prime players—owner, designer, CM at-Risk

- Two separate contracts—owner to designer, owner to CM at-Risk

- Final provider selection based on aspects other than total cost

Typical characteristics of the CM at-Risk approach include the following:

■ Overlapping phases—design and build (sometimes called fast-track)

■ Hiring of the construction manager during the design phase

■ Preconstruction services offered by the constructor (such as constructability review, bid climate development and bid management)

■ Specific contractual arrangement determines the roles of players

■ Clear quality standards produced by the contract's prescriptive specifications

Another type of construction management delivery is generally termed Construction-Manager-as-Agent. The AGC of America views CM as-Agent as a variation of the Design-Bid-Build delivery system with the owner hiring a consultant to act as field representative(s). However, many companies in the construction industry perform both general contracting and construction management services. When acting as a CM as-Agent, the CM firm holds no contracts with the trades, does not take financial risk on the project, and does not guarantee the cost of construction. In this manner, it is acting more like architectural and engineering firms on the construction project. Another similarity between CM as-Agent and the A/E firm is the contractual standing each has as agent of the owner. "Agency" is a contractual designation that has legal ramifications. An agent must act in the best interests of the owner and has some decision-making authority on behalf of the owner. In a traditional construction project, the general contractor has an independent, or arm's-length relationship with the owner and is under no legal obligation to act in the best interests of the owner. The agency distinction is critically important from a legal standpoint, as it creates obligations for the construction manager (called "fiduciary responsibilities") not found in other delivery types. The supervisor's role on the project will vary dramatically if his or her company is acting as an agent on behalf of the owner.

Currently, approximately 10% of all non-residential construction in the United States is delivered using a construction management methodology.

Design-Build

In the Design-Build approach to project delivery, the owner contracts with a single entity—the designer-builder—for both design and construction. The Design-Build entity can be led by either an architect or a general contractor and can consist of any number of people. As with CM at-Risk, the timing of agreement on a GMP varies with each project.

Owners interested in single-point responsibility for both design and construction can use the Design-Build delivery system. In Design-Build, a consolidated entity provides both design and construction services to the owner. A single contract is established between the owner and the architect-contractor or Design-Build entity. Design-Build approaches require an explicit determination of the roles and responsibilities of the Design-Build team.

Single-source contracting has gained popularity in recent years in both the private and public sectors. The primary reason for this interest in Design-Build as a viable project delivery option is the owner's desire for a single source of responsibility for design and construction. This approach has the greatest opportunity for resolution of cost/constructability design issues.

The following *defining characteristics* identify Design-Build delivery:

■ Two prime players—the Design-Build entity and the owner

■ One contract—owner to Design-Build entity

■ Either cost, qualifications, or best-value as the basis for selection of the Design-Build entity.

Typical characteristics of the Design-Build approach include these:

■ Project-by-project basis for establishing and documenting roles

■ Continuous execution of design and construction

■ Overlapping phases—design and build (sometimes called fast-track)

■ Carefully crafted legal and procedural guidelines for public owners (see paragraph below for discussion of public sector work)

■ Some construction-related decisions after the start of the project

■ Overall project planning and scheduling by the Design-Build entity prior to mobilization (made possible by the single point of responsibility)

Currently, approximately 45% of all non-residential construction in the United States is delivered under a Design-Build methodology.

For public sector work, statutory purchasing laws frequently dictate which delivery system can be used, and how the award process must proceed. Currently, the federal government and 46 of the 50 states allow some form of Design-Build delivery to be used on at least a portion of public sector work. Virtually all public sector agencies allow for Design-Bid-Build delivery. CM at-Risk and CM as-Agent delivery systems are used in a variety of public sector work and the statutory process for using a CM delivery system varies a great deal across governmental entities. The CM delivery system is particularly popular for the construction of schools and government-owned hospitals.

Activity 3 involves an exercise in delivery system selection. The instructions for Activity 3 are found in Worksheet 3 in the Appendix. Your instructor will tell you when to turn to WS 3 to apply what you have learned about delivery systems.

Interdependence of Project Team Roles

There are hundreds and perhaps thousands of tasks and decisions that must be managed on a typical construction project. The number and types of tasks and decisions that must be managed by the construction team depends on the type of contract and the market in which the project is being built. For instance, a Design-Build project in a merit shop market in which the contractor has limited experience will be managed much differently than a hard bid job in a union market where the contractor has a long-standing reputation and extensive knowledge of the local construction industry.

Once the number and types of tasks for a project are categorized as part of a work breakdown structure, the next step is typically to assign responsibilities for each task to individual members of the construction team. The work breakdown structure is based on items of work depicted in the plans and specifications, categorized either by trades (e.g., carpenter work, electrical work, etc.) or by CSI Specification section (Division 2 work, Division 3 work, etc.). For instance, the tasks involved in building a concrete deck might be designated as follows:

"Engineer formwork," might be the responsibility of the field engineer,

"Order lumber and panels" might be assigned to the superintendent,

"Build forms" might be assigned to a carpenter foreman, and

"Coordinate mix designs" might be assigned to the project manager.

In general, given projects of similar size, there will be more tasks for the construction team to coordinate in a Design-Build project than in a hard-bid project or CM at-Risk. This is because the project management team on a Design-Build project frequently must supervise and coordinate design issues in addition to construction means and methods. Construction Management projects on which the CM does not self-perform any work might have fewer tasks to coordinate and execute. The specifics of planning for construction tasks will be discussed in more detail in Session 4 (Planning the Work), Session 5 (Working the Plan), and Session 6 (Managing Methods and Materials).

The number and types of decisions are typically spelled out in the contract terms and project agreements. A project management team will identify the processes for which its members are responsible and then make a determination of which processes they want to control, which they want to subcontract, which they want to insure, and which they want to shed by negotiating with the owner or other project partners. The program for managing all these processes is part of the risk management plan. We will further discuss risk management in Session 3 ("Managing and Understanding Risk").

Activity 4 involves an exercise in team roles and responsibilities. The instructions for Activity 4 are found in Worksheet 4 in the Appendix. Your instructor will tell you when to turn to WS 4 to apply what you have learned about project team interdependence.

How Delivery Systems and Team Strengths Change the Role of the Supervisor

The contract arrangement with the owner and the composition of the project team affects the role of the project supervisor. For instance, on a Design-Build project, the superintendent will typically have much more input on design issues. He or she can give advice early in the design phase on details, materials, and methods that can be designed into the project to create a more efficient and cost-effective project for the owner without sacrificing design aesthetics. On a hard-bid project, the superintendent's role will not involve much design input, as the design is more or less completed. The supervisor's role shifts to clarifying design intent, identifying and resolving design conflicts, and documenting additional work required. On a Construction Management at-Risk project, the superintendent's role will involve much more subcontractor coordination and schedule control. Because of these shifting roles, good project supervisors need to be able to change their approach to construction to fit the situation.

The composition of the project team also affects the project supervisor's responsibilities. For example, an experienced project supervisor on a job with a relatively inexperienced project manager may be asked to perform more of the expediting and work planning activities, review subcontractor pay applications, and provide more assistance in defining claims.

For some suggestions for improving your ability to work within various types of project teams and delivery systems, see Session 9 (Understanding People) and Session 8 (Working with Project Partners).

To Implement What You Have Learned

Write down one concept or idea from the introduction and/or Session 1 that you think everyone in your company should know to improve the way your company does business.

Write down one thing you learned in the Introduction or Session 1 that you think should be included in your company's project management training program for entry-level project managers.

Write down one thing you learned in the Introduction or Session 1 that you intend to use on your next project to make the project more successful.

Before the next session, develop the three ideas you listed above into a short memo, and schedule a meeting with your sponsor to discuss your ideas and develop an action plan. Remember: When trying something new, it is important to have the support of your sponsor and other champions in the organization, and to make small, incremental changes. Your sponsor has received an executive summary of this session and will be expecting your report and your phone call to set up a meeting with him or her to discuss your ideas for the company.

If you would like to learn more about construction contract relation-ships and delivery systems, we suggest you register for STP Unit 10, *General and Specialty Contractor Dynamics.*

Managing Information

Goal and Performance Objectives of Session 2

The goals and objectives for participant learning in Session 2 are:

■ To create an awareness of how information flows throughout the project life cycle

■ To understand the types of information the project supervisor is typically responsible for generating, coordinating or managing

■ To appreciate how other project team members use information created and managed by the project supervisor

■ To broaden the project supervisor's awareness of the scope and nature of information management, and how it may vary based on project contracting method, team strengths and weaknesses, and means and methods

To Get Ready for Session 2

Read Session 2 and complete any preparatory assignments given by your instructor. Spend some time thinking about the types of information you receive and distribute on projects. Create a list of documents you receive and documents you are responsible for distributing.

Project Life Cycles

Projects have a typical life cycle, from the owner's recognition of need (feasibility) to occupancy. In the very early stages of a project, an owner may do a feasibility study to determine the need for a new facility. It could be a study of population trends, birthrates, and technology changes to determine whether a new elementary school is needed in the community, or a market study of existing low-maintenance housing options for active retired people. If the feasibility study proves the need for a new facility, the project conception stage begins. After determining whether a new building is needed, or just a facility upgrade, the owner typically will develop a program to decide the most effective scope (size, location, relationships, etc.) of the new facility. Along with the program, the owner will begin arranging for financing, studying potential sites, determining environmental and regulatory issues, and so on. All of this occurs during the project's planning phase. Once the project has been adequately planned, the owner can approve a conceptual design.

The project will then move through schematic design, design development, and final design. This substantially completes the design phase. Once design has at least begun, the owner can acquire the construction services needed to build the project, thus starting the construction phase. In Design-Bid-Build, the design phase is completed before the construction phase begins. In Design-Build, the construction and design phases overlap, sometimes significantly. In Construction Management, the design phase is usually complete before construction begins, but it does not necessarily have to be. Near the end of the construction phase, the close-out, audit, and commissioning phase will take place, after which the owner will take occupancy of the building and begin maintaining the facility until it becomes too small, too outdated, or too inefficient—at which time the process starts all over again. At the end of the project life cycle, the project team involved in construction and design is disbanded, and individuals are assigned to another project team.

Over the course of this project life cycle, information must flow from one part of the project team to another. During the construction phase on Design-Bid-Build projects, the project supervisor is a critical generator, coordinator and manager of information. On CM at-Risk and Design-Build projects, the project supervisor's role in managing information may begin earlier in the project life cycle (perhaps as early as the schematic design phase) with input on constructability and design-for-safety issues.

At each stage of the project life cycle, there is substantial documentation that must be shared with other project team members. The documentation takes different forms and serves a variety of purposes, but the project supervisor is usually involved in the documentation flow.

Documentation

The supervisor must manage many forms of information:

- Information given verbally
- Information given graphically
- Information given in written text
- Information given in standard forms and policies
- Cost information
- Schedule information (delay documentation)
- Safety information
- Quality assurance

Typical information on a project includes

- Requests for information from the field for the designer or the project manager

- Construction changes from the designer for the project manager and the field

- Daily field reports from the field to the project manager

- Quality control logs from the field to the engineer

- Labor productivity and labor hour reports from the field to the estimator

- Toolbox safety talks from the safety director to the field

- Two-week look-ahead schedules from the field to the shop, subcontractors and suppliers

- Notification of claims from the project manager to the designer or owner

- As-built plans and O/M manuals from the field and subcontractors to the owner

In addition, each contractor will have its own internal reports, meetings, and processes requiring documentation.

Because of the large amount of information that must flow through the project supervisor in the field, an effective system for managing information must be established prior to the start of construction. On Design-Build and CM at-Risk projects, where cost savings can lead to higher margins for the builder, it is common to have an idea management system in addition to an information management system.

An information management system involves planning for the control and tracking of documentation and correspondence on the project site, and between those at the project site and other members of the project team. An idea management system involves creating a system by which skilled craftworkers and others on the site can convey to the project team ideas for cost savings, efficiencies, and improvements in constructability. The idea management and information management systems are depicted below.

Idea Management   Information Management

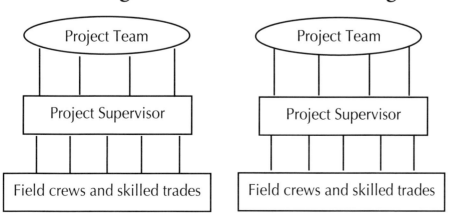

Activity 5 involves an exercise in managing information and ideas. The instructions for Activity 5 are found in Worksheet 5 in the Appendix. Your instructor will tell you when to turn to WS 5 to apply what you have learned about information systems.

On projects where field input can be incorporated into the construction documents, an idea management system is intended to create efficiencies, improve worker safety, reduce material waste, and increase profitability. On projects with an information management system, documentation is typically used to control risk, as further discussed in the following section.

The Importance of Documentation

Except for labor production and worker safety, the greatest risk to a project comes from conditions that are said to be "beyond the contractor's control:" conditions that cause a project to go over budget or beyond the scheduled duration, and expose the contractor to lawsuits and/or the threat of liquidated damages being assessed by the owner.

The best way to reduce or eliminate potential threats is to do a complete and professional job of planning, controlling, and documenting every project activity. Otherwise, conditions beyond the contractor's control will include conditions the project team could have controlled if the team had done a good job of managing the project from the start.

Even the most thorough planning, however, cannot prevent the project team from being affected by outside forces. Any event or occurrence that affects the scope of the work is said to cause "impact." Logistics of the project (the movement of personnel, material and equipment), the flow or sequence of the work, and the duration of the work are all subject to impact.

The first step in controlling the risk of impact is to thoroughly understand the contracts and documents. Impacts are changes that affect time and cost performance of the contractor. They are caused by deviations from the conditions and standards set forth in the plans, specifications, contracts, and other written project documents. The first sign of any such deviation should signal the project team to bring matters back into control.

We will discuss risk management in more detail in the next session, but it is important to understand risk in order to understand the importance of documentation. Once the deviation between actual documentation or work and the contracted documents or work has been identified, the changes must be documented in order to have legal standing. Therefore, documentation is the critical element of a risk control system for contractors, especially on a Design-Bid-Build project.

Once the project team understands the contract documents and is alerted to the potential impacts or risks, the team can decide what documentation is needed for the project.

Types of Documentation

Documentation should include the regular taking of project pictures. Job pictures should be signed and dated by the photographer and include a brief description of the activity shown in the picture. Documentation also should include daily field reports or logs, including the location of the work within the project. This report should identify what occurs on the project each day and describe the impact: size of crew affected, time delayed, cause of impact and a short description.

A more detailed description of an occurrence or impact can be made in an occurrence report. Note that the occurrence report will give the project team ample information with which to price the occurrence or impact, if necessary.

Another type of documentation is notifications of delays, disruptions or other types of impact that are communicated to the owner, architect, subcontractor or vendors. These notices should be transmitted on a timely basis (as defined in the general conditions and/or the construction contract) as part of the documentation to the appropriate parties.

Timecards should be included; they should reflect any extra or additional work done so that these costs can easily be substantiated, if necessary, at a later date. Any overtime or shift work can be noted.

The schedule is another important document on construction projects. The schedule should be updated periodically (schedule update requirements are frequently spelled out in the general conditions and/ or construction contract) and should clearly show the result of impacts. The minutes of planning meetings or schedule review sessions should be kept with the schedule updates as part of the documentation.

Document clarification requests/requests for information (RFIs) should be used to clarify a discrepancy or lack of information in the plans and specifications. This report forces any and all changes or clarifications to be in writing. Quality control reports are another important type of document that can be used to prove the quality of construction if a lawsuit should develop over workmanlike standards.

The project manager will use the documentation from the field to create other types of documents, such as contract change orders, notification letters, audit and closure documents, etc. The project manager will also create a separate set of documents such as subcontracts, purchase orders, and minutes from meetings with owner/architects, etc., and share these documents with the field supervisor.

Information and Project Control

As noted above, documentation is frequently the final step in a risk control process. There are many control processes on a construction project, such as quality control, cost control, schedule control, and scope control. The control documentation is important as both an administrative and historical record. Control processes are intended to help reduce risk, and documentation communicates the efforts taken to reduce risk to other members of the project team. We will discuss risk

SESSION 2

in more detail in the next session, but we cannot emphasize enough the importance of documentation in controlling risk. Contractors who are better able to control their risk are typically more profitable and more competitive in the industry. Therefore, effective documentation, as the final step in the control process, can be viewed as a critical function in the continuing operation of the company. From this viewpoint, then, it can be said that the ability of the project supervisor to adequately and effectively administer project documentation is a key factor in the profitability and long-term viability of the overall company.

Effective Control Systems

- Begin with a clearly understood goal or objective. What is the **scope** of the project, and what **standard** is to be achieved? Project objectives are reflected in the plans, specifications, contracts, quality assurance plans, and instructions to bidders. Some standards are established by the contractor (schedule, budget, and overhead requirements) based on the objectives outlined in the construction documents.

- Secondly, the system must include an **accurate reporting of what is happening**—and when it is happening—on the project. This is where field reports, QA logs, and requests for clarification from the field are important.

- Next, a control system must **compare** past performance with the planned standard. In a cost control system, the project team objectively and collectively reviews the cost report and compares it with the budget. The report not only reviews past performance, but helps the team predict the future.

- Finally, an effective control system provides a responsive means by which to take **corrective action** when necessary. The whole purpose of the control system is based on this last step. If the project team decides that corrective action is required, but fails to see that this decision is carried out, the costs will go uncontrolled. You, the supervisor, will be responsible for taking corrective action—in this case, to control costs.

In addition, a control system can be only as effective as the level of understanding possessed by the people within the organization. When a control system is introduced into an organization, it should be designed around the organization and should be understood and agreed upon by all members of the organization.

Control systems can be designed for virtually every facet of the project. Schedule, cost, safety, quality and risk all can be controlled. However, the control system should always be as simple and as straightforward as possible. Information produced by a control system can be used for future planning. This is especially true for cost records. Most construction companies rely heavily on cost reports to estimate future work. As mentioned earlier, cost records also can be used by the contractor for documentation to substantiate claims.

The type of control system, the nature of documentation, and the routing of information will vary depending on the type of construction delivery system being used. In general, Design-Build projects have more comprehensive internal risk controls, while Design-Bid-Build projects have more external controls (i.e., documentation of scope changes).

Conducting Effective Meetings

In addition to attending to project administration and documentation, field supervisors will need to conduct coordination meetings. It is important that these meetings be run as effectively and efficiently as possible, while still ensuring that critical coordination information is clearly communicated. Meetings should begin with the easiest tasks and discussions, move to the more difficult, and as the meeting moves toward an end, return to easier issues.

One best practice for conducting an effective meeting is to have an agenda published in advance. A standard agenda can be used for weekly field coordination meetings, so that participants know at what point they will need to provide information and at what point they may ask for clarifying information. Meetings should be used to coordinate work and solve problems, not necessarily just to report on the progress made since the last meeting. Accordingly, place near the top the issues requiring the widest participation for coordination and problem solving, and work down to the issues requiring the fewest participants. In this way, attendees whose participation is not required can return to work as soon as their agenda items have been discussed.

Before discussion of any agenda item is concluded, the project supervisor should ensure that everyone understands the scope and schedule of work, or the agreed-upon solution. One of the best ways to ensure understanding is to clearly and concisely repeat the information to the participants and attendees, then ask if there are any questions or concerns before moving on to the next agenda item. Address any clarifications or questions before moving on to the next item, and document the agreed-upon solutions or procedures in meeting minutes to be published and distributed within two days of the meeting.

Sometimes it can be difficult to get everyone to participate in problem solving discussions or coordination meetings. In such situations, project supervisors must use good interpersonal skills to get people talking and contributing to the meeting agenda. If you suspect that an attendee may have critical information or a good idea for solving a

Activity 6 involves an exercise in working with control systems. The instructions for Activity 6 are found in Worksheet 6 in the Appendix. Your instructor will tell you when to turn to WS 6 to apply what you have learned about control systems.

SESSION 2

SESSION 2

problem but is unwilling to speak up, you may need to call on that person directly and ask for his or her input. A technique for opening the discussion could be something like this:

> "Jim, I know your company has done a lot of this kind of work. What do they usually do in this situation?"

or

> "John, your crew's work is critical to the schedule. What do you need to get ahead of the other trades so we can get back on schedule?"

In general, Design-Build meetings will include more members of the project team at earlier stages of project development. In Design-Build, there will be design clarification and review meetings in addition to trade work and subcontractor coordination meetings. Design-Bid-Build projects will usually involve more trade work and subcontractor coordination meetings.

Types of Meetings

For a well-planned and coordinated project, you can hold any of several types of meetings:

- Preconstruction planning meetings

- Pre-award conference meetings with each sub

- Kickoff meeting

- Weekly project meetings

- Bimonthly management meetings

- Design review meetings (for Design-Build delivery)

Preconstruction Planning Meetings

As discussed earlier, subcontractors should be involved in preconstruction planning and in the discussion of such items as scope of work, long-lead items, material storage requirements and activity durations.

If the job schedule is to be realistic and subcontractors are to commit to it, this type of meeting is a must!

Pre-Award Conference Meeting with Each Subcontractor

The project manager may schedule a pre-award conference meeting with each subcontractor and invite the project supervisor to participate. The pre-award meeting will be used to review the bids for compliance with construction documents, to finalize subcontract prices and terms, to define the scope of work, and to verify insurance and bonding requirements.

Kickoff Meetings

The construction phase of each project typically includes a kickoff meeting to discuss assignment of material storage and lay-down areas, scheduling of hoisting, pay application procedures, routing of submittals and clarification requests, safety program requirements, cleanup expectations and waste removal systems, and introductions and creation of the project roster.

Weekly Project Meetings

A schedule and coordination meeting should be held each week. Those attending should include the job superintendent, key supervisors or assistants, and the superintendents for each active subcontractor.

The meeting should be centered primarily on scheduling and coordination, but can also cover cleanup, safety and quality.

For example, it is suggested that each contractor submit a two-week schedule each Thursday morning. These schedules can be reviewed, copied and bound in time for a Friday afternoon meeting. It is extremely important that these short-interval schedules comply with the job schedule.

An Action Items form is also useful at these meetings. Any problems that need solutions can be shown on the Action Items list. Set a date by which a solution is needed and record who is responsible for the solution. This list can be filled out after each meeting and distributed with the two-week schedules at the next meeting.

Bimonthly Management Meetings

Bimonthly management meetings should be well thought-out with a prepared agenda given to each participant ahead of time.

It is recommended that the meeting include the project manager and superintendent, subcontractors and engineer/architect representatives. (By being present, engineers/architects should gain a better understanding of some of the problems encountered on the project.)

This meeting should consist of a complete in-depth job status review. Topics should include a job progress and schedule review, change order review, submittal status review, safety and quality status review, and any special project problems. It should allow time for each subcontractor to comment on material delivery or storage problems, scheduling problems and workforce problems.

Have someone take the minutes. They should be typed and mailed to all attendees before the next meeting.This form is ideal for improving coordination and for showing potential material delivery or storage problems. It is an excellent tool for getting subcontractors committed to the dates they are to have solutions to these problems.

Hold your meeting in a room large enough to seat everyone comfortably and away from phones and other interruptions. The room should be equipped with a large plan of the project, a complete set of up-to-date drawings and specifications, a copy of the total job schedule and a chalk board that shows the two-week schedule form.

Use a black marker on a white board to make the forms. Mark up the form during the meeting and then transfer the information to the meeting notes later on.

Design Review Meetings

For Design-Build delivery systems, the project supervisor may be asked to participate in design review meetings. These meetings verify that design remains within project budget and schedule parameters, while still adhering to the owner's scope. The project supervisor may give advice on design-for-safety and constructability, as well as opinions on best practices for efficient production and material use.

Purpose of the Meetings

The purpose of job meetings is to help the project team manage the overall effort on the project. These meetings, if effectively run, will:

- Help keep communication between the general contractor and the subcontractors open and candid

- Help maintain communication among subcontractors

- Give all contractors a chance to discuss their problems and learn about problems others are facing

- Help contractors schedule and coordinate the entire project

Use of Technology for Managing Information

As communication technology such as cell phones, e-mail, and fax machines have been developed, we sometimes communicate more information to more people than we need to, just because we can. It is important for all members of the project team to remember that everyone is very busy, their time is valuable, and they have many important decisions to make on the project. Cluttering their brains with unnecessary e-mails and faxes, and calling them on the cell phone with information that can wait until the weekly coordination meeting, can become a real nuisance for many project team members. It is a good idea to discuss with each member of the team how they prefer to be contacted, and what the rules are for cell phone use. Many people have chosen to use the cell phone for emergency contact only, and use e-mail, fax, and onsite meetings as the primary means of regular communication. Document any phone calls or decisions in writing.

Another trend in communication is the reduction of face-to-face meetings as a result of the increased use of communication technology. Having the project manager call every day on his or her cell phone is not the same as having him come to the field to see the work being done. If it is important to a project supervisor to have the project manager come to the site on a regular basis, that request should be made at one of the earliest pre-construction planning meetings.

A newly developing trend in communication technology that may even further reduce face-to-face personal communication is the use of web-cams and real-time digital photographs to communicate variances and impact conditions between the field and office. We are not sure where the growth in communication technology will take us, but project teams should carefully consider how much personal communication and face-to-face they need in order to develop the types of relationships necessary for project teams to function at their highest level.

Protocols and Chains of Command

One of the important functions of a preconstruction planning meeting is to establish the lines of communication each of the project partners expects to use. The communication protocols and chain of command may seem cumbersome, but they serve an important purpose: to prevent information from bypassing the project members who have critical risk-management functions to perform. On many projects, the protocols are spelled out in a responsibility matrix that identifies each system, risk area, or other project function that must be managed on the project. Then an individual from the project team is assigned primary responsibility for that system, risk, or function. Many times, a different team member is assigned secondary responsibility in case the primary individual is away from the project (on vacation or traveling, for instance) when a decision must be given. The use of a responsibility matrix allows everyone on the project team to know who to call for certain questions or to deliver information. It is up to the responsible person to make sure the information is communicated to all affected parties. The responsibility matrix will look different for Design-Bid-Build projects than it will for Construction Management at-Risk and Design-Build projects because of the contractual assignment of different types of risk under each system.

Activity 7 involves the design of a responsibility matrix. The instructions for Activity 7 are found in Worksheet 7 in the Appendix. Your instructor will tell you when to turn to WS 7 to apply what you have learned about assigning responsibilities.

SESSION 2

What Who—	Proj. Mgr	Proj. Sup.	Field Engr.
Shop drawings			XX
Pay applications	XX		
Labor timecards		XX	
Daily reports		XX	

To Implement What You Have Learned

Write down one concept or idea from Session 2 that you think everyone in your company should know to improve the way your company does business.

Write down one thing you learned in Session 2 that you think should be included in your company's project management training program for entry-level project managers.

Write down one thing you learned in Session 2 that you intend to use on your next project to make the project more successful.

Before the next session, develop the three ideas you listed above into a short memo, and schedule a meeting with your sponsor to discuss your ideas and develop an action plan. Remember that when trying something new, it is important to have the support of your sponsor and other champions in the organization, and to make small, incremental changes. Your sponsor has received an executive summary of this session and will be expecting your report and your phone call to set up a meeting with him or her to discuss your ideas for the company.

If you would like to learn more about documentation, we suggest you register for STP Unit 4, *Contract Documents and Construction Law.*

Understanding and Managing Risk

Goal and Performance Objectives of Session 3

The goals and objectives for participant learning in Session 3 are:

■ To create an awareness of how risk changes over the life of a project

■ To understand the types and sources of risk in the construction phase of the project life cycle

■ To develop techniques for managing risk, specifically risks that are the primary responsibility of the project supervisor

■ To broaden the project supervisor's awareness of how the scope and nature of risk management may vary based on project contracting method, team strengths and weaknesses, and means and methods

To Get Ready for Session 3

Read Session 3 and complete any preparatory assignments given by your instructor. Spend some time thinking about the types of risk with which your company must deal. Create a list of construction project issues that you think create the biggest obstacles to completing a project safely, on time, and within budget.

The Project Team's Role in Risk Control

To control risk on a construction project, the project team must:

■ Understand the contract and the scope of work

■ Establish early in the project the level of documentation required, based on the anticipated potential risk and type of delivery system/ contract in use

■ Document project activities

■ Constantly check job progress, production, and quality and conditions for variations or deviations from the originally contracted work

- Keep logs of important conversations, including phone logs, meeting minutes, and notes on field visits by project managers or designers

- Keep an up-to-date schedule and keep relevant members of the project team aware of it

- Discuss any potentially significant impact with project management

- Intensify the documentation effort when necessary to control large risks

When carrying out these functions, the project team must remain as objective and honest as possible. Falsifying information or generating slanted data does not help recover losses, and may even lead to criminal prosecution and the necessity of awarding civil damages. Remember, it is tough enough to win a lawsuit or be successful in negotiations when you are totally in the right and accurately documented. To be only partially right with spotty, falsified or extremely biased documentation makes success unachievable. (Success, in this case, is recovering all costs and expenses rightfully due the contractor, or associated with the defense against others' unjust claims against the contractor.)

General Sources of Risk

In any project delivery system, the construction contractor is exposed to a variety of risks from different sources. The type of delivery system used may increase or decrease the degree of risk within broad categories, but the overall nature of risk is largely determined by contract terms and conditions unique to each project. In the following section, we will describe four broad categories of risk in general, and then narrow the discussion to project-specific sources of risk. Then we will further narrow our discussion to project risks typically assigned to the field. However, it is important to remember that the project manager and the project supervisor must work together to effectively manage risk on a project, regardless of the contract terms or delivery system utilized.

Money

Every construction project carries financial risk for all partners. The project can end up costing more than the owner had expected, and therefore may not be profitable (e.g., an apartment complex may cost more to build than can be recovered in monthly rental payments). The contractor and subcontractors may not be able to complete the work within the budgeted labor hours, resulting in reduced margins or even monetary losses. Material prices can escalate rapidly and unexpectedly after the contract is signed, resulting in lost profits. The designer can end up using more hours than anticipated in completing the design. All partners on a project face financial risk. The degree to which each partner assumes financial risk depends on the type of delivery system and the language of the construction contract.

Time

Every construction project carries schedule risk for all partners. The project start can be delayed, moving work into winter months and extending durations of activities such as masonry or flatwork concrete. Even in summer, the contractor and subcontractor may face severe weather, which can delay the project. The architect may not be able to complete the drawings in sufficient time to meet procurement deadlines for long-lead items. The owner may face the loss of business or loss of use if the project is not completed on time (e.g., a school that is not open in time for the return of students or a shopping mall not completed in time for holiday season shopping). How schedule risk is shared among the project partners is determined by the type of delivery system and the contract language.

Design

The biggest factor in design risk is that the project will not perform the function for which it was intended. For example, a factory may be designed to produce 1,000,000 widgets a week, but can only produce 800,000 after it is completed. The factory may be profitable at 1,000,000 units per week, but lose money at 800,000 per week, which would be a loss to the owner. A design defect that results in property damage, personal injury, or death (such as a bridge collapse or mis-routed gas lines) can result in significant judgments against design firms. Contractors who knowingly install or construct an insufficient design may also be brought into the lawsuit (the legal term is to proceed with a patently obvious design error). Most of the design risk is borne by the architect and engineer in a Design-Bid-Build project. In Construction Management at-Risk, the CM may face some design risk, and in Design-Build, all design risk is taken by the Design-Build organization, which may be led by the contractor.

Quality

If poor-quality materials or workmanship are allowed on the project, its usefulness as a structure may be limited. The annual maintenance costs may be considerably higher than anticipated, making the project less attractive to the owner. Poor-quality work can also damage a designer's reputation and lead to lawsuits against the contractor. In severe cases, poor quality can result in a project that is unusable by the intended occupants, resulting in severe risk for one or more project partners.

Activity 8 involves an exercise in risk tradeoff between the general sources of risk discussed in this section. The instructions for Activity 8 are found in Worksheet 8 in the Appendix. Your instructor will tell you when to turn to WS 8 to apply what you have learned about general risk.

Safety

When construction workers use unsafe methods, or when a contractor allows unsafe conditions to persist, accidents are more likely to occur. Accidents lead to loss of time, loss of health, or in the worst case, loss of life. Aside from the ethical considerations, these types of losses expose the company to financial and schedule-related risk. The most effective method of managing safety risk is to implement a loss-reduction plan and have an ongoing safety management program.

Project-Specific Sources of Risk

As discussed in the previous session, a project life cycle extends from the owner's recognition of need (feasibility) to occupancy. In the very early stages of a project, virtually all of the risk is assumed by the owner. If the owner hires a consultant to perform a feasibility study, and the study determines that there is insufficient need to justify a new facility, the owner will not recover the cost of the feasibility study. If the feasibility study is done poorly, the owner could also over-build or under-build the project and suffer economic losses because of it.

As the project becomes more defined, the owner is able to contract with other partners on the project (such as the architect, engineer, contractor, insurance company, sureties, or bankers) to have them assume some of the risk. The point at which other project partners assume a portion of the risk depends on the contracting and delivery method used for the construction of the project.

Before we discuss how different contract types and delivery methods affect assignment of risk, let's take a brief look at the sources of risk. The major types of risk on a project are associated with various losses, including economic losses, property losses, time losses, value losses, and losses due to injury or death. The general rule of thumb is that each of the project partners is responsible for losses under its control. In other words, the contractor is responsible for its own property, the owner for its property, etc. Likewise, the architect and engineer are responsible for preventing injury and death to building occupants after completion of construction. The contractor is responsible for providing a safe workplace for the construction trades and jobsite visitors. Despite the general rule, there are exceptions in most construction projects. For instance, even though the owner technically owns all of the work it has paid for under progress payments, the contract documents usually stipulate that the contractor will insure the project in its entirety until completion.

The risks for which the builder is responsible are typically spelled out in the Supplemental, Special and General Conditions of the project specifications (Divisions 0 and 1). The Supplemental, Special, and

Activity 9 involves an exercise on risk allocation in supplemental conditions. The instructions for Activity 9 are found in Worksheet 9 in the Appendix. Your instructor will tell you when to turn to WS 9 to apply what you have learned about risk allocation.

General Conditions should be read carefully before any construction agreement is finalized, to make sure all the project partners understand the risks they will be assuming on the project. Within the General and Special Conditions, the project manager is generally concerned about insurance requirements, bonding requirements, liquidated damages clauses, allocation of risk, payment terms, errors and omissions clauses, delay claim processes, and notification language. In general, the primary areas of risk that are the project supervisor's responsibility are field labor hours and schedule maintenance (for self-performed work), worker safety, and quality of workmanship. Depending on how the project team is structured, the supervisor may have assistance from a field engineer, a safety officer, or a quality control agent in the field. With that understanding, we can identify four areas of risk that builders will encounter on most projects.

The Location of the Project

The risks for the builder can vary based on project location. For instance, projects located in high-crime districts or densely populated areas are generally more risky. Neighbors are also a risk factor. A project built in a mostly residential neighborhood where many young children play outdoors is more risky than a project located in a secured industrial park where all the neighbors will be similar industrial buildings with controlled traffic. The regulatory policies and inspection processes can also vary by location, which may pose more or less risk for the builder depending on how well the process is understood and agreed upon by all parties. Topography, climate, and soils also can influence project risks for the builder. Imagine your ability to control schedule, costs, and quality on a flat site in a dry climate with firm, well-drained subsurface soils and a constant temperature of 70 degrees. Compare that to the uncertainty you would feel about the budget or the schedule for a winter project in mountainous terrain with pockets of highly organic soils mixed between layers of rocky clay soils. The location can determine labor and material costs as well. Locations with a surplus of skilled labor and good local suppliers of high-quality materials will generally have lower costs and faster schedules than locations where skilled trade workers are in short supply
and most of the material must be transported to the site from distant suppliers.

One of the biggest risks a contractor can face is differing site conditions. The contractor can be responsible for unanticipated subsurface conditions if contract language is not included to transfer risk to the owner. If the construction documents indicate one condition, and another is discovered, then the owner is obligated to compensate the contractor for additional costs. However, if the construction documents do not call out a specific condition (as is typically the case for subsurface conditions or renovation of existing construction), then the contractor may be forced to bear the cost of additional work without compensation from the owner. Therefore, it is critically important that the project manager assess the risk of differing and unforeseen conditions and ask for inclusion of appropriate risk transfer language. If risk transfer language is not included, some bid contingency may be necessary to mitigate the risk of unforeseen conditions.

The Nature of the Project

Another risk factor the builder must consider is the type of project under construction. Under a Design-Build contract, a single firm takes on design risk, schedule risk, quality risk, and some measure of financial risk. Under a CM at-Risk project for which the CM is not performing much of the work itself, the CM may face only schedule risk, quality risk and some cost risk. The point to remember is that each project will have a unique risk profile depending on how the contract has been structured.

Other project factors that will affect the builder's risk:

■ Very complex projects like hospitals and process-piping plants are inherently riskier than warehouses and distribution centers

■ The type of technology to be incorporated into the project (automated conveying systems, special fire-protection systems, etc.) will expose the builder to more risk, especially schedule risk if the technology is untested

■ The types of finishes and materials incorporated into the project. Stone that is sourced from non-U.S. quarries exposes the builder to schedule risk because of the long shipping time and inability to control production schedules in many countries of the world. Very high-end finishes such as carved wood and three-dimensional or template work will be riskier for builders to manage

■ The type of mechanical, plumbing, electrical, and conveyance system will alter the risk profile for the builder

The Construction Process

Risks for the builder do not abate with the construction process. On projects that need government appropriations to be passed before each phase, the certainty of project funding is frequently a concern. An owner's inability to secure interim financing for a private project may slow the start of a project as well. The timetable for completion, the sequencing of tasks, and the release of long-lead-time items for purchase are concerns. Fast-track projects, where construction starts before design is completed, are risky if they are not properly managed and coordinated. In addition, the availability and reliability of pre-construction information is a risk factor on many projects, especially remodeling and rehabilitation projects, or earthwork projects requiring substantial excavation. In general, the more unknowns there are when construction starts, the more risk is faced by all project members.

One of the major issues facing contractors today is how to deal with uninsurable risk and the exposure to financial catastrophe that comes from litigation for excluded conditions. Recent examples of uninsurable risk include

■ Asbestos

■ Mold

■ Volatile organic compounds (VOCs) from curing paint, adhesives, and solvents

A contractor's ability to control these types of risk is somewhat limited. The best practices are to be vigilant in reviewing evolving legal trends and proceedings, to use well-established vendors and subcontractors, and to pay close attention to installation procedures and quality of workmanship.

The Project Organization

The sophistication and knowledge of the owner, designer, subcontractors, and consultants will play a role in defining the risk of a project. An owner or designer with a dense, hierarchical bureaucracy can make it difficult for the builder to get timely answers or clarity of direction on Design-Bid-Build jobs. Lean organizational structures with well-defined project roles make for better decision making, and result in better risk management.

Risks Primarily Assigned to the Field

Now that we have discussed general and project-specific risks, let's turn our attention to the areas of risk that are the primary responsibility of the project supervisor: safety, quality, and field labor productivity.

Safety Requirements

As with other support activities, planning for safety is often ignored until safety (or the lack of it) has become a problem. Just as in planning any other project activity, the more effective the plan, the safer the project will be. You should fold planning for safety into all the operations on the project. This is clearly one of your most critical responsibilities as a field supervisor. Putting a safety plan together requires three activities:

■ Continued inspection of the project for safety hazards

■ Planning the incorporation of safety features and devices such as handrails and nets

■ Administering an effective ongoing safety program, including holding safety meetings and processing the required paperwork

All these phases of the safety plan should be reviewed and planned for by the team before job start-up. Not only will this ensure a safer project, but it also will reduce the cost of safety by planning it into the project ahead of time. On a Design-Build or CM at-Risk project, the field supervisor can give input during the design phase to improve constructability and design-for-safety issues.

The project supervisor needs to be current with OSHA regulations, and should know the company policy or philosophy regarding OSHA inspections. More information is available on the OSHA web site at www.osha.gov.

Quality Assurance and Customer Satisfaction

In order for a company to remain on invited bidders' lists and pre-qualification lists, and to secure repeat clients for negotiated work, it must maintain its reputation for quality and ability to satisfy clients. Because long-term revenue generation is a risk factor for the financial viability of the company, quality assurance and customer satisfaction fall under the area of risk management.

The project team should also plan for quality assurance and customer satisfaction. The project agreement and construction documents will identify the level of quality required on the project. Just as with safety, the assignment of responsibility and authority relevant to quality control should be clearly understood and planned for. Plan for quality control and emphasize its importance, or you could face major problems as the project develops.

If the customer asks for changes, there may be a change order to your contract. As a supervisor, you probably are not responsible for making sure a change order is issued, but it is your job to know about it and to notify your project manager of the situation. You also must know the requirements for notifying and executing change order work. If you are not careful, you could do extra work at the owner's request and not get paid for it.

If the project team feels a significant impact has occurred—or that a potential negotiation or lawsuit may result—the team should immediately ensure that every aspect of the situation is properly documented, as discussed in Session 2. The team members should also consult with project management. The documentation becomes a critical resource in the event of subsequent negotiations or litigation. Remember, poor documentation will weaken any case—even a case in which the facts were strong and positive.

Labor Cost Control

Project labor cost control is one of the most important control systems within a construction company. Some labor cost control systems are complex; others are relatively simple. However, most systems are alike in that they report costs incurred and work completed (units in place), and compare this information with the original estimate. The units in place divided by labor hours or labor costs generates a productivity report.

Before a cost control system is set up, decisions must be made about what is to be included in each budget, what work should be charged to each activity (or code) in the budget, whether labor cost includes taxes, etc. Everyone who will be filling out timecards and making quantity reports must fully understand the cost control system.

The basic information produced by the system comes from the time-cards, which show hours worked, and the production report, which shows total units produced. During the step called report processing, all this information is assembled and analyzed.

Again, the project team has the most important step in this process. It directs changes in the labor activities as necessary. Without these changes, this whole process is a labor cost reporting system but has nothing to do with control. Controlling labor costs and productivity requires accurate information, reliable projections of cost *and* actions to correct problems if profit erosion is forecast.

An Overview of Risk Management

Ron Prichard and Steve Davis, working with the Risk Management Committee of the Associated General Contractors of America (AGC), have prepared an excellent resource manual on risk management entitled *Risk Management, Insurance & Bonding for the Construction Industry*, AGC Publication # 3520. The following is an excerpt from the introduction to that publication that gives an excellent overview of the changing nature of risk management, and why contractors must change their philosophies of risk.

Overview of Construction Risk Management

The construction industry has grown to recognize the relationship between risk management and sustained profits. Now considered a serious management initiative, risk management in today's insurance market requires "beyond-the-edge" thinking if a contractor is to maintain a competitive advantage. The risk management methodologies outlined here offer contractors the means to generate additional earnings while reducing and leveling out losses.

It's apparent that lean and fit organizations represent a platform for long-term survival. This is true for any business enterprise, especially contractors. Additionally, contractors have also recognized the importance of imagination, vision, and competitive information if they are to succeed in a global market. In this respect, risk management has emerged as an additional source of creativity and vision that is enhancing the competitive edge of many contractors, despite the conditions of the construction insurance market. At long last, managing risk has been transformed from a once-a-year insurance bidding frenzy with the local agent into a serious profit initiative having the ability to boost returns, reinforce quality, reduce costs, and permanently change the way construction firms compete. In today's environment, risk management and management practices are integrated and support identical goals: increased profits. They have changed from buyers of insurance to sellers of risk.

This knowledge shift of recognizing and managing risk has occurred as a result of the construction industry's enlightened perspective on risk and its integration with the overall cost to fund losses. This cost is no longer viewed as an expense item, but as an opportunity to make a reasonable return on risk dollars that currently are being consumed to protect and preserve the assets of the construction firm.

The risk management technology available today has long passed the traditional insurance policy buyer in favor of sophisticated construction firms, large and small, that are astute enough to put each and every *risk* dollar to work for the company, generating additional earnings while leveling out the losses on bad projects.

The insurance industry has changed dramatically over the past few years. Fueled by consolidations in the insurance company and the broker ranks, fluctuations in the financial markets, customers demands, and competition, contractors are beginning to partner with specialists, understanding the value that exists with professionals who are skilled at designing a risk management program that effectively manages the cost of risk.

Every construction project faces a full spectrum of risks. The level, depth, and scope of those risks vary from project to project and are tied directly to the context and content of the project. The context relates to the environment in which the project will be built, such as geography, owner, regulatory environment, labor force, transportation, etc. The content of the project relates to the physical elements of the project itself, such as intended purposes, budget, materials, etc.

Contractors' understanding of the areas that have an impact on costs has broadened dramatically over the past few years. For example, the following areas affect costs:

Workers Compensation Losses
- Medical costs
- Indemnity payments
- Expenses for legal, witnesses, and adjusting

Pollution and environmental costs
Risk management administrative costs
Risk transfer costs for insurance
Premium taxes
Safety management services
In-house claims personnel costs

Liability Losses
- Damages for bodily injury
- Damages for property damage
- Litigation expenses
- Adjusting

Deductibles and self-insurance
Broker and agent fees/commissions
Uncovered losses/legal expenses
Interest rate and exchange rates
Surety bond premiums and credit risk costs
Performance losses not covered

Property losses
- Direct losses
- Indirect losses
- Business interruption

Subcontract certificate exposures
Indirect cost of claims
Educational programs and training costs
Productivity of labor crews
Management philosophies on risk

Current insurance underwriting methodology generally is structured around lagging indicators, such as historical losses, litigation, and court decisions. Insurance coverage is designed around events that have already occurred. In effect, the insurance industry has traveled down the highway with eyes focused on the rearview mirror, unable to anticipate the new dangers that lurk ahead. This has allowed pieces of the risk puzzle to remain unidentified and mismeasured, and in essence, handled by default. This default management feeds on hope, luck, and chance. And in today's competitive environment, hope, luck, and chance are poor strategies for generating lasting profits.

Relying solely on traditional methods of risk management, that is, buying insurance, compels contractors to be reactive to the insurance market cycles. Things will never remain stable for an extended period of time. Volatility is a characteristic element of a dynamic and fluid world. Changes in markets, competitors, consolidations, and other factors in an evolving economy demand that businesses make adjustments and innovate—now.

This risk management approach recognizes that staying in the game is difficult. Going out of business can occur more rapidly than ever. In this environment, what one doesn't know can actually hurt; therefore, contractors remain committed to capitalizing on new methodologies that improve their ability to manage and finance risk. Contractors now understand that being a buyer of insurance is an extremely expensive technique and they should capitalize on the insurance market only as a ballast tool in equalizing cost over a period of time.

Below is a table comparing "risk management" to "insurance management." Through the years, contractors have improved their focus on safety management; however, much of the impetus for this focus has grown from compliance with regulations. While such regulations are important, they should not become the benchmark of practices. Our aim should be much higher. The potential will create new practices that will have long-term payoffs.

Consider the following:

"World-class contracting organizations do not use best practices
. . . . they create them."

RISK MANAGEMENT	INSURANCE MANAGEMENT
• Active	• Reactive
• Dynamic	• Passive
• Risk/protection oriented	• Security oriented
• Financially/analytically oriented	• Administratively oriented
• Seeks responsibility	• Seeks safety
• Broad-based—includes safety, claims analysis, insurance	• Narrow in scope
• Creative	• Responsible to others
• Must be involved in the construction activity of the company	• May be involved or may rely on others

Risk cannot be avoided on a construction project. However, there are several options available to contractors that want to manage the risk of construction so that the company is protected from losses that could put it out of business. In general, the contractor can try to get one of the other project partners to take the risk. Contractual language is the method for assigning risk to another party, and we will not concern ourselves with that type of risk management tactic, as it is usually the job of top management and the legal team to work out risk assignments. For risk assigned to the contractor, the techniques for managing risk are:

1) To pass the risk along to someone with technical expertise or specialty equipment better suited for the task (subcontracting)

2) To pay a professional risk-taker to bear the risk (bonding and insurance)

3) To carefully manage the work yourself (self-perform)

Each of these techniques will be discussed briefly in the following sections.

Bonding and Sureties

Sureties are companies that are paid to take risk. If the owner requires it as part of the bid or negotiating process, a contractor will ask a surety company to guarantee the quality of its work to the owner (the performance bond) and will also ask the surety to indemnify the owner against claims if the contractor fails to pay its vendors, suppliers, and subcontractors (the payment bond). Bonding a project is one method for passing along some of the quality risk and financial risk to a professional risk manager.

The contractor's relationship with the surety is an important one if the contractor does a large volume of public work, where bonding is usually required. The relationship is built on the experience and history of the contractor and its management personnel. Any single project forms a piece of the profitability picture for your company. If a company is not profitable or marginally profitable over a number of projects, the surety company that issues the bonds may increase the amount it charges the contractor for the bonds, or reduce its bonding capacity. Therefore, each individual project contributes not only to the current, or short-term, profitability, but also plays an important role in the long-term cost of doing business, and therefore the ongoing, overall profitability of the company.

Overall company profitability and financial management affects bonding rates. Rates are established as a percent of volume, so the cost of bonding is usually spread across all construction projects as a percent of contract value. The cost of bonding a project can vary from 0.5% to 2.0% or more.

Bonding rates affect overall company competitiveness in the bidding market. This is why it is important to keep accurate historical cost records and strive to control scope on projects. For example, if a company has a 1% lower bonding rate, it can bid $100,000 lower on a $10 million dollar project with the same overall cost structure.

Insurance

Insurance companies are similar to sureties in that they are professional risk-takers. The primary difference is that sureties are paid to guarantee the performance and payment of the contractor, and any claim is paid to the project owner. Insurance companies are also paid to take risk, but they pay the contractor for losses they may incur on the project, whereas sureties pay the owner for the contractor's failure to perform. These contractor losses can be property losses (whether the property is owned by the contractors or others), worker injuries and loss of life, and the loss of partially completed work on the project. Just as project profitability relates to the overall financial health of a company, any single project represents a small portion of the company's overall safety and (insurance) loss picture.

Your company's safety performance and loss history affects the cost to the company of insurance, especially in the area of worker injury and loss of life. The company's loss history is compared to industry-wide baselines by worker category to establish a MOD rate, and that is used to calculate the cost of insurance to be paid by the contractor. Just as with bond rates, the cost of insurance is usually charged to the contractor based on overall volume, and then charged to individual projects based on contract size. Insurance can cost between 2 and 6 % of contract value. Just as with bond rates, a company with a very high MOD rate may be at a significant competitive disadvantage if it must pay 4% of project costs for insurance when bidding against a company that only has to pay 2.5%.

Construction companies cannot sign a contract without proof of insurance, and the specific requirements for insurance are usually spelled out in the general conditions. Therefore, a construction company has limited flexibility in changing the amount of coverage and types of insurance it carries. In many ways, insurance rates represent a cost of doing business (as opposed to a project cost) and are difficult to control. That is why safety and property protection are so critical to the long-term profitability of a company. The only way to control insurance costs is by lowering loss rates and implementing better loss-prevention plans. As a result, your company will be more competitive in the bidding market.

Subcontracted Work

One of the primary benefits of subcontracting portions of the project is that it locks in the cost of doing work and shifts the risk of labor cost overruns, material price increases and (some) of the safety/quality responsibility to other firms. However, the general contractor or design-builder also forfeits some return or profit potential when work is subcontracted to others. In general, work is subcontracted when it requires special expertise, special equipment, special vendor arrangements, or specialty labor classes. Therefore, firms that act primarily as subcontractors to general contractors are frequently called "specialty" subcontractors.

Subcontracting by the general contractor can alleviate some of the GC's risk associated with labor and material costs, but the overall project responsibility remains with the general contractor. Therefore, subcontracting carries some performance risks for the general contractor. If a subcontractor fails to properly staff the job, the work for which it is responsible may progress too slowly and cause the entire project to fall behind schedule. If a subcontractor uses inferior products or inexperienced workers, poor-quality work could result. If a subcontractor were to default on its payment obligations to its vendors or second tier subcontractors, this too would be the general contractor's problem. In any of these situations, the general contractor would have to take steps to get the project back on schedule, bring defective work back to specifications, or ensure payment to vendors and suppliers.

If a general contractor has a sufficient volume of work, subcontracting can be an effective strategy for maximizing margins. The company can assign its own employees the work with the highest profit potential, while subcontracting out the lower-profit tasks.

Another benefit of subcontracting is that it helps reduce OSHA and Workmen's Compensation exposures for the general contractor. These benefits are somewhat limited by the fact that safety on a project is the overall responsibility of the ~~project manager~~ General Contractor, but the risk can be spread across more companies if subcontractors are utilized.

Self-Performed Work

When a contractor decides to keep some of the tasks for itself, it takes the risk of labor cost and productivity as well as material prices and availability. Therefore, contractors generally self-perform work with which they are familiar in markets they understand very well. When self-performing work, the contractor's final cost of a section of work (slab-on-grade, CMU walls, etc.) will depend upon labor productivity, and may vary from the estimated cost of the work included in the bid. Positive variances increase margins while negative variances cause margins (and profitability) to decrease.

When general contractors or design-builders self-perform, they have greater control over the progress of the work, the overall schedule and the quality of workmanship and material. However, if the prime contractor fails to properly staff the job, the entire project could fall behind schedule. Poor-quality work could result if the prime contractor uses inferior products or inexperienced workers. In addition, a prime contractor may default on its obligations to its vendors or subcontractors.

On projects using a cost-plus contract, self-performing work may enhance job profit. Many cost-plus contracts allow for higher profit-and-overhead markup on self-performed work than on subcontracted work. If properly managed, this can result in higher project margin.

The more work that is self-performed, the more employees a contractor will have on a project. This increases OSHA and Workmen's Compensation exposures for the general contractor.

Another important consideration in deciding to self-perform or sub-contract is to consider the image and perception of quality. Self-performing high-quality work will increase a company's reputation for craftsmanship and thereby improve the chances for repeat business. However, if a company chooses to self-perform unfamiliar work, or if the company over-commits its labor resources, the resulting work may be of low quality and create a perception in the marketplace of low-quality workmanship.

Site Management

As mentioned above, subcontracting can reduce a general contractor's exposure to certain types of risk and losses on a project. However, the general rule of law is that the general contractor or design-builder is liable for anything that happens onsite. In addition to the risks discussed above, there are other loss exposures or risk areas, including:

■ Injuries to the public

■ Damage to property of others

■ Environmental contamination

■ Soil erosion and runoff

■ Losses due to theft

■ Stored materials

■ Traffic control

■ Utility problems

An effective site management plan can help you manage the risks associated with these factors. Site management will be discussed in detail in Session 6.

To Implement What You Have Learned

Write down one concept or idea from Session 3 that you think every-one in your company should know to improve the way your company does business.

Write down one thing you learned in Session 3 that you think should be included in your company's project management training program for entry-level project managers.

Write down one thing you learned in Session 3 that you intend to use on your next project to make the project more successful.

Before the next session, develop the three ideas you listed above into a short memo, and schedule a meeting with your sponsor to discuss your ideas and develop an action plan. Remember that when trying something new, it is important to have the support of your sponsor and other champions in the organization, and to make small, incremental changes. Your sponsor has received an executive summary of this session and will be expecting your report and your phone call to set up a meeting with him or her to discuss your ideas for the company.

If you would like to learn more about risk management, we suggest you register for STP Unit 7, *Accident Prevention and Loss Control* and Unit 6, *Understanding and Managing Project Costs.*

SESSION 3

SESSION 3

Notes

Planning the Work

Goal and Performance Objectives of Session 4

Goal: After this session, you will understand how the construction work is planned during the preconstruction phase of the project.

Performance objectives:

- To learn how preconstruction planning is defined and how it should be done

- To learn what planning tasks are required of the project supervisor

- To learn the basics of site planning in preparation for a future session

- To learn how to set up a system to manage information

- To learn basic scheduling techniques

To Get Ready for Session 4

Read Session 4 and complete any preparatory assignments given by your instructor.

Preconstruction Phase Planning and Management

For the purposes of this session, the "preconstruction phase" consists of the time between the signing of the owner agreement and the notice to proceed. On a negotiated project, this period may be several months long. At the other extreme, it may be as little as a few days on a hard-bid project. Either way, there are key functions that must be addressed in order to ensure a smooth, successful project:

1. Preconstruction project planning

2. Preconstruction site planning

3. Preconstruction information planning

4. Preconstruction project scheduling

Each of these functions will be discussed in more detail in the pages that follow. When the preconstruction phase is too short to allow full development of all of these areas, the project supervisor should consider delaying the start of work a few days in order to complete the appropriate planning. A well-thought-out project plan will more than make up for the few days lost at the beginning of the project, because it may save thousands of dollars in overall construction cost.

SESSION 4

Activity 10 involves an exercise in breaking down the scope of work into manageable units for planning. The instructions for Activity 10 are found in Worksheet 10 in the Appendix. Your instructor will tell you when to turn to WS 10 to apply what you have learned about understanding scope of work in project planning.

If delaying the start of a project even a few days is unacceptable to the owner or the contractor's upper management, you still should complete the project plan, even if you have to do so during the clearing and grubbing or demolition. The main point is to complete the plan!

Preconstruction Project Planning

The basics of project planning consist of answering the what, how, who, why, where and when questions for the project:

- What do you need to do?

- How are you going to do it?

- Who is going to do it?

- Why are you assigning the work the way you are?

- Where on the project are you going to work first?

- When are you going to do the work?

What you need to do is usually dictated by the contract documents and the drawings and specifications defining the scope of work. Care must be taken to consider items modified by addenda (plural form of "addendum"), supplemental instructions, and change orders to the contract. While a general contractor, design-builder or construction manager is usually responsible for the entire scope of work, it is important to know what work is being done under separate contracts with the owner or by the owner organization. If you work for a subcontractor or a separate prime, your scope will be significantly less than the entire scope of the project. You must have a thorough understanding of your firm's responsibilities. Understanding the project scope forms a basis for determining the work tasks for project scheduling, which will be covered later in this session.

After you understand the scope of the work, you must decide how you are going to complete the work. Most construction contracts leave the means and methods (the "how") up to the contractor. There are many factors to consider in determining how to do the work. Soil conditions, weather conditions, labor or material availability, and schedule constraints are but a few of the considerations. In addition, your previous experience, as well as that of your employer, will influence how you choose to do the work. If you choose to subcontract the work, you likely will give up some of the control of how the work is completed.

Several options are available in deciding who will do the work. The most fundamental decision is whether to self-perform or subcontract it. If you choose to self-perform, you need to decide who the crew foreman and crew members will be and how many there will be in the crew. It is helpful to delegate specific responsibilities to each foreman and crew team. If you subcontract the work, you will either already have subcontractor bids to review (in the case of a hard-bid project), or you may need to solicit subcontractor quotes (in the case of a negotiated project).

The options available in terms of **how** and **who** will drive the decision process and help clarify **why** you choose the way you do. The overriding factor in making the **how** and **who** decisions is risk management. If, for example, you self-perform the work, you have more control over schedule but run the risk of exceeding the estimate. If you subcontract the work to a reliable firm, then you lose some schedule control but reduce the risk of exceeding your estimate (assuming a lump-sum subcontract arrangement). In nearly every project there will be resource constraints, such as a lack of skilled craftworkers. Prioritize which tasks get the necessary resources when the demand for resources exceeds the supply. If you can explain **why** you made the allocations, it will improve your working relationship with the owner, the subcontractors, and your own crew.

Determining the **where** and the **when** is part of the scheduling function, which will be covered in detail later in this session.

Preconstruction Site Planning

Site planning usually comes first, as the contractor needs to know where the office trailer(s), storage trailer(s), portable toilets, etc. will be set up and where workers will be able to park. The location of existing utilities (if any) helps determine where to place the office trailer. Otherwise, it is important to locate the office trailer near visitor parking and close to the worksite, as field foremen will be using the trailer amenities such as plan tables and fax machines.

In site planning you also must consider the approach to the project. For example, storage trailers should be located near the work for which they are storing tools and/or materials, but out of the way of other work to be done. Storage trailers are often used as mobile billboards, so locating the storage trailer to maximize visibility from the highway is often a consideration.

Other considerations include delivery routing and lay-down areas for temporary material storage. In general, the smaller the site, the more planning will be needed for truck circulation and allocation of storage areas. Security fencing and gates to control public access or to provide labor access need to be carefully thought out to protect the public and to minimize travel time for employees between work and parking areas. In addition, plan to place temporary utility routing out of the

Activity 11 involves an exercise in preconstruction planning. The instructions for Activity 11 are found in Worksheet 11 in the Appendix. Your instructor will tell you when to turn to WS 11 to apply what you have learned about preconstruction planning.

SESSION 4

way of construction activities, but make sure it provides utilities where they are needed.

Detailed site layout planning will be addressed in Session 6.

Preconstruction Information Planning

In addition to managing resources and risks, competent supervisors need to be able to effectively manage information. Some information, such as daily reports and timesheets, will be generated by the project supervisor. Other information, such as change order estimates and clarification requests, will be generated by others with the assistance of the project supervisor. Additional information will be generated by others and given to the project supervisor to assist in getting the project completed.

There are many options available to help manage information: job files, project websites, trailer set-up and computer set-up are only a few examples. It is important for the field office to have a filing system that is similar to the home office's filing system. The contents do not need to mirror each other directly, but it helps if the project supervisor and project manager have a common framework for referring to documents. Project websites are a relatively new tool, but are available to facilitate information exchange between co-workers. Websites also can enable quicker communication between owner, designer and contractor teams.

Even the arrangement of the furniture in the job trailer can facilitate the management of information. In addition to file cabinets or bins, there should be a system for organizing drawings, specifications, shop drawings and samples. A project supervisor quickly will be buried with paper and plans if he or she doesn't take steps to effectively manage information.

Preconstruction Project Scheduling

The project schedule is the written documentation of the project planning. The schedule will address the following factors:

- Sequencing of work
- Duration of activities
- Predecessor and successor activities
- Resource loading/responsibility
- Critical path calculations
- Contract compliance (milestone dates)

The project schedule is a "living" document that requires periodic updating during construction. There are several accepted techniques for scheduling; indeed, scheduling is the subject of entire textbooks! The most important scheduling techniques include Gantt charts and precedence diagramming. Gantt charts are simply time-scaled bars that represent the duration of an individual activity.

Precedence diagramming is a technique that considers predecessor and successor activities. Predecessor activities are those that must be completed before a given activity can start. Successor activities are those that cannot be started until the given activity is completed. For example, the predecessor activity "pour footings" must precede the successor activity "form foundation walls." A precedence diagram is similar to a flowchart, in that it consists of a box for each activity, and the various activities are connected by arrows at the start and finish of each activity to indicate predecessor and successor relationships.

The precedence diagram is not time-scaled, and the Gantt chart does not show activity relationships. However, many scheduling software products do allow the user to print a diagram that combines the strengths of both systems. The user can view what looks like a Gantt chart, but it also shows arrows for the various activity relationships.

The project schedule is developed using the work tasks identified in the **what** portion of the planning exercise. First crew sizes are assigned to each task. The quantity of work is determined from the project cost estimate and productivity information from the company's cost history. From these activity duration can be generated. Or, in the case of sub-contracted work, the subcontractor is consulted for activity durations.

Next, link all the project activities to reflect the predecessors and successors. The final step is calculating the critical path. This calculation involves analyzing the various paths through the project to determine the one with the longest duration. All activities on this path are critical. "Critical" activities are the ones that will delay the completion of the project if they are not completed within the planned duration. Say for example that the activity "pour foundation walls" is a critical activity is scheduled to take 14 days. If the activity "pour foundation walls" takes 19 days instead, the project will be delayed by five days. (When referring to "workdays," contractors usually are not including Saturdays, Sundays and holidays.)

The project supervisor will use the overall project schedule as a guide-line for developing two-week look-ahead schedules. These schedules should be distributed to all parties scheduled to work in the next two weeks and should be discussed at the weekly foreman's meeting.

For more on project scheduling, please see AGC's Construction *Planning & Scheduling Manual,* Item no. 3502 in the AGC Products and Services Guide at www.agc.org/e-STORE.

Activity 12 involves an exercise in scheduling. The instructions for Activity 12 are found in Worksheet 12 in the Appendix. Your instructor will tell you when to turn to WS 12 to apply what you have learned about scheduling.

SESSION 4

SESSION 4

To Implement What You Have Learned

Write down one concept or idea from Session 4 that you think everyone in your company should know to improve the way your company does business.

Write down one thing you learned in Session 4 that you think should be included in your company's project management training program for entry-level project managers.

Write down one thing you learned in Session 4 that you intend to use on your next project to make the project more successful.

Before the next session, develop the three ideas you listed above into a short memo, and schedule a meeting with your sponsor to discuss your ideas and develop an action plan. Remember that when trying something new, it is important to have the support of your sponsor and other champions in the organization, and to make small, incremental changes. Your sponsor has received an executive summary of this session and will be expecting your report and your phone call to set up a meeting with him or her to discuss your ideas for the company.

If you would like to learn more about planning and scheduling, we suggest you register for STP Unit 5, *Planning and Scheduling.*

Working the Plan

Goal and Performance Objectives of Session 5

Goal: After this session, you will understand how to start up a project and to ensure that the field crews get the materials, equipment, and approvals they need in a timely manner.

Performance objectives:

- To learn how to mobilize and organize a project in the field

- To learn the basics of field purchasing for commodity materials

- To learn how to expedite material and equipment orders

- To learn how to manage the inspection and approval processes

- To understand the importance of keeping plans and schedules up-to-date

- To learn the basics of closing out a project in the field

To Get Ready for Session 5

Read Session 5 and complete any preparatory assignments given by your instructor.

Construction Phase Tasks

After the project plan and schedule have been developed and you have received the notice to proceed, it is time to begin work. In addition to overseeing and helping to direct the work, the project supervisor must ensure that the craftworkers performing the direct labor have the information, materials, equipment and approvals necessary to perform their jobs efficiently. These items can be addressed under the following categories:

1. Mobilization

2. Purchasing

3. Expediting

4. Approvals

5. Closeout

Activity 13 links Sessions 4 and 5 through an exercise in team planning. The instructions for Activity 13 are found in Worksheet 13 in the Appendix. Your instructor will tell you when to turn to WS 13 to apply what you have learned about team planning.

SESSION 5

You often can accelerate the project schedule by adding more workers to crews, but it is impossible for them to perform the work if the required materials and equipment are not delivered on time to the site. The project supervisor may receive assistance from the project manager, or may delegate many of these items to the project engineer, but someone must take the lead in ensuring that the workers have what they need to do their jobs.

Mobilization

Activity 14 involves an exercise in mobilization. The instructions for Activity 14 are found in worksheet 14 in the Appendix. Your instructor will tell you when to turn to WS 14 to apply what you have learned about mobilization.

Mobilization is the beginning field activity on any project. Some of the tasks that may need to be completed during mobilization:

- Identify team members (foremen, field engineer(s))
- Install temporary utility connections
- Hook-up computer data link and network
- Move-in trailers
- Installation project sign
- Erect temporary fence and gates

Together the supervisor and project manager should review the project specifications and the cost estimate to determine who (owner, contractor, other contractors, subcontractors) is responsible for temporary facilities. Often there is a distinction between who installs a temporary utility such as power to an office trailer and who pays for the electricity consumed.

The mobilization activities should be focused on setting up the infrastructure required to effectively perform the work of the project. Site layout will be addressed in detail in Session 6.

Purchasing

The project manager and project engineer (if assigned to project) often take primary responsibility for the purchasing (subcontracts and purchase orders) for the project. Nevertheless, the supervisor is at the center of many purchasing decisions and activities. Especially on a remote (in a geographic sense) project site, the supervisor will be involved in establishing local accounts for consumables such as gasoline, loose lumber, hardware, small tools, etc. In other situations, supervisors may need to become familiar with the standing purchase orders and accounts that are already available.

The supervisor must read and study the subcontracts and purchase orders written by others, comparing these to the project's scope of work. If a supervisor inadvertently has the company's workforce perform work meant for a subcontractor or other contractor, it is usually difficult to recoup satisfactory funds. If there are any "gaps" or overlaps in scope among the various subcontractors, the supervisor should notify the project manager immediately so that corrections can be made.

The supervisor's next important task is to contact all suppliers and subcontractors to obtain delivery dates for materials and equipment. It is a good idea to collect the contact information for manufacturers and sub-suppliers so that you can confirm that orders have indeed been placed and that project delivery information is correct. The supervisor must compare promised delivery dates to the project schedule and work with the various vendors and project manager to resolve any conflicts.

Supervisors may be asked to call lumber yards, ready-mix plants and other businesses to obtain unit pricing on locally available commodity items that do not need to be custom-made for the project. They may also work with the project manager (or other boss) to analyze make, rent or buy decisions on equipment such as forklifts and concrete formwork.

Expediting

Procurement

Expediting is the process of getting all the materials delivered to the jobsite on time. After the buy-out, or purchasing process, the next step from a paperwork point of view is **submittals.** Submittals are typically required by the project specifications, either to verify the design professional's material and equipment selections, to allow selection of color and finish options, or to confirm compliance with the design's intent for items such as reinforcing steel or wood roof trusses.

Ideally, the project manager and/or engineer bought out everything. However, change orders, clarifications and field conditions often require some buy-out to occur on the fly in the field. Since the project supervisor knows the project better than anyone else does at this point, he or she is sometimes called upon to work with vendors to order these items that were not apparent during the buy-out process. It is very important for the supervisor to know what has been purchased for the project, so that these overlooked items can be identified as early as possible. It is often best for the supervisor to delegate these items back to the project manager or engineer so that he or she can focus on putting work in place.

Activity 15 is an exercise in purchasing involving a "rent or buy" decision. The instructions for Activity 15 are found in Worksheet 15 in the Appendix. Your instructor will tell you when to turn to WS 15 to apply what you have learned about purchasing.

SESSION 5

SESSION 5

Activity 16 involves an exercise in purchasing and expediting. The instructions for Activity 16 are found in Worksheet 16 in the Appendix. Your instructor will tell you when to turn to WS 16 to apply what you have learned about purchasing and expediting.

While the project supervisor may not be primarily responsible for tracking submittals, he or she can often help the office in this function. The supervisor may hear concerns voiced by field crews that realize they are waiting for materials that have not been approved. Expediting submittals is often necessary to ensure that materials and equipment can be ordered with adequate lead time so that these items will arrive on the jobsite in advance of their installation. Once the submittals have been processed and approved, it is important to confirm with each subcontractor or vendor that the appropriate orders have been placed with the manufacturer or fabricator. It is sometimes advantageous to speak directly with the maker of the goods. Once shipment has been confirmed, there are various methods of tracking shipments, including "PRO" numbers and the Internet. Ronald Reagan's "trust, but verify" slogan applies to construction just as much as it does to arms reduction treaties.

The project supervisor is primarily responsible for monitoring subcontractor progress, and has the most influence in ensuring that subcontractors perform. Some non-performing subcontractors may offer excuses, but it is the supervisor's job to dispel excuses. Sometimes excuses are legitimate, and the supervisor must determine who is delaying the work. Is it the design professional's inadequate response to a request for information? Is stored material from another trade in the way? Is it the failure of the contractor's office to issue a subcontractor change order? The supervisor must find out what the holdup is and who is causing it, then tactfully address the delay.

Approvals

We have already discussed the review and approval of submittals. There are several other related issues, such as inspections and testing. EPA and OSHA are two federal agencies that concern themselves with construction projects.

Inspections are numerous in construction. Governmental agencies, as well as design professionals, often require inspections. The best way to determine which inspections are required is to thoroughly review the specifications as well as the building permit. The building permit will usually detail what the building code official needs to inspect; for example, the footings before the concrete is poured. The specifications will describe what the design professional, the owner, or their designated testing agency will need to inspect or test. A design professional may want to see and approve a mock-up of a masonry wall before masonry starts. An owner may want to confirm that the color scheme for pipe-painting is consistent with the rest of the plant. The testing agency may be asked to take slump tests and cylinders from each concrete pour. The project supervisor must know what inspections are required and take steps to schedule these at the right times so as to facilitate job progress.

In recent years, the EPA has instituted stormwater runoff standards for construction sites. Permitting, planning and physical barriers are now required on projects exceeding a certain number of acres. You should check with your project manager to determine whether these standards apply to your project. If they do, you will probably be in charge of making sure that the barriers remain in place throughout the construction period.

We all know that OSHA can show up unannounced on our jobsites at any time. The project supervisor usually will be the point of contact for the OSHA representative. It is important to know what your company's policy is regarding OSHA inspections. In some jurisdictions (there is either a state program or the federal program), you may be allowed to ask the inspector to wait while your company's safety director comes to the site to accompany the inspector. Safety is covered in depth in Unit 7 of the STP series.

Updating

A big part of "working the plan" involves updating the plan (schedule, budget, material quantity estimates, etc.). Several factors cause plans to change on construction projects, including weather, labor conditions, incomplete or conflicting design information, or owner's changes in scope. The project supervisor must update the plan to keep information current and expectations realistic. Some of the updates may even be spelled out in the supplemental and general conditions as contractual requirements. For instance, many projects have clauses in the supplemental general conditions requiring the contractor to submit updated schedules on a periodic schedule (every two weeks, monthly, etc.). Corporate policy may include a monthly budget update for the top executives in the company. Changing or unexpected site conditions (such as heavy snowfall, or high water tables in spring) may result in the need for a different site layout and truck routing plan.

The reasons for changing the plan are many and have a variety of sources (the contract, Mother Nature, the home office). One thing is certain on a construction project—some things will not go as planned. Because of this, project supervisors need to update the project plan frequently, and communicate these updates to the project team. The frequency and formality of the updates can vary from project to project, but the need for continual review of the original plan is constant on every job.

Closeout

Quickly and successfully closing out a project is almost as important as the actual construction of the project. When you consider that the retainage on the project is often more than the contractor's profit, being able to close out the project and have the final payment request approved is a vital part of overall contractor success. While it may not be common, it is possible to have final payment delayed for months or even years due to lack of attention to detail during closeout.

Successful closeout of a project is similar to the construction phase. It takes a unified and coordinated effort of the contractor's office, project supervisor, subcontractors and suppliers, design professional and owner. Usually the project supervisor is at first focused on completing the final inspections with government authorities, but the completion of the punch list is not far behind. The project supervisor also will assist with any owner training required.

Another way the supervisor can help is with the identification, collection and proper transmission of any attic stock items to the owner. "Attic stock" is simply extra materials and spare parts kept for future owner maintenance or repair work. "Proper transmission" means that the project supervisor must carefully document everything that is turned over to the owner. The owner signs a transmittal indicating receipt. As the owner is often going through a hectic move-in process at this point, it is very important to be able to document who received attic stock, in case it is misplaced or inadvertently discarded.

The supervisor will also be called upon to work with the project engineer and the various subcontractors on the project to coordinate a set of "as-built" drawings. These drawings are not to be drawn at the end of the project, but rather developed over the course of the project to document specific routings of concealed items, such as piping and conduit. The project specifications will often state what form these record drawings must take. CAD or reproducible drawings are sometimes required. It is best to identify the requirements for the as-builts before construction begins, so that the proper information is recorded in the proper format as the work progresses.

The project manager, engineer and coordinator will often work from the office to obtain operation and maintenance data; warranties and guarantees; and final lien waivers and pay requests or pay applications. The project supervisor and manager should coordinate efforts so that each subcontractor is presented with a full list of requirements for closing out the project. Closeout of the project is a crucial part of working the plan, and closeout requires a coordinated effort of the field and office.

To Implement What You Have Learned

Write down one concept or idea from Session 5 that you think everyone in your company should know to improve the way your company does business.

Write down one thing you learned in Session 5 that you think should be included in your company's project management training program for entry-level project managers.

Write down one thing you learned in Session 5 that you intend to use on your next project to make the project more successful.

Before the next session, develop the three ideas you listed above into a short memo, and schedule a meeting with your sponsor to discuss your ideas and develop an action plan. Remember that when trying something new, it is important to have the support of your sponsor and other champions in the organization, and to make small, incremental changes. Your sponsor has received an executive summary of this session and will be expecting your report and your phone call to set up a meeting with him or her to discuss your ideas for the company.

If you would like to learn more about the construction phase tasks, especially as they pertain to general and specialty contractor interaction, we suggest you register for STP Unit 10, *General and Specialty Contractor Dynamics.*

Notes

Session 6

Managing Methods and Materials

Goal and Performance Objectives of Session 6

Goal: After this session, you will better understand methods selection and materials management.

Performance objectives:

- To learn the details of site layout

- To understand factors influencing equipment selection

- To learn material handling, storage and protection techniques

- To be able to analyze prefabrication vs. onsite fabrication options

To Get Ready for Session 6

Read Session 6 and complete any preparatory assignments given by your instructor.

Site Layout

Site layout involves determining how the space on the construction site will be allocated. As mentioned in Session 4, the site planning is usually one of the first steps in planning the execution of the project. In this part of the process the contractor figures out where to place office trailer(s), storage trailer(s), portable toilets, lay-down areas, parking for employees and visitors, stockpiles, dumpsters, break areas, security fences and gates, project signs, temporary utilities and field fabrication areas. On a greenfield project, the contractor often has much flexibility in site layout; however, for a remodeling or addition project, the contractor must work around the owner's existing operations. Accommodating the customer's use of the site increases the challenge of generating an efficient site-use plan.

Office trailers should be placed close to the work area to minimize the time field personnel must spend walking back and forth to the office; however, the placement of the field office must not interfere with any of the work. There are also advantages in placing the office trailer close to the security gate (if present) or entrance to the site so that visitors may easily check in with the project supervisor or attend meetings in

SESSION 6

the trailer without interfering with production activities on the site. The field office will need, at a minimum, temporary electric power and telephone service. The tie-in location for these utilities must be considered when locating the field office, to facilitate hook-up. It is also important to minimize the number of trailer moves that will be required, as it is often costly to unhook and reconnect these utilities. (Temporary utilities were also discussed in Session 4).

Many contractors use their job trailers to advertise the company. Locating the trailer at a point on the site that is clearly visible from the adjacent thoroughfares has its advantages. If you can find a location that is illuminated at night, or flood the trailer with temporary lighting, the advertising works around the clock. Nighttime lighting also deters thieves, as do high-quality locks and burglar bars or screens over the windows. Many subcontractors want to bring trailers onto the site. The project supervisor should be as accommodating as possible in order to foster teamwork on the project, but whether a subcontractor can be allocated trailer space on the site is ultimately decided by the project leaders.

Portable toilets should be located close to the work, break areas and office trailers. The required number of portable toilets is determined by the number of workers on the site, per OSHA regulations. Separate facilities for male and female employees are often required, as are handicapped-accessible units. Depending upon the nature of the work, particularly in situations involving abatement of hazardous materials, wash facilities may be required so that the employees can cleanse their hands and face before eating. Some abatement activities may require change rooms and showers. Temporary toilets should be regularly inspected for graffiti that may be offensive to other employees and create a hostile work environment. If present, such graffiti should be removed immediately. Employees' break areas should be located as close to the work as possible to maximize labor efficiency.

Like the office trailer, storage trailers can be used for advertising. Storage trailers are used to store everything—tools and equipment, concrete blankets, custom casework, wood doors. Since storage trailers are often purchased second-hand with more than a few problems, care must be taken to ensure that materials that must be kept dry are kept in trailers with sound roofs! Storage should be kept as close as possible to the location at which the tools will be used or materials will be installed. A large portion of the inefficiency in construction operations stems from workers needing to walk long distances for tools and materials.

Lay-down areas are often insufficient, especially on building projects, and are almost non-existent on high rise projects in urban areas. There is often fierce competition among trades for lay-down space. Special care should be taken to secure materials that have significant scrap value such as copper wire, aluminum and steel. When scrap steel pricing is high, it is not unthinkable for bar joists to be stolen and sold for scrap. Protection from the elements is another concern for materials stored in lay-down areas.

Another source of production inefficiency on construction projects is excessive handling of materials. Therefore, it is important to design lay-down areas so that materials stored in them do not need to be moved again. It is also important to plan how trucks delivering materials will be routed to the lay-down area and out of the site. Ideally, materials in lay-down areas should be hoisted directly from the lay-down area into their final place in the finished project. Stockpiles of soils or fill materials are essentially another form of lay-down area, and the same analysis should apply.

Parking for employees and visitors ideally will be located close to the worksite and office trailer respectively. On many industrial and urban projects, parking on or near the site is impossible. Depending upon work rules or union agreements, the project supervisor may need to arrange for shuttle transportation for workers.

Waste containers (dumpsters) must be located where they are easily accessible by waste haulers, but also as close as possible to the source of waste.

Project signs should be posted at a location that provides maximum visibility for the project.

Security fences and gates are often specified in the contract documents as to location and form. Think carefully about where gates are needed for material and equipment access during construction. Another function of security fences is public access control. For liability reasons, it is important to limit access to the project to those that are part of the project's execution. However, it is often necessary, in remodeling and addition projects, for the public to have access to certain portions of the project area. Protecting the public from the construction operations becomes a key area of concern in such a building project. Yet another challenge is how to protect the workers on a road project from highway traffic.

Just as work is saved when you put materials directly in place, it is often advantageous to construct assemblies in the field for erection as a unit. These field fabrication areas should be carefully located close to the relevant material storage areas and near the area in which the assemblies will be installed into the project. Also consider how easily the required hoisting and hauling equipment can access the assemblies. Cranes, especially fixed tower cranes, must be located in the optimal spot to maximize their use.

Activity 17 involves development of the construction site layout for Sure Fresh. The instructions for Activity 17 are found in Worksheet 17 in the Appendix. Your instructor will tell you when to turn to WS 17 to apply what you have learned about site layout.

SESSION 6

Equipment Selection

To learn more about equipment selection, we recommend you take STP Unit 9, *Productivity Improvement.*

The first issue in equipment selection is determining the method that will be used to execute the work. For example, wood-framed walls can be stick-built in the field, or panelized offsite. If panelization is chosen, a decision has to be made on how to handle the wall panels. A small mobile crane, an all-terrain forklift or other equipment might be used to erect the panels. The decision regarding what type of equipment to use may depend upon what the company owns or what it can economically rent.

After determining the type of equipment, choose the needed size and/or capacity as well as the quantity of the equipment. Often these characteristics must be matched with complementary equipment on the site. For example, the quantity and hauling capacity of dump trucks should be matched to the excavator and haul time required to cycle the trucks. Neither the dump trucks nor the excavator should have excessive waiting time. Although a tower crane is not usually subject to another piece of equipment's productivity, the crane's downtime should be minimized in order to maximize economies of scale.

Especially with hoisting equipment such as tower cranes, there can be a high demand on the site for its use. Depending upon the constraints of the site and availability of lay-down areas, the controlling contractor may have to allocate hoisting time to best serve the overall project schedule. At times during the project, certain trades will need to be flexible with their hoisting requirements. Hoisting of materials may need to occur before or after regular working hours or on weekends in order to use the tower crane. If there is no lay-down space on the site, and the city restricts lane closures during certain hours, the hoisting schedule will have to work around the constraints imposed by the city.

Activity 18 will give you an opportunity to design your "dream" yard for your company, but you have to "pay" for it. The instructions for Activity 18 are found in Worksheet 18 in the Appendix. Your instructor will tell you when to turn to WS 18 to apply what you have learned about equipment selection.

Several trades might each have a minimal requirement for use of a certain piece of equipment. It is sometimes advantageous for the controlling contractor to rent the equipment and then have each trade to agree to a voluntary backcharge to pay for their portion of the rental. This approach requires careful coordination of schedules, but it may save money for all, as a longer rental period usually results in a lower rental rate. However, arrangements such as these may have liability and insurance issues that first should be reviewed with the company safety officer. Another option is for trades to cooperate to rent a piece of equipment back-to-back, so that one company incurs the cost of the equipment delivery and another incurs the cost of the pick-up at the end of the rental period.

Safety should play an important role in equipment selection and use. Careful selection of equipment not only can achieve enhanced labor productivity, but also improve safety performance on the project. In general, using equipment, instead of "muscle," tends to lessen the exposure of workers to injuries such as strains and pulled muscles. Another advantage of using the proper equipment is that fall hazards can be dramatically reduced. Using the proper lift can eliminate the need for scaffold construction and reduce the likelihood of a fall. It is important, however, that all workers are trained in the proper usage as well as the unique hazards posed by certain types of equipment. Operators of equipment must be able to effectively communicate with the other workers on the site using radios, hand signals or some other method.

Other issues to consider in the selection of equipment include the ventilation of exhaust gases for equipment used indoors, storage of fuel, and scheduling maintenance downtime.

Material Handling, Storage and Protection

We have discussed storage trailers and the allocation of lay-down space, but another option is to store materials offsite. There are several things to consider when using offsite storage. First, the storage facility must be properly insured for its contents. Next, the contract documents regarding payment procedures will usually specify that the materials in offsite storage be clearly labeled for the project. It also is good practice to understand how secure the materials are at the offsite storage facility, but you can reasonably expect that an insured warehouse is a safer location for the materials than the jobsite.

Security and protection for materials stored onsite is of utmost importance. In addition to protecting materials from the weather, storage trailers should be secured with heavy-duty locks to deter thieves. For materials stored outside, pallets, tarps and good surface drainage can help to minimize the effects of precipitation and sunlight. Effectively controlling mud may require the stripping of topsoil and the placement of stone base. Ideally, areas being prepared for paving can be used as clean lay-down areas.

Deliveries often must be coordinated with:

■ The availability of hoisting or unloading equipment

■ The availability of storage space (unless materials will be directly incorporated into the work from the delivery truck)

■ Access to the site or security personnel (in the case of a secured facility such as a nuclear plant or military installation)

Once onsite, the delivered materials should be carefully inspected for damage and to ensure that the quantity and quality delivered are consistent with the bill of lading or packing slip.

If materials cannot be directly incorporated into the work, they should be unloaded to an area from which they can be directly incorporated into the work the next time they are handled. Another option is to work out a rental agreement (demurrage charge) for the trailer in which the materials were shipped. The materials may then be left on the trailer until they can be directly incorporated into the work. Again, the goal of effective material handling is to minimize the handling of materials.

Onsite Fabrication vs. Modular Units/ Panelization

There are three possible rationales for determining the value of onsite fabrication vs. offsite fabrication. The most obvious one is cost. In general, materials fabricated offsite will cost less to make than those items constructed onsite. There are several reasons for this cost difference. Many of the variables affecting productivity are better controlled in the factory or shop environment. For example, it never rains or freezes in the shop. The shop floor doesn't get muddy. There is ample power located conveniently to the work. Workmen's Compensation insurance premiums are less than for comparable field work. Wage rates in the factory or shop tend to be less than those of field workers. The work station in the shop is often designed for the specific tasks, leading to higher productivity.

The next consideration in the decision process is schedule. Prefabricating materials offsite earlier than the work could be completed onsite accelerates the project schedule. Prefabrication also reduces the time spent in the field, further improving the schedule. Since field work is generally more hazardous than shop work, workers are exposed to fewer hazards. The third rationale is quality. While it cannot be said that shop or factory workers inherently produce better work, the elimination of the weather variable, for example, may improve the quality of the work. In addition, high quality levels with certain materials may be easier to attain in the factory than in the field, for a variety of reasons.

The compatibility of field fabrication with weather conditions may also drive the onsite vs. offsite decision process. For example, it may be difficult to lay concrete masonry units (CMUs) in International Falls, Minnesota in January, but it may be considerably easier to erect precast wall panels. On a Design-Build project, the contractor can direct the design professional to use precast wall panels to improve constructability for winter conditions. On a Design-Bid-Build project, the contractor will have to bid the CMU wall that has been drawn and provide a voluntary alternate bid to entice the owner to use precast, or negotiate a change in materials after the contract award. On a CM project, the contractor can suggest the precast wall to the architect during the design phase.

Another reason to consider different design alternatives is to improve the compatibility of the project with the local labor climate. The CMU wall again serves as a good example. In recent years, there has been a major shortage of bricklayers in many metropolitan areas. The ability to change from a CMU wall to a precast concrete wall can have a positive influence on the overall project schedule. The ability to make this change depends upon the project delivery system, as discussed in the previous paragraph.

Another aspect to consider in the onsite/offsite debate is how the decision will affect compliance with applicable codes, specifications and design intent. Some building codes, for example, may be suspicious of new approaches to construction from a risk management viewpoint. As a way of protecting the union trades, other building codes may resist anything that reduces the amount of labor expended in the field. In other cases, it may be difficult to meet the specifications in the field or in the factory, and this aspect will drive the decision process. Another factor to consider is delivery constraints. Sometimes offsite fabrication is not possible because of weight restrictions on area roads, material restrictions through tunnels, low-clearance overpasses on the route, or width constraints. In addition, the contractor must always comply with the designer's intent. Field construction may be able to achieve a scale that is just not possible with prefabrication. For example, the designer may dislike the many joints inherent to a precast wall and may insist on field-casting of the wall.

Determining what to prefabricate and what to construct in the field is a complex decision process that involves cost, schedule and quality tradeoffs. It is best to make these decisions early in the design phase of the project, if possible. This minimizes the design rework necessary to effect changes later, promotes the best price during bidding, and maximizes quality during construction.

Activity 19 asks you to compare and contrast tilt-up vs. precast for the walls on the Sure Fresh project. The instructions for Activity 19 are found in Worksheet 19 in the Appendix. Your instructor will tell you when to turn to WS 19 to apply what you have learned about onsite and offsite fabrication.

To Implement What You Have Learned

Write down one concept or idea from Session 6 that you think everyone in your company should know to improve the way your company does business.

Write down one thing you learned in Session 6 that you think should be included in your company's project management training program for entry-level project managers.

Write down one thing you learned in Session 6 that you intend to use on your next project to make the project more successful.

Before the next session, develop the three ideas you listed above into a short memo, and schedule a meeting with your sponsor to discuss your ideas and develop an action plan. Remember that when trying something new, it is important to have the support of your sponsor and other champions in the organization, and to make small, incremental changes. Your sponsor has received an executive summary of this session and will be expecting your report and your phone call to set up a meeting with him or her to discuss your ideas for the company.

If you would like to learn more about the construction phase tasks, especially as they pertain to managing materials and methods, we suggest you register for STP Unit 9, *Productivity Improvement.*

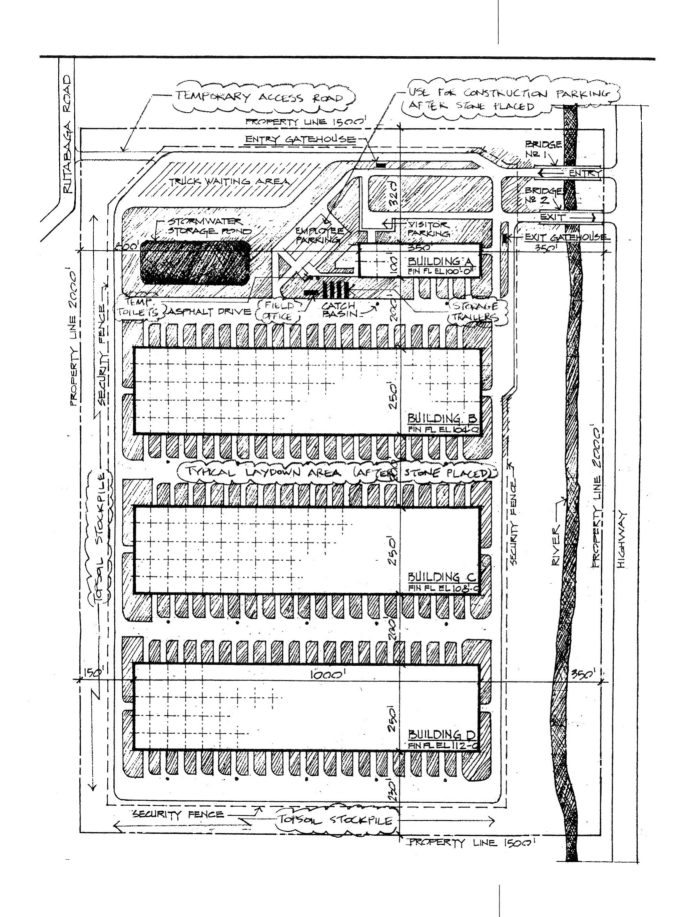

Notes

Understanding Finances

Goal and Performance Objectives of Session 7

The goals and objectives for participant learning in Session 7 are:

- To create an awareness of how cost information cycles through companies and projects

- To understand project cash flows

- To develop knowledge of the uses and importance of accurate cost coding

- To broaden the project supervisor's awareness of how retainage affects financing costs and cash flows

To Get Ready for Session 7

Read Session 7 and complete any preparatory assignments given by your instructor.

Cost Information Cycle

The ability of a contractor to secure new work at a profitable rate depends on the contractors' access to accurate historical records. The information on costs runs in a cycle, which can be represented in the following diagram:

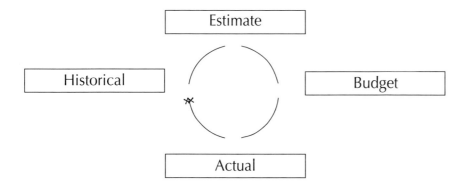

Every project, whether it is a hard-bid job using Design-Bid-Build delivery or a negotiated Design-Build project, must have an estimate of total cost. Part of this estimate will include labor hours, equipment

Activity 20 involves an exercise on the labor cost cycle. The instructions for Activity 20 are found in Worksheet 20 in the Appendix. Your instructor will tell you when to turn to WS 20 to apply what you have learned about the cost cycle.

usage, and material used in specific work tasks (concrete columns, rough framing, etc.). If the builder is successful in obtaining a contract, the estimate will form the basis for developing the project budget. The estimate-to-budget portion of the cost information cycle occurs during project award and start-up.

As the work proceeds, labor hours are tracked on timecards, equipment usage is tracked on yard tickets or rental slips, and material usage is tracked on purchase orders or delivery tickets. Each cost on the project is coded to a certain category of work as it occurs, and is periodically compared to the budget. The budget-to-actual portion of the cost information cycle occurs during the project execution phase of the project.

As each task is completed, or when the project is audited, the actual labor, equipment, and material costs for each category of work are recorded and moved to a historical archive. The actual cost-to-historical cost portion of the cost information cycle occurs during the project closeout and audit phase of the project.

When the contractor is asked to bid or submit a proposal on a similar project, the estimator can go to the historical records to determine the costs of tasks and work categories for use in preparing the estimate for the new project. The historical-to-estimate portion of the cost information cycle occurs during bidding and proposal (pursuit of new work).

Information Flows

Information first flows from the office to the field as budgets are developed for labor hours, equipment usage, and material costs. Then, as the work progresses, information flows back to the office from the field in the form of actual costs. Accurate and timely communication in both directions is critical to both short-term profitability and long-term capability to secure new work. Cost and schedule information also must flow between the contractor and subcontractors/suppliers to both the contractor's field and the office. When the scope of work changes, or when additional costs are incurred because of design errors, conflicts, or omissions, the project manager will compile a list of actual costs related to new work from the field and each of the subcontractors. The project manager also will communicate the cost of changes to the Architect/Engineer and the owner. When change orders are issued to increase or decrease the contract amount, budgets should be changed to reflect the new scope of work.

Value engineering is another important information-sharing function of contractors. Project teams should develop the skill of reviewing plans and specifications and comparing different systems in order to determine which combinations provide the best value for the owner. An owner who believes a contractor is adding value to the project is more likely to choose that contractor again for future building needs.

Cost Coding Accuracy

Each work task is assigned a budget, developed from the estimate. Usually each work task is also assigned a cost code, which can be used to track budgets and actual costs. It is important that each cost code reflect a distinct task with easily identified units and task boundaries. The level of detail required in the cost coding system depends in part on the delivery method used and the contract type. For instance, if the project is using a cost-plus contract, it is important to have clarity in the work categories and very accurate records. Lump-sum Design-Build projects may aggregate cost codes into systems (concrete columns, masonry walls, etc.) with much less level of detail.

Direct work vs. indirect work can also affect the cost coding necessary for accurate records. Direct work refers to labor hours, equipment charges, and materials that can clearly be associated with a discrete work task, such as concrete formwork or installing wood doors. Indirect work refers to tasks that result from general needs, such as cleanup, hoisting, or moving material. For instance, the cleanup and disposal of waste lumber from building formwork should be charged against the formwork code, but such level of detail is difficult to achieve, as labor costs for cleanup and trash removal usually cover waste from a number of tasks.

Because historical records are so crucial to promoting long-term contractor success and short-term profitability, supervisors should cooperate with project managers in making sure that the cost codes provided in the budget reports reflect the actual breakdown of the work tasks. Project supervisors should ask for more cost codes when necessary, and should take primary responsibility for accurate assignment of work to appropriate codes. Project managers should take primary responsibility for assessing the impact of change orders on cost codes and budgets for work tasks. Changes in budgets and cost codes must be communicated to the supervisor in a timely manner in order to be effective. If budgets and cost codes are not coordinated and updated, accuracy will suffer.

If supervisors do not pay close attention to the allocation of labor, equipment, and material to appropriate codes, historical records will result in bad estimates for future projects. In other words, if you put garbage in, you'll get garbage out (GIGO). GIGO is a term left over from the early days of computer programming and automated payroll systems. The logic was that the ability of the computer program to produce accurate results was dependent on the quality of the data being input. For instance, if the payroll clerk did not accurately input hours worked, the payroll program would not print out an accurate paycheck. The same logic holds for cost records—if accurate information is not collected during projects, the historical record will be worthless. Bidding accuracy is highly dependent upon timesheet accuracy and appropriate allocation of costs.

Activity 21 involves an exercise on developing an ideal cost coding system. The instructions for Activity 21 are found in Worksheet 21 in the Appendix. Your instructor will tell you when to turn to WS 21 to apply what you have learned about cost coding.

SESSION 7

Project Cash Flow

Cost codes also assist the project manager in preparing the schedule of payments and applications for payments, which in turn is used by corporate executives to project cash flow for the company. The application for payment should reflect all the labor, material, and equipment put in place on the project, and the work completed. The expenses incurred in one month are not typically reimbursed by the owner until the following month (assuming a 30-day pay cycle). Because of this lag in contractor payments of material invoices, payroll, equipment charges, and subcontractor applications for payment, the contractor actually self-finances the first portion of work. In other words, the contractor works for 30 days, pays his or her bills, and bills the owner for the value of the accumulated work completed. The owner takes another 30 days to pay the contractor, so the contractor has another 30 days of payroll, equipment charges, and material payments. Therefore, the contractor works for 60 days (typically) before receiving payment from the owner. If the contractor is self-performing a large proportion of the work, the self-financing costs could be quite high, and cash management will be critical at a corporate level. All these factors are made easier if project managers and corporate financial officers have accurate information from the field on actual costs and work completed.

If reports of work completed are given on a percentage-of-total basis, the percentage complete must be accurate, or else projected costs to finish that task could become skewed. It is always better to report work completed in terms of units of work in place, which can then be compared to the bid/estimate quantities to determine a projected final cost.

The project manager will use the field cost reports to prepare the monthly progress pay application, based on percentage of work completed. The monthly payment schedule, if plotted as a percent of total project costs, will usually resemble an S-curve. In other words, if there are 10 payments, the first few payments and last few payments will be for less than 10% each while the middle payments will be for more than 10% each. A typical project S curve of payments is shown below.

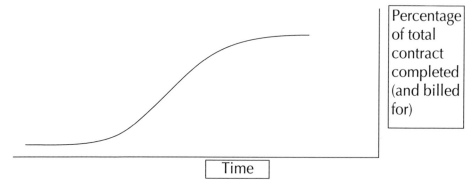

SESSION 7

In order to reduce the cost of self-financing the first 60 days of work, many contractors try to have much of the mobilization, insurance, and other up start-up costs included in the first pay application. Aggressive, early billing for all work completed is good business practice, but contractors must be careful not to bill for work that is not completed. They also must not bill for material not onsite, nor in bonded storage. Aggressive billing at the beginning of a project is sometimes called "front-end loading," and although a common practice in the construction industry, the use of front-end loading must not become so aggressive as to be dishonest, abusive, or unfair to the owner.

Use of cost-loaded schedules helps the owner, construction financing company, and corporate financial officers to understand the relationship between time and money on a construction project. The cost-loaded schedule integrates budget/estimate information into the progress schedule so project team members can see how much money is to be spent by activity and by time period.

Contract form and language can affect how budgets, cost information, and payment requests are utilized. For instance, cost-plus contracts will frequently require more detailed cost information and may have cost codes for some indirect project functions that might otherwise be considered part of project overhead. Examples would be project management time, field engineer time, and project coordinator (project secretary) time. Unit-price contracts require close attention to units produced, moved, installed, etc., with contract prices applied to each unit. Lump-sum contracts are more likely to aggregate data with less detail, and will typically not include non-site indirect costs such as project management, office rental, and a project secretary.

Activity 22 involves an exercise in planning for cash flow needs on a project. The instructions for Activity 22 are found in Worksheet 22 in the Appendix. Your instructor will tell you when to turn to WS 22 to apply what you have learned about project cash flow.

Retainage

Contractors do not receive 100% of their pay requests. Owners "retain" a small percentage to ensure project completion and to make sure that the contractor will handle callbacks, rework, and punch list items in a timely manner. The amount of money withheld from the application for payment is called retainage, and is typically between 5 and 10% of the total billing in the early phases of the project. Many contracts call for a reduction in retainage once a project has reached a certain percentage of completion. A common contract term allows the owner to retain 10% of application for payment until the project is 50% complete, at which time the retainage is reduced to 5% of the overall project cost until the punch list is completed and the owner accepts substantial completion of the project.

Some contractors have attempted to use **pay-when-paid** clauses in their subcontracts. Pay-when-paid clauses inform the subcontractor that it will not receive payment from the general contractor until the

SESSION 7

general contractor receives payment from the owner. Although this reduces the self-financing cost for the general contractors, it can work a hardship on small subcontractors. Before enforcing a pay-when-paid clause, the project manager should ensure that the subcontractor has the financial strength to accept one.

To Implement What You Have Learned

Write down one concept or idea from Session 7 that you think everyone in your company should know to improve the way your company does business.

Write down one thing you learned in Session 7 that you think should be included in your company's project management training program for entry-level project managers.

Write down one thing you learned in Session 7 that you intend to use on your next project to make the project more successful.

Before the next session, develop the three ideas you listed above into a short memo, and schedule a meeting with your sponsor to discuss your ideas and develop an action plan. Remember that when trying something new, it is important to have the support of your sponsor and other champions in the organization, and to make small, incremental changes. Your sponsor has received an executive summary of this session and will be expecting your report and your phone call to set up a meeting with him or her to discuss your ideas for the company.

If you would like to learn more about understanding finances, we suggest you register for STP Unit 6, *Understanding and Managing Project Costs.*

Working with Project Partners

Goal and Performance Objectives of Session 8

Goal: After this session, you will appreciate the importance of working with people outside of your organization and how to effectively interact with individuals whose goals on the project may not exactly align with your own.

Performance objectives:

- To learn how your actions on the project may affect future work with the client

- To learn how to work effectively with subcontractors

- To understand how to work with design firms in different types of projects

- To appreciate the importance of working with inspectors and government agencies

- To understand how to work with trade union representatives (if applicable)

- To understand how to work better with other internal stakeholders (co-workers)

To Get Ready for Session 8

Read Session 8 and complete any preparatory assignments given by your instructor.

Working With Owners (The Supervisor as the Salesperson)

The project delivery system affects the working relationship between the owner's representative and the project supervisor. There are two forms of a Design-Bid-Build project: the competitively bid general contract and the negotiated general contract. In the former, the relationship will sometimes be adversarial, as the owner may seek to extract as much value as possible from the general contractor, and the general contractor may try to give as little value beyond the contract documents as possible. In the negotiated form, the relationship may be friendlier because the initial basis for the business relationship is derived from more than just a low price. However, in both forms, the supervisor must limit the work to that indicated in the contract documents and must insist on a change order for any work required or requested beyond the drawings and specifications. The project supervisor also will help make the case for subcontractor change orders.

In the Design-Build system, the owner and the contractor must have a high degree of mutual respect and trust. The owner has entrusted the contractor with the roles both of builder and of designer. The project supervisor has a different relationship when it comes to the drawings, specifications and change orders. Because the contractor owes the owner a certain scope of work regardless of the thoroughness of the drawings and specifications, a change order may be sought only if the owner changes the scope of the project from that in the agreement. Because owner change orders are not readily forthcoming, the supervisor must dissuade subcontractor change orders that might reduce the contractor's profit. In the construction management system, the project supervisor is something of an owner's agent, and must help critique prime contractor change order requests and maintain fairness to all.

Regardless of the project delivery system used, the project supervisor must always be a professional. Communication must always be suitable for broadcast television. The project supervisor is his or her company's day-to-day representative on the site, especially on addition and remodeling projects. It is likely that the performance of the project supervisor will either cloud or enhance the reputation of the contractor in the eyes of the client. The supervisor also is the first line of defense on the project when it comes to solving problems and achieving difficult objectives. A can-do attitude will help to earn respect from the home office, the designer and the owner.

Everyone has heard the phrase "The customer is always right." In construction, the customer is *almost* always right. Many owners seldom, if ever, commission a construction project. Their knowledge of how to conduct a project may be limited at best. It is important for the project supervisor to help guide the owner when necessary. For example, the owner may become frustrated with a mistake in the field and insist on a change of personnel. As project supervisor, you may recognize that the specific task was very difficult and that the odds of outright success were small. You may need to help coach the owner and explain that the results may have been even worse with another foreman.

Many owners will designate an individual with limited authority to represent their interests on a day-to-day basis. The project supervisor must recognize how much authority this person has to authorize extra work, approve installed work, etc. The owner' chain of command must be respected. It is crucial to understand how approvals are granted within the owner's system so that decisions have the proper underlying support. A construction project is a constantly changing landscape; therefore, the supervisor must be able to manage change. If the project supervisor excels at working cooperatively with the owner, solving problems and managing change, he or she will give the contractor an advantage in securing the next contract with the owner. Most owners recognize the value of a competent, professional project supervisor, and will strive to keep one working on their projects.

Working With Subcontractors in the Field

Subcontractors, just like owners and designers, are an important part of the project team. By specializing in certain aspects of the work, subcontractors bring expertise and economies of scale to a project that would be difficult for the contractor to replicate in many cases. However, subcontractors are separate business entities and have their own goals and objectives for the project. Chief among these goals and objectives for some is the realization of a profit on the project. Sometimes this goal competes with minimizing schedule or maximizing quality or making safety a top priority. In such cases, the supervisor must be firm with a subcontractor in order to ensure that the schedule, quality and safety needs of the project are adhered to closely.

Just as there is a difference between competitively bid and negotiated contractors, there is a difference between bid and negotiated subcontractors. A competitively bid subcontractor will not want to go beyond the scope of its contract unless it is issued a change order. On the other hand, a negotiated subcontractor (or Design-Build subcontractor) may have a more general scope of work, which should limit its ability to seek change orders if the scope of work has not changed.

To have a successful project, it is imperative for the project supervisor to plan and schedule the work with the input of the subcontractor. The involved subcontractor will buy into the project, ensuring better performance. However, there still may be times when a supervisor must be firm and demand that a subcontractor adequately staff the project to meet the schedule. It also is the supervisor's responsibility to monitor subcontractor progress. The supervisor may be called upon to assess the percentage complete for each subcontractor as a part of the monthly pay application process. It is important to be accurate so that the subcontractor is neither under- nor overbilled.

Another source of concern may be periodic and daily cleanup of the worksite. It is important that this responsibility be clearly spelled out in the subcontract agreement. If the subcontractor is contractually

Activity 23 involves working through a conflict resolution activity. The instructions for Activity 23 are found in Worksheet 23 in the Appendix. Your instructor will tell you when to turn to WS 23 to apply what you have learned about conflict resolution.

SESSION 8

obligated to provide cleanup, then the supervisor must enforce this clause.

Working with Designers

As with owners, the project delivery system affects how the project supervisor will interact with design professionals (architects and engineers) on the project. On all project delivery systems except Design-Bid-Build, the contractor is afforded at least some input during the design process. The project supervisor may be able to suggest improvements to facilitate constructability or to enhance safety during construction. The project supervisor is the key field contact for the designer in both change and punch list management. In addition, most of the quality assurance sampling and inspections will be closely coordinated with the project supervisor.

The supervisor's relationship with the designer as it pertains to change management will vary, depending upon the project delivery system used. On a Design-Bid-Build project, the designer works for the owner and is less likely to seek the owner's approval for change orders, especially those that are a result of a design oversight. On a Design-Build project, the designer may be a consultant to the contractor and may be left out of the change order process entirely, except in cases where the designer's knowledge of the relevant code is needed. On the construction management project, the project supervisor and field representative for the designer will almost be partners in change management.

Designers and contractors will often work together to provide value engineering services to the owner. Designers will prepare ideas for different systems (e.g., concrete frame and steel frame) and then ask the contractor to provide cost estimates of each system. In this way, the owner can be assured of receiving the best value on the construction project. A project supervisor who works with the designer to solve problems, acts professionally, and appreciates what the designer brings to the project in terms of a skill set, will likely help the contractor succeed in the future by getting his or her employer recommended for short lists for bidding and negotiated work.

Working With Inspectors/Government Agencies

Part of successfully completing a construction project is completing all the required inspections. Unlike owners, designers, and contractors (who all want a project completed in the least amount of time possible), the government agency representative might not have any stake in the project other than protecting the safety of the public. For example, the building inspector typically issues the certificate of occupancy (C. of O.) for a building project. While the contractor is almost

Activity 24 challenges the group to respond to a hypothetical OSHA inspection at the Sure Fresh project. The instructions for Activity 24 are found in Worksheet 24 in the Appendix. Your instructor will tell you when to turn to WS 24 to apply what you have learned about working with government agencies.

SESSION 8

desperate to get the C. of O., the building inspector is not necessarily interested in issuing it. Therefore, the supervisor must take great care to remain on good terms with the inspector.

It should be noted that in many small towns, the building inspector might not have much formal training in codes or construction techniques. This type of inspector likely will focus on ensuring that the installed work matches the approved drawings exactly. If changes are made in the work after the permit is issued, it is important to sit down with the inspector and explain the changes that have been made so that the inspector has time to confirm that the code is being met.

One way to simplify the relationship with the building department is to carefully coordinate inspections between the subcontractors and the inspectors. Inspectors don't like to waste their time any more than anyone else does. Therefore, an inspector should not be called out to the jobsite unless the work is truly ready for inspection. The supervisor also must allow adequate time for the proper sequencing of the inspections leading up to the issuance of the C. of O.

Working with Unions

Working with unions can be complicated at times. For example, two or more trades may claim a certain type of work, such as metal roofing. In this example, depending upon the type of roof, the ironworkers or the sheet metal workers might claim the work—but the contractor must assign the work to only one of them. Typically, if the trade to which the work has been assigned accepts the assignment, then the issue is concluded unless the other union wishes to challenge the assignment. At this point, the only recourse is the National Labor Relations Board (NLRB).

Unions can wield significant political clout. If you work for a union contractor, you may be able to leverage the union's political base to get onto bidders' lists. Alternatively, your firm may be allowed to work in unionized factories where merit shop contractors are shunned. Or your firm may not be allowed into a merit shop factory. On other occasions, the union may create difficulties for the company with the aforementioned jurisdictional disputes, with strikes, or by the imposition of productivity-hindering work rules.

In right-to-work states, the subcontract clause of the union agreement can hurt the union contractor's competitiveness by limiting its ability to compete with merit shop contractors that may have lower wage costs. For example, a union contractor may travel for a project into a town with few union subcontractors—perhaps none for certain trades. If the contractor has an agreement with the carpenter's union, there undoubtedly will be a clause prohibiting the hire of non-signatory

Activity 25 deals with a jurisdictional dispute between two trades. The instructions for Activity 25 are found in Worksheet 25 in the Appendix. Your instructor will tell you when to turn to WS 25 to apply what you have learned about working with unions.

subcontractors for any work that the union would claim. However, what if the contractor doesn't do drywall work itself, and there are no union drywall subcontractors in the area (or willing to travel into the area)?

One option is for the union to be happy with the doors, cabinets and trim work being completed by union carpenters and to look the other way while the drywall work is completed by a non-signatory subcontractor, as there are no signatory subcontractors available. Another option is for the union to flex its muscles and insist that the drywall work be done by union employees. This demand may be met by working with the subcontractor to hire some union employees via a project agreement. Or you may have to institute a dual-gate system, whereby union employees enter (and picket) at one gate, while merit shop employees use another. Whenever tensions are running high with a union, it is best to involve contractor upper management or the local AGC executive director to help resolve the issues. This step will keep the project supervisor out of the fray.

Working With Internal Stakeholders (Co-workers)

Working effectively with owners, designers, inspectors and subcontractors is important, but even more so is having ongoing, long-term working relationships with your co-workers. In the classic economic sense, the construction company's production floor is the jobsite, where product is produced, wealth is created and profits are realized. It is easy to fall into the mindset that the only thing that matters is the jobsite, and everything else supports the project. However, the rest of the organization is more than just a cost center.

While the project site is the profit center for the construction company, it takes marketing, sales and estimating to obtain contracts. In other words, salespeople and estimators make it possible for the company to have profit centers. Since projects are by definition of finite duration, a company will die without new projects. Accountants are necessary to make payroll, pay bills and to "keep score." Without accountants, it would be difficult to know whether individual projects were making or losing money. Project engineers and managers work to keep the field supplied with information, materials, equipment, and subcontractor forces. Operations officers work to ensure that adequate labor is available for each project. Company executives often provide the working capital and bonding capacity as well as overall leadership for the direction of the company.

Just as the office works to support the field, the field often needs to support the office. Occasionally a payroll clerk may need a timesheet clarified so that payroll checks can be issued on time. The project supervisor must appreciate that this one question may be holding up the entire payroll system. Ignoring the cell phone because there's a concrete pour today is not acceptable. Similarly, a project manager may be drafting the monthly pay application and need the supervisor's opinion on subcontractor completion percentage. Or a project engineer might need some field measurements to complete a request for information that needs to be resolved in order to keep the steel fabricator moving.

While the project supervisor is often the ultimate company authority on the jobsite, there will be times when the supervisor must cede to the company executive. If the company executive decides to abandon a request for change order, the supervisor must follow the executive's lead and proceed with the work even though he or she might think that a change order is justified. The executive may have a "big picture" reason for abandoning the request. Perhaps the owner has just handed the company a large negotiated project, or perhaps the executive has realized that, in the whole scope of the project, the change order is a battle not worth fighting.

The project supervisor and project manager are often at similar levels of authority on projects. The supervisor and manager should work to complement each other's strengths and weaknesses. It is usually more efficient for the two co-workers to divide the work of the project and to avoid duplication of efforts. This approach also presents a unified front to the outside world, which reinforces the solidarity of the company team. It is common-sense that the supervisor should determine crew sizes, and the manager should process owner change order documents, but the there are many tasks that are not so obvious. For example, it may be more effective to team up on the punch list and job-closeout management activities.

To Implement What You Have Learned

Write down one concept or idea from Session 8 that you think everyone in your company should know to improve the way your company does business.

Write down one thing you learned in Session 8 that you think should be included in your company's project management training program for entry-level project managers.

Write down one thing you learned in Session 8 that you intend to use on your next project to make the project more successful.

Before the next session, develop the three ideas you listed above into a short memo, and schedule a meeting with your sponsor to discuss your ideas and develop an action plan. Remember that when trying something new, it is important to have the support of your sponsor and other champions in the organization, and to make small, incremental changes. Your sponsor has received an executive summary of this ses-

SESSION 8

sion and will be expecting your report and your phone call to set up a meeting with him or her to discuss your ideas for the company.

If you would like to learn more about working with other stakeholders on the project, especially in the area of solving problems and implementing solutions, we suggest you register for STP Unit 3, *Problem Solving and Decision Making*, as well as Unit 10, *General and Specialty Contractor Dynamics.*

Session 9
Understanding People

Goal and Performance Objectives of Session 9

The goals and objectives for participant learning in Session 9 are:

■ To create an awareness of how relationships affect project performance

■ To understand various leadership styles

■ To develop techniques for motivating and rewarding project team members

■ To broaden the project supervisor's awareness of how the appropriate leadership style may vary, based on the project contracting method and the nature of the team

To Get Ready for Session 9

Read Session 9 and complete any preparatory assignments given by your instructor. Spend some time thinking about the types of people you deal with on projects. Create a list of the types of people with whom you usually enjoy working, as well as a list of the types of people you find difficult to work with on a construction project. List adjectives to describe your preferred co-workers and non-preferred co-workers.

The Project Team

Any project team, whether it is a construction project, a church project, a school project, or even a family planning a vacation, will consist of various individuals with unique skills, knowledge, personality, experience and values. This diversity is necessary for a successful project, but it does put pressure on project leaders to develop a leadership style that is flexible and adaptable, and to understand the various needs and preferences of the project team members. To maximize their effectiveness, project leaders should develop a large tool kit of ideas and approaches for working with team members. In the following sections, we will introduce some of the factors that can improve a supervisor's ability to understand and lead people on construction projects.

It is important to understand that **the leader** is more of a role than a position on a project. On a project responsibility matrix or work plan, the tasks necessary to complete the project are assigned to the individuals best qualified (and available) to complete those tasks. For instance, on a Design-Build project, responsibility for completing structural drawings may be assigned to a senior structural engineer, while responsibility for building post-tension deck forms may be assigned to an experienced carpenter foreman. Leading the effort to make sure those two tasks are coordinated and completed on time with superior quality is not so much a task to be delegated as it is a role to be assumed. The role of leader on a team is typically assumed and shared by a field superintendent and a project manager, but anyone on the team can lead at certain times or for certain tasks. The leader's role on a construction project is to:

■ Motivate and reward team members to do the best job possible

■ Communicate and coordinate tasks

■ Develop relationships of trust and cooperation among team members

These issues will be discussed in more detail below.

Motivation and Rewards

Most people work because they have to. The most basic reward for performance is the paycheck, which allows workers to afford a home for their family, put food on the table, have a vehicle or two, and take a vacation. The motivation to go to work every day is the lifestyle that is afforded by working. Benefits are increasingly important in compensation and reward systems. Some companies try to motivate employees to stay by vesting retirement payouts or offering more vacation at longer terms of service. Compensation (hourly pay or salaries) and benefits (life insurance, healthcare insurance, retirement, etc.) are set largely by the local market conditions and the policy makers in the organization, and may be beyond the influence of the project supervisor. However, the project leaders do have means at their disposal to reward and motivate team members beyond their compensation and benefits.

There are many different ideas about the best way to motivate and reward individuals. The ability to motivate and reward is partially linked to the supervisor's power and position, and partially linked to his or her level of control over resources (time, money, promotions, etc.). For the purposes of this unit, we will assume that project supervisors and project managers have some authority over other team members and have access to some resources that can be distributed as rewards. Many of the means for motivating and rewarding project team members are simple enough that the pool of available resources does not have to be large in order to be effective.

The position of project supervisor or project manager usually carries some power, including (within limits) the power to reward and the power to punish and enforce (e.g., fire an employee, reduce pay or hours, or take to court). Motivating through punishment or enforcement can be effective over the short term, and sometimes it is necessary to motivate non-performers, but research has shown that these negative reinforcements lose their effectiveness if they are used too frequently. Therefore, motivation though threats, intimidation, and coercion should be used as a last resort. These methods should not be relied upon as a continuing source of motivation.

The power to reward is a very important part of motivating team members, and most project leaders have more power to motivate than they realize. There are personal or intrinsic rewards that can be very motivating and rewarding, such as recognition in a project meeting, compliments on the quality of the work, or a laudatory e-mail to a team member's direct supervisor. These types of rewards require no more resources than a little bit of the project supervisor/manager's time. Some companies have more formal recognition programs, such as "employee of the week" or "good citizen" points. If your company has these types of programs, you should consider nominating your high-performing team members for recognition.

Working conditions can be an important factor in motivation. Allowing project team members some input into working conditions can be motivating. For instance, allowing craftworkers to schedule their own breaks (within reason) or discussing how overtime will be allocated can make the craftworker feel as though he or she is a valued member of the team, increasing loyalty and commitment to the project. Having a safe worksite is also important. Project managers and project supervisors also can improve working conditions through their ability to assign favorable work tasks, days off or early quitting times, and other perks to reward high-performing team members.

> Activity 26 involves a brainstorming session to develop ideas for motivating/ rewarding members of the project team. The instructions for Activity 26 are found in Worksheet 26 in the Appendix. Your instructor will tell you when to turn to WS 26 to apply what you have learned about motivation and reward.

The relationship with co-workers, especially the relationship with the boss, is a critical factor in motivation on the jobsite. Research has shown that workers who respect their boss and admire their co-workers are more productive and have less absenteeism than workers who do not have positive co-worker relations. The project supervisor needs to be aware of the interpersonal factors within a project team, and work to resolve or reduce the tensions that can arise from personality conflicts, value differences, or disagreements. Resolving interpersonal disputes is perhaps one of the most difficult jobs a leader has, and most leaders would prefer to avoid getting involved, but unresolved clashes among co-workers frequently can lead to productivity problems and team decline.

Because the basic needs of most individuals are met through the compensation and benefits package, many of the rewards and motivational tactics used by project leaders should be aimed at personal growth and development. To help workers achieve their personal growth needs, the leader should use motivation tactics and rewards that have value to the team members. In other words, the type of reward you offer must meet a personal need of the team member in order to be motivating. That is all "personal growth" really means; I have a need as a person, and I can't get to the next point in my life until that need is met. If project leaders can help their team members achieve some of those needs, it becomes an important motivator. For example, for a team member who feels as though the quality of his or her work is not appreciated, the strongest motivator will be recognition of the quality of that work. Whenever possible, this recognition should be given publicly in front of co-workers and influential team partners (owner's reps, city officials, etc.). On the other hand, if a high-performing individual on the team needs more time, perhaps because of a change in family status (just married, new baby, sick parents, etc.) then rewards of early quitting time or days off will be more motivating than recognition. Sometimes it is possible to create more time by assigning certain tasks that require only a partial day's work, but which must be completed before the next tasks in a sequence can begin, such as pouring a concrete deck or moving scaffolding.

Many workers would like to know what they must do to move up in the organization. Perhaps you have a journeyman trade worker who is interested in becoming foreman, or a foreman who would like to move up to superintendent. If you can find out who these workers are, you can give them more responsibility or delegate more complicated tasks to them (with appropriate supervision, of course) to help them learn the necessary skills to move to the next level. The fact that you, as a project leader, were willing to take a chance on them, will be very rewarding and motivating to these workers.

Perhaps the most important thing to remember about rewards is that they must be tied to performance in order to be effective. Your goal as a project leader is to shape the behavior of your team by rewarding high-performing members. This should motivate everyone on the team to higher performance. If rewards are distributed without regard to performance, the best performers may become cynical and de-motivated to continue their high-performance work. At the same time poor performers may try to "fish for the bottom," continuing to under-perform until they find the point at which rewards stop and enforcement/punishment begins. On the other hand, while rewards should be differential based on performance, it may be counter-productive to have a reward system that is overly competitive. You want to reward all performers and not have a system of competitive, selective rewards that discourages team members from sharing resources or information in order to maximize their own rewards.

Leadership Skills

Some people believe that leadership is a trait, and that some people are born to lead. This may be somewhat true, in that research has shown a few (very few) genetic traits that are linked to leadership. The types of leaders that are born to lead are sometimes referred to as charismatic leaders, who motivate others through the power of their speeches, appeals to common values, and by describing a set of shared goals that guide the actions of the team. Charismatic leadership can be very powerful, but is probably less common in construction than in entertainment, politics and religion. Therefore, most leaders of construction projects are not born leaders (charismatics), but have learned their craft and gained the respect of their co-workers, and are looked to for leadership.

Leaders of construction projects usually develop a leadership style early in their careers. There are many methods of categorizing leadership styles, but most of them are based on whether the leader focuses on task completion or personal relationships with team members. A leader who focuses solely on task completion while ignoring team members' needs might be categorized as a "driver" type of leader. A leader who cares deeply about the satisfaction and needs of the team members, but does not push for task completion, might be categorized as a "country-clubber." In reality, most people have a leadership style that is not at either extreme. In addition, leadership style is usually linked to a leader's personality. For example, leaders with introverted personalities are unlikely to open up in team meetings.

Leadership is a process or a role, more than a position on a project. Leadership involves the leader, the followers, and the situation they are working in. The leader and the followers together form the team. In construction, the situation is usually always a project (building, road, dam, bridge, etc.) defined by project characteristics (budget, schedule, scope, etc.). A good leader must have skills appropriate for the situation (the project) and for the followers (the team) as depicted in the following diagram:

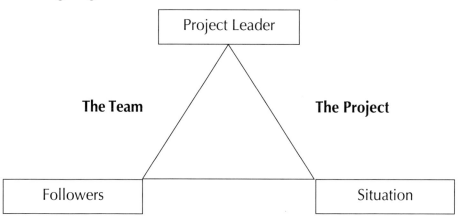

Leadership skills required for managing **the project** are generally technical in nature. These are frequently referred to as task-oriented skills such as planning, estimating/budgeting, project financing, scheduling, producing the work, craftsmanship, organizing and structuring the work assignments, etc. These skills can be acquired through a combination of education, training and experience. A well-developed performance appraisal system will allow you to request additional technical training in areas you feel may need improvement. Technical competence is a very important aspect of project leadership.

Leadership skills required for managing the team members are much more relationship-oriented than the task skills required for the project itself. The ability to effectively manage relationships on a project team is related to the leader's ability to communicate, to listen, to understand the personality and values of the individual team members, and to help them achieve their personal and professional goals.

The key to being a good leader is to try to match your leadership style to the needs of the followers and the situation. Critical to managing the relationship skills on a project is the leader's ability to adapt his/her communication skills, delegation methods, and listening skills to the individual members of the team. For example, some members of the team will be very detail-oriented, whereas others will be very "big picture" types. Giving very specific, detailed instructions to the detail-oriented worker will probably be effective, but using the same leadership style on the "big picture" worker will result in anxiety and frustration. Similarly, some workers react positively to a harsh challenge (the proverbial kick in the rear), while others will retreat from contact with the team if publicly challenged in this way. The most effective leader is the person who knows which of his or her employees need a kick in the rear and which need a pat on the back.

Likewise, situations vary from project to project, requiring the project leader to adjust his or her style to the project characteristics. For instance, a hard-bid industrial project with thin margins going through a tough winter probably requires a leader to push hard for task performance, with close, frequent scrutiny of budgets, schedules, equipment usage, and crew sizes. More patience and a broader view of task completion will be needed in a Design-Build negotiated transportation job with a repeat client who wants the builder to work with the neighborhood in solving problems.

There is a difference between being a leader and being a manager. Most construction projects of any degree of complexity or size require both leadership **and** management. Management is the part of the project supervisor's job that involves controlling risk, coordinating the work, enforcing the rules, working within the company's system, and providing instructions on how to complete work tasks.

Obviously, there is a lot of this type of work required of project supervisors on a construction project. Leadership involves creating opportunities for others, energizing the team to do the work, improving the system, and helping others learn. The most effective project supervisors, and those who add the most value to their employers, are good leaders as well as good managers. Project supervisors should know what type of power they have over the project team. Project supervisors usually have **legitimate power** that comes from their position in the company. They are positioned in the organization chart or the project matrix as the direct supervisor of a number of workers, so their position gives them some power over some of the workers on the project, at least if some of the work is self-performed. Another form of legitimate power is that spelled out in the contract. Most contracts include language out-lining the steps to be taken if another party is not performing adequately. Project supervisors can begin the process, as spelled out in the contract, to exercise legitimate power over a non-performing party. **Reward power** is the power to distribute resources such as time, money, or work tasks. This type of power was discussed in the earlier section on rewards and motivation.

Referent power is achieved when team members admire and respect the leader and want to behave like the leader. Workers refer to the leader as a role model and try to emulate his or her behavior. Referent power comes from the individual regardless of position or access to resources. **Expert power** comes from special knowledge or skill that is required by the team. If someone has expertise or highly specialized skill or knowledge that is required by the team to complete the project, that person has power over the other members of the team. Many project supervisors and project managers have expert power because of their experience in a variety of construction projects. **Coercive power** is the power to punish or even physically harm. As mentioned earlier, most project supervisors have some power to punish (withhold payment, dock hours, reject work). However, the use of coercive power becomes less and less effective the more it is relied upon.[i]

Technical competence is another requirement of good leaders. A construction project supervisor could be very good at adapting his or her style to the individuals on the team and to the situation, very good at managing budgets and schedules, and understand the use of power. However, put this same individual in charge of a software development team, and the results would probably be disastrous, even though there is a team, a project, a schedule, a budget, and so on. Good leaders must understand the goals and objectives of their particular team in order to lead, and for the construction project supervisor that requires a strong understanding of the construction process.

Activity 27 involves a self-assessment of leadership style. The instructions for Activity 27 are found in Worksheet 27 in the Appendix. Your instructor will tell you when to turn to WS 27 to apply what you have learned about leadership styles.

Personality Styles

One of the most common personality style descriptions is the Myers-Briggs Type Indicator (MBTI)®, which describes four attributes of personality that indicate an individual's preferences in how to communicate, interpret, and perceive information[ii].

There are other good descriptions of personality style available, and your company may have a professional development or management training program that utilizes a different system for describing personality styles. If that is the case, the names or categories of personality styles may differ, but the basic principles and their application to project teams are probably very similar.

The first dimension of the MBTI® describes how a person prefers to interact with the outside world to generate new ideas or innovative solutions. Extroverts prefer to "talk out loud" in face-to-face conversations in order to sort through their ideas. They are energized by being around other people and enjoy the opportunity to share in an interactive dialogue to produce a workable solution. Introverts, on the other hand, prefer to have time alone to reflect on the problem before offering their ideas. They need some time alone to think things over before giving a solution, and they are energized by quiet surroundings that allow them to work through the issues internally.

The second dimension involves how people approach problems. Some individuals have a personality type that prefers to gather a great deal of information before making a decision, and would rather have concrete issues defined. They act based on the present situation as it is understood and live in the here-and-now world of practical solutions. Other individuals have a personality style that prefers a much more abstract and conceptual approach to problem solving. People with this personality type will make a decision quickly and then gather information to see if the decision is working out. They are quickly bored by details and prefer to deal with future possibilities rather than current problems.

The third dimension of the MBTI® involves the process people use to make decisions. Some people are very objective and logical in their approach to problem solving, preferring to make decisions based on which of the available options will get the job done most efficiently. Other people use a process that is more subjective and emotional, preferring to make decisions based on which of the available options will be perceived as most fair, or will best support the personal values of the team members.

The final dimension involves how people organize their lives. Some people prefer highly structured and planned lives, while others are comfortable with change, spontaneity, and flexibility. The personality

Activity 28 is an exercise for determining personality styles of other members of your team. The instructions for Activity 28 are found in Worksheet 28 in the Appendix. Your instructor will tell you when to turn to WS 28 to apply what you have learned about personality styles.

type that prefers order and structure will likely ask what the deadline is or what the plan is, while the personality type that prefers keeping all options open will be much less concerned with these details.

The cause of much of the conflict in teams can be traced to personality differences. If you understand your own personality, and can make some observations about the personality styles of other team members, you can communicate better. The most effective leaders understand how to tailor their communication to the personalities of their team members. As one small example, a good leader might send e-mails to introverts, asking for a response within two days, whereas he or she might meet an extrovert face-to-face and ask if they can talk over some ideas. The more styles you can incorporate into the problem solving aspects of a project team, the more likely you are to find the best solution.

To get a better understanding of personality styles and to take a short, free self-assessment, visit the following website: http://www.personalitypathways.com/type_inventory.html.

Please be aware that on-line personality or cognitive style assessments are meant as general guides to better understanding, and should not be considered replacements for a professionally administered and facilitated assessment. If you are interested in learning more about your style and how it affects your ability to work in teams, ask your supervisor or the human resources department in your company to arrange for a professionally administered assessment, with follow-up discussion on the meaning of the assessment.

To Implement What You Have Learned

Write down one concept or idea from Session 9 that you think everyone in your company should know to improve the way your company does business.

Write down one thing you learned in Session 9 that you think should be included in your company's project management training program for entry-level project managers.

Write down one thing you learned in Session 9 that you intend to use on your next project to make the project more successful.

Before the next session, develop the three ideas you listed above into a short memo, and schedule a meeting with your sponsor to discuss your ideas and develop an action plan. Remember that when trying something new, it is important to have the support of your sponsor and other champions in the organization, and to make small, incremental changes. Your sponsor has received an executive summary of this session and will be expecting your report and your phone call to set up a meeting with him or her to discuss your ideas for the company.

If you would like to learn more about managing people, we suggest you register for STP Unit 1, *Leadership and Motivation.*

[i] The five forms of power were first described by John French, Jr. and Bertram Raven in a monograph entitled "The Bases of Social Power" (pp. 607-623) in the book *Group Dynamics,* edited by D. Cartwright and A. Zander, published in 1960 by Harper and Row of New York.
[ii] The MBTI was developed in 1943 by Isabel Myers and Katharine Cook Briggs. CPP, Inc (Consulting Psychologists Press) currently holds the rights to the personality type indicator instrument.

Understanding Corporate Policies/Procedures

Goal and Performance Objectives of Session 10

Goal: After this session, you will understand how to recognize corporate policies and procedures and to incorporate this knowledge into how you do your job.

Performance objectives:

■ To learn how local governments and state and federal agencies affect the execution of your project and how corporate policies affect your actions as a supervisor

■ To understand some of the rationale behind why a company might take a certain project

■ To appreciate why you might be assigned to a particular project

■ To learn how construction companies approach the sales function

■ To understand what corporate overhead is and how it is recovered through projects

■ To learn how each construction company is somewhat unique based upon its culture and personality

To Get Ready for Session 10

Read Session 10 and complete any preparatory assignments given by your instructor.

Compliance Issues

Whether project supervisors like it or not, local, state and federal governments play a significant role in the execution of construction projects. In an earlier session, we discussed the impact on the project of permit-issuing agencies, inspectors and other government workers. In this session, the focus is on the employment policies that the federal government imposes upon the company and, in turn, upon the supervisor.

While nearly every contractor has a home office location, the government considers the project site a place of employment. Accordingly, all the compliance issues that apply to the home office apply to the jobsite office. Just a few of the issues that fall into this category are equal employment opportunity (EEO) notices, Right-to-Know notifications, OSHA 300 log postings (lists of injuries suffered by employees), and others. The project supervisor may be required to have new employees complete job applications, W-4 forms for tax withholding, and citizenship verification forms. The supervisor may also be required to examine driver's licenses and Social Security cards presented by employees as proof of citizenship, as part of the I-9 Employment Eligibility Verification process.

Many companies have an employee handbook or manual that describes the policies and procedures that employees are expected to observe. Certain fringe benefits such as sick leave, vacation time and health insurance also may be described in the handbook or manual. Many companies have "at-will" employment and termination policies, which explicitly indicate that there is no guarantee of employment and that either party may terminate the relationship at any time. Nearly all companies will have a human resources (HR) department or at least an HR officer who is in charge of administering (and in some cases, developing) employee-employer policies.

If you or your field employees are members of a collective-bargaining unit, all or parts of the employee handbook or manual may not apply to you. Many of your work rules and details will be dictated by the labor agreement.

A company may or may not have explicit regulations when it comes to hiring and promotion policies. However, it is to your advantage to understand how employees are identified and developed for promotion. If your employer is sponsoring your participation in this STP course, chances are that the company has already decided to invest in you and your skill set.

It also is important to note that many companies will have detailed rules about what may and may not be done with company resources. Failure to observe and follow these regulations can result in disciplinary action, termination, or even prosecution. To reduce liability exposure, many companies do not allow personal use of company vehicles. However, many companies will allow personal use of vehicles, tools, and equipment as long as it is not for personal gain. If in doubt about your company's policy, it is best to read the handbook or to ask your supervisor. Theft of useable building materials, tools, or equipment from your employer can result in jail time. Some companies even have policies against employees salvaging materials from demolition projects.

Many of the compliance issues discussed above apply to supervisors who work for companies that self-perform work. In these situations, the project supervisor is typically in a direct supervisory position over the workers on the jobsite. This employee relationship is different from a subcontractor relationship. The project supervisor must follow company policy and governmental compliance issues for employees. The supervisor's relationship with subcontractors on the jobsite will be much more contractual. The expectations and obligations of the project supervisor and subcontractor employees will typically be spelled out in contract language, rather than dictated by governmental regulations or company policies. Make no mistake, there are certain compliance issues specific to subcontractors (like federal prompt payment guidelines), but in general, the relationship between the project supervisor and subcontracted workers on the site will be different from the relationship between the supervisor and employees of the company for which he or she has direct supervisory responsibilities.

Project Portfolio/Risk Diversification

As discussed previously, the construction company will fail if it is unable to procure and to execute profitable work. However, the project supervisor may wonder from time to time, "Why did we take this project?" The answer to the **why** question can be quite complicated sometimes; at other times, the answer is very simple. The simplest answer is that "we were the low bidder," but this response often hides a complex thought process that resulted in the company bidding the project. Projects are often bid because the company needs a certain level of revenue to ensure that it will have a high enough level of job profit to cover company overhead and to provide some corporate profit. Contractors almost never have the luxury of dictating what projects are available to bid.

Sometimes, projects are bid in order to give the contractor the opportunity to develop new expertise. What better way is there to learn how to build post-tensioned concrete parking decks than to build one or two? After the company constructs a few projects of a certain type (assuming the experience was profitable), the company will want to reinforce the developed expertise by continuing to do that type of work. Similarly, the type of work sought will provide employment opportunities to help keep skilled workers in the company from being lost to competitors.

Contractors may also seek certain projects to keep competitors out of a market or out of a sector of the market. The best illustration of this concept is the owner who often negotiates work with a certain contractor, but occasionally bids out some work to keep the preferred contractor honest. The preferred contractor typically will bid the work very competitively to keep other contractors from working for the owner. Because a large portion of company overhead is expended in the sales, marketing, and bidding effort, repeat clients are highly valued.

A contractor also may pursue a project to help average out the risk in its project portfolio. Adding some low-risk projects to balance out a high-risk project helps the company to ensure that it will at least break even if the riskier project does not turn out as planned. Construction contracting, like any business activity, usually is based upon the principle of "the higher the risk, the higher the return." Having a diversity of projects from a risk perspective helps a contractor ensure its consistent profitability.

Project Staffing Decisions

Closely related to the question "Why did we take this project?" is "Why am I on this project?" Many of the answers are similar to those just given. For example, you might be on the project because you were the one supervisor who was available, or the physical location is close to your home or to another project that you are running. The rationale is usually more detailed, however. You might be on the project because your prior experience or existing technical expertise matches the project needs. Or, your manager wants to give you the opportunity to develop new expertise.

Another reason you might be on a project is that your strengths and weaknesses complement those of the rest of the team. Your weakness might be paperwork, so you are assigned an assistant supervisor or project engineer who is very good with paperwork. On the other hand, you might be very good at being assertive while your assistant may not be. Your past working relationship with a repeat client or designer may be why you were selected. Your participation may have been requested by a repeat client or promised during the sales and negotiation phases of the project. The bottom line is that there are numerous reasons a particular project supervisor may be assigned to a particular project.

Sales Prospecting

Activity 29 designs a system for bouncing up sales leads from the field to the office. The instructions for Activity 29 are found in Worksheet 29 in the Appendix. Your instructor will tell you when to turn to WS 29 to apply what you have learned about sales prospecting.

Sales are what fuel the engine of the construction company. Some companies are large enough that they have dedicated sales representatives. Others are so small that the primary shareholder is the main salesperson. At any size company, all employees may be empowered to be salespeople. If your company employs the "everyone sells" approach, you need to know when to hand off the sales lead to the people qualified to scope the work, to provide cost estimates and to negotiate contract terms. Even if you are not part of the formal sales strategy for the company, your everyday performance helps to sell the company's professionalism, competence and reputation for quality. As project supervisor, you may have everyday contact with owner representatives. Your performance has a direct effect on the likelihood of the owner either asking your company to bid the next project or selecting your company to negotiate the next project.

If you are asked to be involved in the sales effort, think about all your networking opportunities. To what clubs and organizations do you belong? Do you have relatives or close friends in decision making positions at local businesses? Do you know realtors in the commercial sector? All these contacts could help you obtain valuable information about the building plans of various entities. These leads should be followed up quickly or passed on to the sales staff of the organization. Usually there are more leads than the company has time to chase. It is important to qualify these leads so that the projects that are most likely to happen are targeted. The same is true with cold calls and mass-mailings. It is often best to take a focused approach in lieu of a "shotgun" approach. If there are more leads than there is time to follow up on all of them, why not try to identify the best leads and focus on those?

The preceding discussion is largely directed at privately owned entities that have the legal capability of selecting any project delivery system they wish. With most public organizations, such as school districts and municipalities, the delivery system is often prescribed or limited by statute. Most of these projects will use the Design-Bid-Build system. There are several ways to learn about competitive bidding opportunities, and the people in the estimating department are most likely to follow these sources. The most basic is staying in touch with local design firms to learn what they have coming out for bid. Another method is to watch the public notice section of the newspaper, as many government bodies are required to advertise in this manner. There are a number of commercial reporting services that research and issue information about projects to be bid. Plan rooms are another avenue by which to learn what is out for bidding.

Corporate Overhead

All construction companies in the United States (and other free-market economies around the world) are in business to make a profit. Very few construction companies are paid to do estimating or preliminary work on projects, so most generate a profit by constructing so that the field costs are less than the owner contract amount. Some companies manage to enhance profit through short-term investment of surplus cash flows, but even this ability depends upon profitable projects. The job profit on any one project is seldom purely profit to the company. Nearly all companies will have overhead or costs that cannot be attributed to specific projects. The company profit is equal to the sum of all the job profits, less the overhead costs for the company.

Overhead consists of many categories:

- Home office, warehouse and yard
- Rent, utilities, property insurance, or property taxes
- Home office employee salary and benefit costs such as officers, estimators, sales people, clerical staff, or accountants
- Some types of insurance and office supplies

Although construction equipment is used only onsite, some companies charge equipment maintenance and repairs to overhead accounts, to simplify the accounting for individual projects. Many companies will find that job profits exceed overhead only by a small margin each year. This difference is equal to the profit that is reported to the IRS. Just because your employer has a 6% fee on a negotiated project, it is not true that the company is making a 6% profit.

Activity 30 involves a discussion of how corporate culture drives project selection. The instructions for Activity 30 are found in Worksheet 30 in the Appendix. Your instructor will tell you when to turn to WS 30 to apply what you have learned about corporate culture.

From an accounting point of view, it is preferable to assign as many of the costs (that are directly attributable to the project) as possible to the cost of the project. However, the owner contract on a cost-plus contract may restrict which items can be billed to the owner. In other words, the contractor may choose to allocate certain overhead costs to the project, even though the owner will not reimburse these costs. It is hoped, however, that the project fee would be large enough to absorb these non-reimbursed costs, so that the project is still profitable from the contractor's perspective. After all the job profits are added up and all the overhead costs are deducted, a successful contractor will have a net income (before taxes) of only a few percentage points of its revenue for the year.

Corporate Culture/Personality

Just as there are many kinds of people in the world, every company has its own unique corporate culture or personality. Some companies are built around the concept that the employee is a resource, just as a pickup truck or wheelbarrow is a resource. In general, these companies are having a harder time succeeding, as more and more employees are highly educated and trained and no longer view themselves as commodities. At the other end of the spectrum are the companies that acknowledge employees as individuals with families, lives outside of the work environment, and problems of their own that they need to solve.

Activity 31 challenges you to summarize your implementation notes from each session and to design a personal development plan. The instructions for Activity 31 are found in Worksheet 31 in the Appendix. Your instructor will tell you when to turn to WS 31 to apply what you have learned about professional development.

Some employers are very good about celebrating the individual and providing recognition for achievements made by individuals. In some cases, employees are praised for contributions they make to their community. The company may have a focus on its employees or it may have a focus on the ownership. Many construction companies are closely held, family-owned enterprises, so it is sometimes possible for the personal egos of the owners to overshadow what is right for the company as a whole, or the employee as an individual. In other cases, the ownership may attempt to reach out to the employees to make them feel they have a stake in the company's success. In extreme cases, certain employees may be offered a seat at the ownership table. Both situations have their advantages and disadvantages, and a situation that might be ideal for you when you're 28 might not be what you'd want when you are 45. The key thing is to recognize what situation you are in and to act accordingly.

Some companies hold decision making authority very close to the top of the organizational chart, while others delegate it to very low levels. The project supervisor must recognize how much decision making authority has been delegated to him or her. On one hand, a supervisor can be criticized for failure to make a timely decision for which authority has been delegated. On the other, the supervisor can get into trouble for making a decision that he or she did not have the authority to make. The supervisor must be able to quickly determine whether the decision at hand is one that he or she should make, or if the decision is one that must be directed to higher management authorities. If it is a decision that the supervisor should make, it is usually best to formulate a reasonably informed decision, to make the decision, and to move forward. Time lost waiting to make a fully informed decision or thoroughly investigating all the possible alternatives is rarely recovered, and that loss could delay the project completion beyond what could have been achieved with a faster decision making process.

Professional development of the individual in the form of training and self-improvement exercises has an effect in building the supervisor's skill set. Expansion of skills and capabilities, coupled with experience, enhances the likelihood of promotion, additional responsibilities, and higher income. Many companies invest heavily in the individual, taking the attitude that improving the employee improves the company. Other companies will expect the employee to take the initiative to improve. Professional development support is only one aspect of an employee compensation and benefits plan. Benefits can include paid time off (sick leave, vacation time); flexible work hours; health, dental, life and disability insurance programs; retirement/pension programs; and flex benefit programs. Depending upon your current life circumstances, you may prefer better benefits to higher pay. Again, what works well for you at age 28 may not be what you want at age 45.

If you or your field employees are members of a collective-bargaining unit, all or parts of the company compensation and benefits plan may not apply to you. Most of your compensation and benefits will be dictated by the labor agreement.

Whether one wants to acknowledge it or not, the professionalism and reputation of the project supervisor reflects upon his or her employer. At the same time, the professionalism and the reputation of the company reflects upon the supervisor. If you are a fair and honest person, but the company treats subcontractors poorly, the presumption about you will be that you will not be fair to subcontractors. While many people both inside and outside the company will separate the attributes of the company and supervisor, some will let their opinion of one be colored by the other. The bottom line is that your character and that of the company you work for should be compatible.

To Implement What You Have Learned

Write down one concept or idea from Session 10 that you think everyone in your company should know to improve the way your company does business.

Write down one thing you learned in Session 10 that you think should be included in your company's project management training program for entry-level project managers.

Write down one thing you learned in Session 10 that you intend to use on your next project to make the project more successful.

Develop the three ideas you listed above into a short memo, and schedule a meeting with your sponsor to discuss your ideas and develop an action plan. Remember that when trying something new, it is important to have the support of your sponsor and other champions in the organization, and to make small, incremental changes. Your sponsor has received an executive summary of this session and will be expecting your report and your phone call to set up a meeting with him or her to discuss your ideas for the company.

We have noted what the other numbered STP units cover at the end of each session's narrative. If there is another STP unit that you would like to take, please contact your sponsor or ask your instructor about enrolling in another STP offering.

Unit 8 Summary

The next 12 pages include a summary of each session of Unit 8, *Managing the Project: The Supervisor's Role.* Use these summaries for the in-class review and for quick reference in course planning or reference after classes.

Session 1   Understanding Delivery Systems

The goals and objectives for participant learning in Session 1 are:

■ To create an awareness of how the type of delivery system or contracting method affects the roles and responsibilities of the project management team

■ To understand how different strengths and weaknesses of the individual project team members may affect the delegation of project management responsibility

■ To develop an appreciation for the interdependence of the project management team and the various roles and responsibilities that must be coordinated to achieve optimum project performance

■ To broaden the project supervisor's awareness of his or her roles and responsibilities on the project, and how they might change based on project contracting method, team strengths and weaknesses, and market conditions

Session 1 includes the following topics:

General Contracting

- Design-bid-build (Hard bid)

- Negotiated

Construction Management

- At risk

- Agent (not at risk)

Design/Build (and Assist)

The supervisor's roles and responsibilities change under each delivery system

The supervisor's roles and responsibilities can also change under different team characteristics (experience, staffing level, leadership, etc.)

In a broad sense, the project supervisor has three basic responsibilities on every project:

- Managing tasks

- Managing people
- Managing risk

Session 2   Managing Information

The goals and objectives for participant learning in Session 2 are:

■ To create an awareness of how information flows throughout the project life cycle

■ To understand the types of information the project supervisor is typically responsible for generating, coordinating and/or managing

■ To develop an appreciation for how information created and managed by the project supervisor is used by other project team members

■ To broaden the project supervisor's awareness of how the scope and nature of information management may vary based on project contracting method, team strengths and weaknesses, and means and methods

Session 2 includes the following topics:

Information Flows

- To the superintendent
- From the superintendent

Project Life Cycle

Effective Control Systems

Documentation

- Requests for information
- Construction changes
- Daily field reports
- Quality Control logs
- Labor production and labor time
- Toolbox safety talk attendance
- Two-week look-ahead plans
- Speed-memos (performance problem notifications)

Types of Meetings

- Preconstruction planning meetings
- Pre-award meeting with each sub
- Kickoff meeting

- Weekly project meetings
- Bimonthly management meetings
- Design review meetings (for design-build delivery)

Purpose of Meetings

- Communication
- Problem solving
- Coordination

Effective Meetings

Use (and Abuse) of Technology

Protocols/Chain of Command

Responsibility Matrix

Session 3   Managing & Understanding Risk

The goals and objectives for participant learning in Session 3 are:

■ To create an awareness of how risk changes over the life of a project

■ To understand the types and sources of risk in the construction phase of the project life cycle

■ To develop knowledge of techniques for managing risk, specifically risks that are the primary responsibility of the project supervisor

■ To broaden the project supervisor's awareness of how the scope and nature of risk management may vary based on project con-tracting method, team strengths and weaknesses, and means and methods

Session 3 includes the following topics:

The Project Team's Role in Risk Control

Risk Management

- Owners "delegate" risk
- Contractors "delegate" risk
- Subcontractors further "delegate" risk

General Sources of Risk

- Budget/cost (money problems)
- Time (schedule problems)
- Design (design flaws)

- Quality (construction defects)
- Safety (loss of life, loss of time, loss of property)

Managing the Risks

- Bonding and sureties (monetary risk/construction defects)
- Insurance (safety)
- Subcontract vs. self-perform (cost risk, schedule risk)
- Site management (safety)
- Budget and cost controls (monetary risk)
- Quality Control plan (construction defects, design flaws)
- Schedule (time)
- Safety plan (loss of life; loss of time)

Project Factors Affecting Risk

- Location of project
- Nature of project
- Construction process
- Project organization

Risks Managed in the Field

- Enforcement of safety requirements
- Quality assurance
- Labor cost control

Costs Associated with Poor Risk Management

The Future of Risk Management

Session 4   Planning the Work

The goals and objectives for participant learning in Session 4 are:

■ To learn how preconstruction planning is defined and how it should be done

■ To learn what planning tasks are required of the project supervisor

■ To learn the basics of site planning in preparation for a future session

■ To learn how to set up a system to manage information

■ To learn basic scheduling techniques

Session 4 includes the following topics:

Preconstruction Phase Planning and Management

Preconstruction Project Planning

- Determining work tasks (what)
- Means and methods selection (how)
- Delegating primary responsibilities (who)
- Allocation and prioritization of resources (why)
- Sequencing of the work on the project (where)
- Scheduling of the work (when)

Preconstruction Site Planning

- Delivery routing
- Lay-down areas
- Parking areas
- Public access control
- Storage trailers
- Office trailers
- Temporary utilities

Preconstruction Information Planning

- Job files
- Design clarification and communication
- Daily logs
- Time sheets
- Job trailer set-up
- Computer set-up

Preconstruction Project Scheduling

- Sequencing of work
- Activity durations
- Predecessor and successor activities
- Resource loading (balanced crew sizing)
- Critical path calculations
- Contract compliance

SESSION 10

Session 5   Working the Plan

The goals and objectives for participant learning in Session 5 are:

■ To learn how to mobilize and to organize a project in the field

■ To learn the basics of field purchasing for commodity materials

■ To learn how to expedite material and equipment orders

■ To learn how to manage the inspection and approval processes

■ To understand the importance of keeping plans and schedules up-to-date

■ To learn the basics of closing out a project in the field

Session 5 includes the following topics:

Construction Phase Tasks

Mobilization

- Identify team members (foremen, field engineer)
- Temporary utility hook-ups
- Data link and networking
- Move-in trailers
- Project sign
- Install security fence and gates

Purchasing

- Setting up accounts
- Standing purchase orders
- Reviewing POs and subcontracts for scope
- Scheduling deliveries
- Pricing of commodity items
- Make-or-rent decisions (e.g., formwork)
- Own-or-rent decisions (e.g., all-terrain forklift)

Expediting

- Assist project manager in tracking submittals
- Assist project manager in buy-out
- Track subcontractor progress
- Verify deliveries (e.g., PRO numbers)

Approvals

- Building inspections
- Owner/architect inspections
- Testing agency inspections
- EPA/surface water
- Closeout
- Operation and maintenance data
- Warranties and guarantees
- Attic stock
- Training
- Punch list
- Final inspections
- Final pay application
- Final lien waivers

Session 6   Managing Methods and Materials

The goals and objectives for participant learning in Session 6 are:

■ To learn the details of site layout

■ To understand factors influencing equipment selection

■ To learn material handling, storage and protection techniques

■ To be able to analyze prefabrication vs. onsite fabrication options

Session 6 includes the following topics:

Site Layout

- Delivery routing
- Lay-down areas
- Parking areas
- Security fences
- Public-access control
- Storage trailers
- Office trailers
- Temporary utilities

Equipment Selection

- Equipment type
- Equipment size and capacity
- Equipment quantities
- Safety (wind, indoor exhaust, hand signals)
- Minimization of downtime (equipment sharing)
- Maintenance
- Allocating equipment time

Material Handling, Storage, Protection

- Storage trailers
- Offsite storage
- Security
- Other protection (sun, weathering, etc.)
- Coordinating deliveries
- Allocating lay-down space
- Inspecting deliveries
- Minimizing handling

Onsite Fabrication vs. Modular Units/Panelization

- Cost
- Schedule
- Compliance with specifications/design intent
- Compatibility with weather conditions
- Compliance with codes
- Compatibility with local labor climate
- Control of quality

Session 7   Understanding Finances

The goals and objectives for participant learning in Session 7 are:

■ To create an awareness of how cost information cycles through companies and projects

■ To understand project cash flows

■ To develop knowledge of the uses and importance of accurate cost coding

■ To broaden the project supervisor's awareness of how retainage affects financing costs and cash flows

Session 7 includes the following topics:

Cost Information Cycle

- Measures
  - ◊ Estimate to budget
  - ◊ Budget to actual
  - ◊ Actual to historical
  - ◊ Historical to estimate
- Information flows
  - ◊ Field to office
  - ◊ Subcontractor/supplier to office
  - ◊ Office to A/E/owner
  - ◊ Office to field (feedback)

Cost Coding Accuracy

- Understanding cost codes
  - ◊ Level of detail
  - ◊ Direct work vs. indirect work
- Asking for more cost codes when necessary
- Accurate assignment of work to code(s)
- Assessing impact of change
- Garbage in, garbage out (GIGO)
- Bidding accuracy depends highly upon timesheet accuracy

Schedule of Payments/Project Cash Flow

- Contractor self-finances first portion of work
- Monthly progress pay application
  - ◊ Project S curve
  - ◊ Aggressive billing
  - ◊ Cost-loaded schedules
  - ◊ Cost-plus/unit-price/lump-sum
- Retainage
- Reduction in retainage
- "Pay when paid" clauses

Session 8   Working with Project Partners

The goals and objectives for participant learning in Session 8 are:

■ To learn how your actions on the project may affect future work with the client

■ To learn how to work effectively with subcontractors

■ To understand how to work with design firms in different types of projects

■ To appreciate the importance of working with inspectors and government agencies

■ To understand how to work with trade union representatives

■ To understand how to work better with other internal stakeholders (co-workers)

Session 8 includes the following topics:

Working with Owners (Supervisor as the Salesperson)

- Effect of delivery system
- Professionalism
- "Can do" attitude
- Customer is almost always right
- Respect the owner's chain of command
- Problem solving ability (managing changes)

Working with Subcontractors in the Field

- Hard bid vs. negotiated subs
- Resolve/firmness
- Resolution of performance issues
- Taking excuses away
- Coordinated planning
- Cleanup
- Monitoring sub progress
- Assessing sub completion percentage

Working with Designers

- Project delivery system effect
- Constructability
- Safety
- Change management

- Punch list management
- Quality and inspections

Working with Inspectors/Governments

- Entities with limited or no stake in project having power to bring project to a halt
- Coordinating inspection schedules
- Allowing lead time for inspections prior to Cert. of Occup./Cert. of Comp. and move-in
- Involving inspectors in change as necessary
- Acknowledging limited technical knowledge of some code officials

Unions

- Jurisdictional disputes
- Political power
- Dual gates
- Work rules

Working with Internal Stakeholders (accounting, PM, corporate, etc.)

- Timely response to requests for information
- Respect for other parts of organization
- Setting appropriate boundaries
- Respect of higher decision-making authority
- Profit center vs. cost center

Session 9   Understanding People

The goals and objectives for participant learning in Session 9 are:

■ To create an awareness of how relationships affect project performance

■ To understand various leadership styles

■ To develop knowledge of techniques for motivating and rewarding project team members

■ To broaden the project supervisor's awareness of how the appropriate leadership style may vary based on project contracting method and the nature of the team

Session 9 includes the following topics:

Motivation and Rewards

- Compensation
- Benefits
- Threats/coercion (short-term and infrequent)
- Recognition
- Working conditions
- Co-worker relations
- Personal growth
- Career advancement

Leadership Skills

- Charisma and personality/styles
- Tasks vs. people
- Adjusting style to the individual
- Adjusting style to the situation
- Managing vs. leading
- Power
- Competency

Personality styles (MBTI)

- Extrovert vs. Introvert
- Intuition vs. Sensing
- Thinking vs. Feeling
- Judging vs. Perceiving

Session 10   Understanding Corporate Policies/Procedures

The goals and objectives for participant learning in Session 10 are:

■ To learn how local governments and state and federal agencies affect the execution of your project and how corporate policies affect your actions as a supervisor

■ To understand some of the rationale behind why a company might take a certain project

■ To appreciate why you might be assigned to a particular project

■ To learn how construction companies approach the sales function

■ To understand what corporate overhead is and how it is recovered through projects

■ To learn how each construction company is somewhat unique based upon its culture and personality

Session 10 includes the following topics:

Compliance

- Government policies

  ◊ EEO

  ◊ Right-To-Know rules

  ◊ OSHA 4-in-1 notification

  ◊ OSHA 300 logs

- Corporate policies

  ◊ At-will employment and termination

  ◊ The role of the human resources department

  ◊ Promotion and hiring practices

  ◊ Personal use of company resources (e.g., company truck)

Project Portfolio/Risk Diversification

- Why did we take this project?

  ◊ Repeat client

  ◊ Develop new expertise

  ◊ Reinforce existing expertise

  ◊ Low-risk project to balance high-risk contract elsewhere (or vice versa)

  ◊ Keep competitors out of market

  ◊ Retain skilled workers

  ◊ Need for certain level of revenue to recover overhead

Sales/Marketing

- Sales prospecting

  ◊ Networking opportunities

  ◊ Dedicated sales staff vs. "all-sell"

  ◊ Qualifying leads

  ◊ Targeted cold calls and mailings

- Information sources
  - ◊ Commercial report services
  - ◊ Bid exchanges
  - ◊ Public notices

Project Staffing Decisions

- Why am I on this project?
  - ◊ Prior experience or existing technical expertise matches project needs
  - ◊ Opportunity to develop new expertise
  - ◊ You were available (next-in-line selection)
  - ◊ Past working relationship with client or partners
  - ◊ Physical location of the project
  - ◊ Result of client request or project promises
  - ◊ Compensate for weaknesses of other team members

Corporate Overhead

- Project profits and investing must cover general corporate overhead
- When in doubt, assign it to a project (not feasible for all types of overhead or projects)
- Categories of corporate overhead
  - ◊ Officer salaries and benefits
  - ◊ Support staff salaries and benefits
  - ◊ Office space (rent, light, heat, phone, etc.)
  - ◊ General supplies and expenses
  - ◊ Yard warehouse and storage
  - ◊ Certain types of insurance
  - ◊ General equipment/fleet depreciation

Corporate Culture/Personality

- Employee as a "whole person" vs. a resource
- Employee recognition for achievement
- Balance of employer-focus vs. employee-focus
- Delegation of decision-making authority
- Job descriptions

- Professional development support
- Employee compensation and benefit plans
- Company's professional reputation
- Company's community reputation

SESSION 10

Notes

APPENDIX

Participant Worksheets for In-Class Activities

APPENDIX

WS 1

Ice-Breakers

To maximize the benefit of this course, it will be necessary for you to work in teams on in-class exercises allowing you to apply what you have learned in the sessions. You will be able to work more effectively as a team if you get to know other members of your team before working on any of the activities.

Another goal of this class is to get the participants to share their knowledge with each other through in-class discussions of the topics presented. It will be easier to start this discussion if you know the other individuals in the class.

For these reasons, the instructor may begin the first session with some ice-breakers. There are a number of different ways to get people in the class talking to each other. Use the space below to write down some things you learned about other members of the class.

WS 2

Sponsor's Guide

The sponsor's guide is intended to help you implement what you have learned in the everyday activities of your company. The instructor will work with you on implementation details using the Sponsor's Guide. In the space below, write the details of your Sponsor's Guide.

Sponsor name:_____

Weekly meeting time:_____

Contact information:_____

_____

_____

APPENDIX

WS 3

Best Delivery Method

Design-Bid-Build is the dominant delivery method for public-sector construction such as transportation systems, government office buildings, etc.

Construction Management is a popular choice of delivery for school districts and state prisons (among others).

Design-Build is the preferred choice of real estate developers, and is used for transportation projects involving reconstruction of heavily traveled urban corridors.

Discuss among your team some ideas related to the following question:

Why do you think these different types of owners use different types of delivery systems?

Write down your team's answers in the space below.

Public sector	School board	RE developer

WS 4

Delivery Team Roles and Responsibilities

Review the Sure Fresh documents that came with your STP Unit 8 Participant's Manual. The course instructor will assign members of your team different roles to play during your review of the Sure Fresh project documents.

Team member	Project Role	Experience

You are a project team that has to meet the new project supervisor in an hour. You need to tell him or her what your expectations are for supervisory performance. In particular, you have to tell the project supervisor what the expectations are for managing people, tasks, and risk.

The course instructor will also assign some project attributes for you to consider.

Delivery type	Repeat owner?	Market conditions	Other	Other

What will you tell the new project supervisor when you meet with him/her? Use the Performance Profile on PowerPoint Slide 13 as a guide for thinking about the type of project supervisor you need on the project.

WS 5

Design an Information/Idea Management System

Using the diagram on page 2-3 of your Participant's Manual as a guide, complete the following worksheet. In the left column, list the types of information you manage on a project, including design information, planning information, safety information, cost information, etc. Create as many categories as you need to capture all the different types of information you receive, create, distribute, or archive on a project.

In the next three columns, list where this information comes from, where it needs to go, and where it must be stored. Many types of information must go to more than one member of the project team, so be thorough.

In the last column, list the factors that influence the amount, complexity, and pace of information. This can include factors such as the type of delivery system used, the amount of self-perform work, or the relationship with the owner.

Now draw a diagram of all the sources of information, receivers of information, and keepers of information. **Don't worry, the diagram should be messy!** You should have something resembling a giant spider's web when you are through. The objective is to understand the complexity of information management on a construction project.

After you have shared the diagram with others in the class, and have tried to explain to them the types of information flows your diagram represents, discuss some ideas (e.g., filing systems, electronic archives, back-up files, etc.) for tracking and maintaining information on a construction project. You may use the space below to record your team's ideas.

Info type	Info comes from:	Info goes to:	Info stored at:	Factors influencing info

APPENDIX

APPENDIX

Diagram of Information Flows:

WS 6

Control Systems

In the first column, list all the factors and processes that must be controlled on a construction project (e.g., cost, quality, risk, etc.). The number of factors that must be controlled is probably larger than you might think at first, so take some time to brainstorm among the team.

In the second column, list the type of information needed in order to know whether a process or issue is under control (e.g., concrete strengths, labor productivity).

In the third column, list the type of document that best captures and conveys the required information to the project team members who must be involved in the control function.

Factors to be controlled	Information needed	Documents created

For each of the factors above, discuss where the control standard came from and what type of corrective action you will take if actual performance falls outside the standard.

Factors	Source of standard	Corrective action

WS 7

Responsibility Matrix

Review the Sure Fresh project documents that came with your Participant's Manual. The course instructor may give you some additional information to consider while you review them.

Each of the control factors and corrective actions listed in Worksheet 6 must be assigned to some member of the project team. Such assignments of responsibility are frequently communicated in a responsibility matrix.

The course instructor may give you some information regarding the composition of your project team. If not, assign responsibilities to team members that you would normally consider part of every project team (project manager, architect, project supervisor, lead foreman, etc.). You can use the following blank page to list your team members and any relevant project information. In the matrix below, list each of the control factors in the leftmost column, and then list each team member across the top row. Assign each factor to a specific team member by placing an "X" in the box intersecting factor and team member.

Team member→ ↓ Factor of control				

Note any project information from the instructor.

What types of jobs will be needed on your team? List your team members (by title) in the space below:

WS 8

Risk Trade-off in Schedule Acceleration

Using the Sure Fresh documents as a context for discussion, complete the following worksheet. Your instructor will give you additional information to consider in your discussions.

In the left column, list the types of issues or processes on the project that will create risk. Some of the risk factors will be common to almost all construction projects, and you may think of some that are specific to the Sure Fresh project or other parameters given to you by your instructor. Create as many issues as you need to capture all the different types of risk you think you might encounter on the project. Put a check mark in the category of risk (schedule, cost, safety, design, quality) that you think best describes the issue.

What would happen to the risk issues if the owner of the Sure Fresh project came to you after the contract had been signed (but before the work began) and said he or she needed to take occupancy of the building one month sooner than originally scheduled? Indicate which risk issues would be increased by noting a plus sign (+) next to the check mark in the category columns. How much do you think you should be paid to assume these additional risks?

Issues	Schedule	Cost	Safety	Design	Quality

WS 9

Risk Allocation in Supplemental Conditions

Review the AGC 200 general conditions contained in your Sure Fresh packet and use the information to complete this worksheet. In each of the sections and/or articles of the supplemental conditions, note what types of risk are assigned to each party on the project team. For instance, note who is responsible for replacing the work-in-place in case of a fire or windstorm.

Identify each area of risk described in the supplemental conditions by writing a short descriptor in the first column. Then, put a checkmark in the appropriate column denoting which member of the project team (designer, builder, owner) has responsibility for that risk. The resulting product represents a risk allocation table that project managers and construction executives sometimes use to organize their risk management plans.

Area of Risk	Design-Builder		Owner
	Builder	Designer	

APPENDIX

Copy each of the areas of risk assigned to the builder (in the table above) to the left-hand column in the table below. Then, indicate how you will manage that risk. For example, quality of work may best be managed by subcontracting if special tools or technologies are required for high-quality craftsmanship. Some types of risk are best managed by insuring against their occurrence.

Area of Risk Allocated to (Design) Builder	Best Method of Managing the Risk

WS 10

Work Breakdown Structure for Sure Fresh Project

A work breakdown structure (WBS) is fundamental to developing a detailed project schedule and project labor cost codes, and to tracking the project's cost, schedule and, therefore, productivity performance. On very large projects involving multiple bridges or buildings, a work breakdown structure would begin with major facilities, such as the different buildings or bridges on the project. The smallest unit would be work packages, such as drywall for the offices in a specific building on the project. For the Sure Fresh project, you would start with the facilities level such as site work/building. The next level would consist of trade-specific activities like "electrical work" and "painting." You would next move to the task level with examples like "power distribution" and "priming," followed by a distinct, identifiable grouping of the task, such as office vs. warehouse, or 2nd floor, 3rd floor, 4th floor, etc. The example below provides a graphic illustration of how to organize a work breakdown structure.

```
Facilities:        site work          building
                                      /      \
Trades:                        electrical   painting
                                            /      \
Tasks:                                   priming   finish coat
                                         /      \
Work packages:                     offices    warehouse
```

Using the example above as a guide, break down the work of a trade of your choice on the Sure Fresh project (use a separate sheet of paper).

Now that you have developed a WBS for the trade work, discuss within your group at what level it would be practical to track the cost. For example, you may choose to separate the work by trade (e.g., carpenters, laborers, tinners) or operation (e.g., clean up, hang doors, trim windows, etc).

Also discuss how you would go about determining schedule durations for each of the work packages for the trade. Options may include experience or quantities multiplied by productivity rates.

APPENDIX

APPENDIX

WS 11

Preconstruction Plan for the Sure Fresh Project

Using the Sure Fresh documents for project scope and background information, complete the following worksheet. Your instructor may give you additional information to consider in your discussions.

WHAT: Describe the overall scope of work in terms of site work and building construction required to construct the project:

_____

_____

_____

HOW: Discuss the means and methods that will be used to complete the excavation and foundation work:

_____

_____

_____

WHO: Discuss who will do the work (self-perform or subcontract), and how the choice of project delivery system would affect your options:

_____

_____

WHY: Explain why you have chosen this assignment of work:

_____

_____

WHERE: Discuss where on the project and when you will begin the excavation and foundation work. Also, explain why you have chosen this approach:

_____

_____

WS 12

Summary Schedule for the Sure Fresh Project

The Sure Fresh project is typical of many building construction projects. Develop three summary schedules based upon the project delivery system chosen for the project:

1. General Contracting

2. Design-Build

3. Construction Management

Your summary schedule should include general phases and milestones such as design, procurement, mobilization, construction, substantial completion, and closeout. Use a bar chart format to illustrate your summary schedule, overlapping bars where appropriate. Use graph paper to make your schedule, with a scale of each square equal to one week.

Which project delivery system has the shortest summary schedule duration?

_____

Why?_____

_____

_____

Which project delivery system has the longest summary schedule duration?

_____

Why?_____

_____

_____

_____

Discuss within your group how the choice of project delivery system affects the duration of each phase of the project, as well as how effectively these phases can be overlapped.

APPENDIX

WS 13

Identify Team Members for Sure Fresh Project

Using the Sure Fresh documents for project scope and background information as well as your completed Activity 10, complete the following worksheet. Your instructor may give you additional information to consider in your discussions.

Choose two trades involved with considerable work on the project that your employer might be capable of self-performing:

_____

_____

Discuss how the size of the project relative to your employer's overall organization would affect your ability to get the foremen you desire for this project:

_____

_____

Assume that your employer is the hard-bid GC for the project and that your employer used subcontractors for the two trades of work you listed above. How much input will you have regarding the subcontractor foremen chosen?

_____

_____

Let's say that your employer is the negotiated GC on a cost-plus basis for the project with a conservatively estimated guaranteed maximum price (GMP). How much input do you have now regarding the selection of foremen?

_____

_____

Assume you are the CM's project supervisor on a public project and the CM is not allowed to self-perform any work. Do you have much influence as to who the prime foremen will be?

_____

_____

WS 14

Analyze General Requirements

The general requirements in the specifications for a project (usually Division 1 on a building project) will address who is responsible for temporary utilities and facilities. Examples include temporary electricity and parking for the workers.

Within your Sure Fresh teams, discuss the types of temporary utilities and facilities on some of your recent projects, and complete the following list:

Temporary Utility or Temporary Facility	Provided by	Usage Paid by

APPENDIX

WS 15

Rent or Buy Decision

The first step in analyzing the rent or buy decision for a piece of equipment is to gather data. To gather that data, you must ask questions. The questions will deal with everything from costs to maintenance to insurance. If you have ever looked at leasing a new car instead of buying one, you have thought through some similar questions.

Form a group of three and complete the following lists:

What questions would you ask if you wanted to rent or lease a piece of equipment?

_____

_____

_____

_____

_____

_____

_____

_____

What questions would you ask if you wanted to buy a piece of equipment?

_____

_____

_____

_____

_____

_____

Your instructor will go group to group to compile the lists of the entire class.

WS 16

Develop a Procurement Schedule for Sure Fresh

While we do not have the luxury of time to develop a full-blown procurement schedule in this session, we can identify the types of materials and equipment that would and would not warrant careful tracking during the expediting task. Review the Sure Fresh drawings and provide up to five examples of each classification of materials and equipment:

Custom-made for this project with a long (say a month or more) lead time:

_____   _____   _____

Custom-made for this project with a short (a few weeks) lead time:

_____   _____

Commodity items that are readily available:

_____   _____   _____

Commodity items that are sometimes subject to shortage:

_____   _____   _____

1. Which long-lead item would be the most disruptive to the overall schedule if its delivery date were delayed one month?

   _____

2. If you could change the project delivery system to Design-Build, what design change would you make to have the largest impact on reducing the schedule duration?

   _____

3. Besides price, what criteria might you use to select the supplier of the item you named in the first question above?

   _____

WS 17

Site Layout for the Sure Fresh Project

The Sure Fresh project site plan is typical of many building construction projects. Using your Sure Fresh site plan, develop a site layout for construction. Your instructor may direct you further as to the location of existing utilities, zoning constraints and other challenges to your task.

First, generate a list of all the temporary facilities, ranging from trailers and lay-down areas to parking and utilities, that you will need in order to safely and efficiently construct the project:

_____   _____

_____   _____

_____   _____

_____   _____

_____   _____

Using graph paper, sketch out a construction site layout plan for the project. After you have experimented with the graph paper, transfer your final plan to the Sure Fresh site plan, taking care to keep the trailers, lay-down areas and parking areas to scale.

After you have drawn your site plan, your instructor will go around the room asking each group for an item to put onto the master list of temporary facilities. Add to the list until there are no unique items remaining. Use the input from the other groups to add to your list above and rework your plan to incorporate those items that you believe should be included.

Time permitting, your instructor may ask each group to make a brief (two- to three-minute) presentation of its design.

WS 18

Design the 'Dream' Company Yard

In an ideal world, construction supervisors could focus solely on putting work into place. Making sure that the tools, equipment, and things like concrete formwork are ready to go would be someone else's job. However, the supervisor sometimes lands in the position of playing "go-fer," especially on smaller projects. In other cases, the supervisor is busy calling the rental houses in town to find a concrete chainsaw for a unique demolition task. Yet at other times, the supervisor is playing mechanic or trying to find someone who can fix a plate compactor that's lost its shake.

Wouldn't it be great to have a highly skilled yard person who had the resources and talents to take care of all these requests with the simple press of a push-to-talk button? While some larger companies might have just such a person (or a team of people), most companies are going to have to settle for something less because they simply don't have the economies of scale necessary to pay for a fully stocked yard including dedicated mechanics. Therefore, you need to strike a balance between what the supervisor would like to have available in a yard and what the company can afford to have in a yard.

Team with individuals who work for similar companies. This exercise might require working with a different group than your usual Sure Fresh team. Once you have formed a team of three to five, work with your group to design the dream yard for the type of work you do.

How would you staff your yard?

_____

_____

_____

_____

What would you have in your yard? Make a list on a separate sheet of paper.

What would you plan to always rent? Make a list on a separate sheet of paper.

How did you determine what to own and what to rent?

_____

_____

_____

How would you handle maintenance?

_____

_____

_____

_____

For the remaining questions, the following assumptions apply:

1,000 SF of warehouse per $2,000,000 worth of work in place per year
Warehouse costs $40 per SF to construct, including design
For each SF of warehouse, 2 SF are needed for setbacks, parking, landscaping, etc. (43,560 SF to the acre)
1 acre of outside storage per $24,000,000 worth of work in place per year
Land costs $50,000 per acre
Annual rent is equal to one-tenth of the land and construction cost
Annual property taxes are equal to one-hundredth of the land and construction cost
Annual utilities are equal to $1.25 per SF of warehouse
Each full-time yard person costs $40,000 per year. You will have one yard person until you exceed $40,000,000 in work in place per year, adding another each time you exceed the next multiple of $40,000,000 in volume
Each full-time mechanic costs $70,000 per year. You will add your first mechanic once you reach $40,000,000 in work in place per year, adding another one at $80,000,000, $120,000,000, etc.

Using the assumptions above, the annual cost to build and staff a warehouse at various levels of annual volume would be:

Volume	Annual Cost, $	% of Volume
$20,000,000	$580,973	2.90%
$50,000,000	$1,502,433	3.00%
$100,000,000	$2,964,866	2.96%

How will you account for this cost? (Charge to company overhead or charge to projects)

_____

Let's say that your company averages a 2 to 3% profit before income taxes. Relative to the company profit, is the cost of the warehouse and yard significant?

_____

Therefore, is it feasible to have everything you'd ever want in the warehouse and yard, or do you need to work to minimize this cost?

_____

APPENDIX

WS 19

Compare and Contrast Tilt-up vs. Precast Walls for the Sure Fresh Project

Using the Sure Fresh documents for reference, compare and contrast using tilt-up vs. precast for the wall panels. Your instructor may give you additional information to consider in your discussions.

Which option will require the most field labor? Why?

_____

_____

_____

Which option will require the most shop drawing coordination? Why?

_____

_____

_____

Assume that the project is located in International Falls, MN. Which method would be best for this location? Why?

_____

_____

_____

In addition to cold weather, what other weather phenomena would prove challenging for tilt-up? Why?

_____

_____

Assuming that the weather conditions are cooperative, which method provides you with the most control as project supervisor? Why?

_____

WS 20

Labor Cost Cycle

Break into your Sure Fresh teams. Identify all of the concrete work (CSI Division 3) that must be performed on the Sure Fresh project. You have been asked by the vice president of operations of your company to develop an estimating template that can be used to perform the initial estimate, relate estimate information to the field in the form of budgets (labor, material, and equipment), track actual costs, and store the actual cost information for use in improving estimate accuracy on future bids.

In the table on the following page, list all the concrete work that needs to be estimated for the Sure Fresh project. Think through the level of detail that is best for keeping track of information through the cost cycle.

Next, describe how you will determine the costs associated with each item of work (vendor quotes, historical costs, best guess of the super-intendent or yard foreman, equipment lease rate lists, etc.). Discuss among your team the most reliable (least risky) method for estimating costs.

After you have determined where the cost information will come from, define how the information will be communicated to the field in the form of budgets. Some issues to consider are:
- Should the field supervisors receive material, equipment, and labor budgets expressed as dollars?
- *177   Should the field supervisors receive only unit budgets (labor hours, material quantities, equipment lease peri-ods)?
- What are the tradeoffs between giving budgets in dollars vs. units?
- What level of detail will be used for communicating budget infor-mation? In other words, how far will work activities be broken down for budget tracking purposes?
- How will the budgets reflect "indirects," such as hoisting, cleanup, and temporary enclosures? In other words, if a carpen-ter is assisting in the hoisting of formwork, should those hours be charged to hoisting, or to formwork? What are the pros and cons of assigning indirect costs to items of work rather than using sepa-rate budgets?

Now that you have set up a system for communicating estimate infor-mation to the field, think about how the actual units or costs are going to be communicated back to the office. How are costs going to be tracked? What types of special or unique information should the esti-mator be aware of if he/she is going to use the Sure Fresh project as a basis for future estimates of similar jobs?

Use the table on the following page to guide development of the cost cycle template.

APPENDIX

Work item	Source of cost information	Type of budget to field	Method of tracking actual cost	Special or unique issues affecting cost to be noted on future estimates

WS 21

Ideal Labor Cost Coding System

What would be your ideal cost coding system for tracking actual costs on a construction job? What are some of the issues that need to be considered, such as level of detail, use of technology, value of time spent recording data, etc.? How much detail is needed to give the project manager an accurate picture of the costs incurred on the project and make margin projections? At what point does cost detail lose its effectiveness and become just a waste of time? How will mixed trade work units (e.g., concrete slabs) and indirect work (e.g., cleanup) be coded in such a way as to be useful to the project manager and the estimator?

Discuss these items with your team and present a short report to the class. Consider different ways of categorizing the work (e.g., by specification division, by trade, by system, etc.). Use the space below to list your ideas.

How are we going to categorize the work?

_____

_____

_____

_____

How far are we going to break down records? To what level of detail are we going to record costs?

_____

_____

_____

_____

_____

_____

APPENDIX

How can we track indirect costs such as hoisting and cleanup so that the estimator knows what costs to use for these items on future projects?

_____

_____

_____

_____

_____

_____

WS 22

Project Cash Flow

Break into your Sure Fresh teams. Your team is to play the role of the concrete subcontractor. Your company will come to the site after the excavation is complete. It has received a subcontract for all concrete work, including strip footings for the cast-in-place concrete walls, column pad footings, CIP walls, and slab-on-grade. You are responsible for all formwork, material, labor and equipment to complete the concrete on the project.

Plan the sequence of work and then estimate the cash flow based on the following assumptions:

- You start work on the first day of the month, a Monday
- • Uniform pay rate of $25/hour for all trades and scales, and payday is every Friday
- Material invoices are paid 10 working days after delivery
- Ready-Mix is $70/CY for material
- Reinforcing steel is $10/CY for material
- Equipment rental charges are paid every two weeks, on Friday
- Equipment needs are:
  - one ground crane at $1,000/day, plus
  - one concrete pump at $500/day when more than 15 yards are poured

Use the costs and assumptions above to complete the cash flow table on the following page. The asterisks indicate where you should have a cash expense entry using the assumptions above. Your instructor may have different or additional assumptions that change the dates that cash is needed. Work closely with your instructor on this activity.

		Labor hrs	Labor expense	Material units	Material expense	Equip used	Equip expense
Week 1	Mon	40		10 CY	*		
	Tue	40		10 CY			
	Wed	48		15 CY			
	Thu	48		15 CY			
	Fri	56	*	15 CY			
Week 2	Mon	56		15 CY			
	Tue	48		10 CY			
	Wed	48		10 CY			
	Thu	40		10 CY			
	Fri	40	*	6 CY			*
Week 3	Mon	40			*		
	Tue	36			*		
	Wed	36			*		
	Thu	32			*		
	Fri	24	*		*		
Week 4	Mon	24			*		
	Tue	24			*		
	Wed	16			*		
	Thu	16			*		
	Fri	8	*		*		*
TOTALS			**		**		

WS 23

Sure Fresh Conflict Resolution

The Sure Fresh project is not particularly complicated, but every project is susceptible to conflict. It turns out that your plumbing subcontractor and the plumbing inspector do not get along very well with each other. It can be said that they "have a history." Specifically, the owner of the plumbing subcontractor (who also works with his tools) and the plumbing inspector were partners in business at one time, but had a less-than-amicable separation.

The applicable code for the project is the State Plumbing Code. In the past, the code has been very conservative regarding the adoption of new materials and techniques. Previously, the code required all waste piping, whether above or below grade, to be cast iron. Recently, the code has been revised to permit PVC piping. In the interest of saving money on the project for the owner, the plumbing subcontractor suggested value engineering the waste piping to PVC in lieu of cast iron. The mechanical engineer of record recommended this change to the owner (but did not update the drawings and specifications), and the owner accepted the credit to the contract for this change.

Unfortunately, the plumbing inspector is not aware of the change to the project plans and specifications and is upset when he comes out to do the underground rough-in inspection and sees PVC piping. The inspector has just returned from his annual two-week trip to the family cabin and has not read the amendment to the code from the State Plumbing Commission. He immediately red-flags the project, thinking that the plumber is willfully violating the plumbing code, and threatens to call the sheriff's deputy out to arrest the plumbing subcontractor.

Knowing that your structural steel is set to arrive the next morning, you realize that the inspector's actions are going to delay the progress on the project if the job is shut down. It does not help anything that your plumber has an anger management problem and is ready to go toe-to-toe with the inspector.

Given that the inspector and the subcontractor have this antipathy, how do you go about getting the PVC approved and inspected and getting the project back on track? Remember that you are caught between two individuals who dislike each other, *and* that you'll need cooperation from both of them after this issue is resolved in order to complete the project successfully.

Discuss proposed solutions among your group for about five minutes. Your instructor will then ask each group for its proposed solution to the conflict.

There will be many different ways of resolving the conflict. Which ones will be the most uncomfortable for the inspector? Why might it be a good idea to give the inspector a way out even though he is clearly wrong given the amendment to the code?

WS 24

OSHA Visit to Sure Fresh

Although your project is located in a remote area, the site borders on an interstate right-of-way. Several OSHA inspectors happen to travel past your site each week on their way to another metropolitan area that does not have a local OSHA office. Even though you do your best to comply with all the OSHA regulations, you have a momentary lapse of caution when you climb onto a snorkel-style lift to inspect some work done by the outside sheet metal subcontractor.

Since timing is everything, you manage to pick one of the five times this week that an OSHA inspector is driving by on the interstate to have your lapse of caution. Specifically, you have forgotten to put on a harness and to attach a lanyard to yourself as you zoom up to look at the sheet metal coping that just doesn't look right. The OSHA inspector sees you on the lift without the proper safety gear and says to *herself*, "that just doesn't look right." She exits at the next opportunity and nine minutes later, she is waiting for you to return to earth from your daring adventure.

After completing your inspection, you turn around to lower yourself to the ground and see the OSHA vehicle next to the trailer. You look closer at the base of the snorkel lift and see that the agent wants to take your picture. You feel uneasy, but you still have not figured out what the interest is in your use of the lift until you lower the boom and begin to climb out. The inspector has caught you red-handed, and now wants to inspect the entire project.

What do you do first? How do you interact with the inspector, knowing that your momentary lapse of caution is likely to result in a fine to your employer?

During the whole site inspection, no further violations are noted; however, you know that your lift exercise likely will result in a citation and fine.

Discuss with your small group how to handle the situation. In 10 minutes, your instructor will go around the room to solicit your ideas so that the class can develop a strategy for handling the inspection.

WS 25

Sure Fresh Jurisdictional Dispute Project

The Sure Fresh project has been designed with precast concrete walls. The precaster is from out of state and always quotes its products erected. The precaster's sub-subcontractor employs only steelworkers and equipment operators. The logic in its home territory is that the precast, albeit concrete, erects most like structural steel with the intense use of a crane and welded and bolted connections. Unfortunately, in the locale of the project, the concrete workers claim the precast erection because the panels are made of concrete. To make matters worse, you are also from out of state and have no idea that a jurisdictional dispute is about to occur on your project.

The precast panels are scheduled to arrive on Tuesday next week. It's Friday, and your concrete paving subcontractor is onsite pouring the loading dock slabs. The concrete paving foreman happens to come into the jobsite trailer while you are on the phone coordinating the move-in of the crane for the precast erection crew for Monday. In the course of the conversation, the concrete paving foreman overhears you talking about the steelworkers coming onto the site first thing Tuesday morning. Before you finish the phone call, the foreman is out of your trailer and sitting in his truck calling his union business agent. However, you are oblivious to any potential issue until an hour later (just 30 minutes prior to quitting time for the weekend) when the business agent for the concrete workers arrives at your jobsite.

As you are from out of town, you do not have any experience with this business agent. All you know is that he is making it very clear that he wants his concrete workers to erect the precast panels and if the steelworkers show up to erect the precast, there will be trouble. All of a sudden, your dream of spending the weekend fishing begins to evaporate. You know that the project is going to be delayed unless you can figure out a way to solve the problem quickly. And you know that your weekend is going to be ruined either way.

Based upon your experience, the suggestions in the Participant's Manual and your instructor's comments, how would you proceed? Work with your group to develop possible courses of action to keep the project moving. Your instructor will go around the room after about five minutes to give you the opportunity to share your solution with the class. Again, there are multiple ways to handle the situation, which you must do, as it clearly will not go away on its own.

Your instructor might challenge you by throwing out twists to the scenario:

1. The project is in a right-to-work state. How does this affect your plan?

    What if your firm is merit shop? What if your firm is union shop?

2. The project is not in a right-to-work state. How does this affect your plan?

    What if your firm is merit shop? What if your firm is union shop?

APPENDIX

WS 26

Low-Cost/No-Cost Rewards for Craftworkers

Your instructor will assign you to teams of four and give you a time limit for this activity.

Within the allotted time, come up with as many low-cost or no-cost means of rewarding craftworkers as possible. Feel free to include ideas that you have actually used on some of your previous projects. When you get the two-minute warning from your instructor, narrow your list down to the five ideas you think will be most effective. The instructor will direct you to share them with others in the class.

Low-Cost/No-Cost Reward Ideas:

_____   _____

_____   _____

_____   _____

_____   _____

_____   _____

_____   _____

_____   _____

_____   _____

Top Five Ideas:

1.

2.

3.

4.

5.

WS 27

Matching Leadership Style to Optimal Project Type

If you had to rate yourself on a 1-to-10 scale on working with tasks (budget, schedule, work, coordination, etc.) and 1-to-10 on working with people (motivating, rewarding, communicating, listening, etc.), how would you score yourself? Place your scores in the following grid and think for a moment about your leadership style.

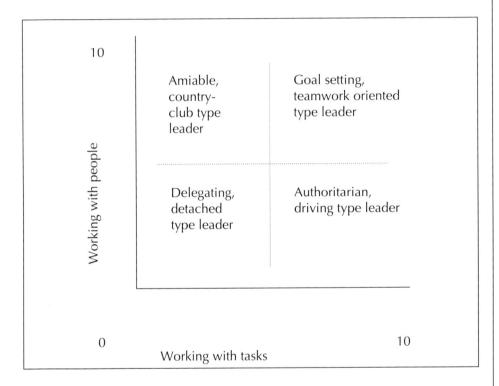

In the space below, list the project characteristics that you think are best suited for your leadership style. Think about issues such as team size, number of people you have to coordinate, complexity of the tasks, schedule flexibility, budget certainty, design completeness, etc.

_____

_____

_____

Which areas of leadership do you think you could improve to make yourself a more effective project leader?

_____

_____

APPENDIX

WS 28

Personality Interaction Exercise

This in-class activity should be fun and straightforward. Your instructor will assign you a partner for this activity. Spend 15 to 20 minutes having a conversation with your activity partner, but instead of just casually conversing, ask questions and listen to answers with the intent of making some assumptions about your partner's personality.

There are many personality tests available from consultants or online testing sites. These can be valuable in understanding yourself and how you relate to others. However, when placed in a team situation, no one comes up and says, "Hi, I'm Bill, and I am an Introverted, Detail-Oriented, Rational, Logical, Planning Personality." (If only it were that simple!) People usually have to spend time with their team members, make observations, and listen carefully to perceive what type of personality they are dealing with. Remember, the goal is not to categorize the other person for the sake of labeling, but to help you communicate better.

Some of the personality traits can be inferred from casual conversation. Asking questions and then listening carefully to the answers is a good practice for leaders to learn. Some examples follow.

To learn whether someone is extroverted or introverted, ask them what they do after work or in their spare time. If the answer is reading books, tinkering in the workshop, or watching TV, they are most likely an introvert. If the answer is going to the sports bar, dancing, or volunteering in the community, then they may be more extroverted.

To try to determine their preference for detail, ask them to describe a vehicle they drive, or tell you about their favorite vacation. If the answer to the first question is "red," you are talking to an intuitive, big-picture personality. If you get color, make, model, year, size of engine, type of transmission, accessories, and upgrades, you are likely talking to a sensing, detail-oriented person. The same would hold true for asking about the vacation. An intuitive type might say "fishing," whereas a sensing personality would give specific details about where they would fish, for what type of fish, whether they would fly-fish or troll, etc.

For the personality dimension involving thinking types (logical, rational, and objective) vs. feeling types (emotional, aesthetic, and subjective), you can ask how your partner feels about their job. If they talk about the processes and the tasks, they are probably thinking types. If they talk about the people and the teamwork, they are probably feeling types.

Organizational types (perceiving vs. judging) can be more difficult to guess at from a conversation. Remember that perceiving types appear unorganized, are unconcerned about deadlines, and prefer creativity and flexibility. Judging types are natural planners, with details, tasks and routines to guide their lives. You can ask some questions about their typical day or have them describe a project they worked on to see if the answers fall more into the perceiving or judging category.

Use the space below to write down the questions you will ask as well as the relevant comments from your partner's answers, then circle the personality type you think best describes them. Remember, this is just practice! You wouldn't actually write down answers during a casual conversation with a team member, but good leaders train themselves to notice the personality types and preferences of their team members through interactions.

Extrovert/Introvert (Circle partner's most likely type)

Question to ask: _____

Relevant insights from the answers:

_____

Sensing/Intuition (Circle partner's most likely type)

Question to ask: _____

Relevant insights from the answers:

_____

Thinking/Feeling (Circle partner's most likely type)

Question to ask: _____

Relevant insights from the answers:

_____

Judging/Perceiving (Circle partner's most likely type)

Question to ask: _____

Relevant insights from the answers:

_____

WS 29

Bouncing Up the Sales Lead

Many companies have a dedicated sales staff, while others have project managers who also sell and bid work. Regardless of how your company handles the sales function, it rarely hurts to have everyone in the company helping with sales. While you don't want your mason tenders leaving in the middle of the day to make sales calls, it wouldn't hurt to have them tell you about their in-law's restaurant that is about to open a second location.

How do you get everyone involved in the sales effort? The first step is probably letting them know that sales leads are welcome. However, you also need to let everyone know that the sales staff cannot physically follow up on all potential leads. How the leads are prioritized will be driven by the corporate culture (see WS 30), the current workload, profit potential, competition, etc.

Work with the same partner that you worked with on the previous activity. Your charge is to develop a system for bouncing up sales leads from the field to the office. Some things to think about include:

- Must leads follow the chain of command (craftworker to foreman to supervisor to office), or do you designate a person in the home office to receive leads?
- Do you provide incentives for providing leads? Or, do you only reward lead providers whose leads result in actual projects? If so, do you calculate the reward based upon project profitability?
  - How do you handle the "reward" aspect if two or more employees submit the same lead?
  - How do you handle the employee who is upset that his or her lead wasn't followed up on aggressively?
  - Do you provide rewards for leads that could have been read about in the paper or heard about on the radio or TV?
  - Do you provide rewards for leads for publicly bid projects?
- Do you provide incentives to people in estimating and sales, especially if they do not currently have a performance bonus system in place? (While sales and estimating might be their main job, these employees might want to rewarded for the leads they generate.)

These are just some of the things to think about in designing your lead generation and incentive program. Using a blank sheet of paper, develop your program. Your instructor will give you approximately 10 to 15 minutes to work on your design. At the end of the work time, your instructor will go around the room and ask you to present your plan.

WS 30

Corporate Culture and Project Selection

While there are some companies that will bid everything in sight, most companies have a culture-driven philosophy or strategy that determines what projects they will bid or not bid (or, in the case of negotiated projects, pursue or not pursue). Some of the factors that contribute to the bid/no bid determination are the client, size of project, location of project, type of work, competition, risk, volume, etc.

Work with a partner and develop a company profile for your hypothetical construction company. Make sure that you include the following characteristics:

Self-performed trades:_____

_____

Annual volume:_____ Bonding capacity:_____

Location of home and branch offices, if any: _____

Type(s) of work:_____

Current/recent clients:_____

_____

Attitude toward risk: _____

Other items of note: _____

Your instructor will describe various projects that your firm could pursue. Work with your partner to determine which projects you will chase, based upon your company's characteristics.

Why did you choose to pursue the projects that you did? Why did you reject the ones that you did?

WS 31

Personal Development Plan

After each session, you have been asked to write down one thing that everyone in your company should know, one thing that your company should include in its project management training program, and one thing that you intend to use on your next project to make it more successful.

At this time, please review the short memos you have developed over the course of STP Unit 8. Focus on the 10 things that you chose to use on your next project. Group together the ones that have related concepts and write a paragraph for each group. Each paragraph should indicate how you can work on or implement the items in the group over the course of the next year. Again, it is important to choose something achievable to work on first, so that you have some early success in your personal development plan. After you enjoy some successes, move on to some of your more difficult goals.

While many of your personal development goals may be implemented on your own, you may need your manager's support to implement some of your ideas. Hopefully you have been working with your manager after each of the sessions and already have his or her buy-in for your development plan. If you do not have this consensus developed yet with your manager, it is important to get it prior to implementing any ideas that are contrary to standard company practice. You probably have shared many great ideas with your classmates over the course of the 10 sessions, but no one in the class has the authority to grant you permission to conduct your job in a manner that is inconsistent with company policy.

If you have been working with your supervisor over the course of the 10 sessions, you might want to help him or her develop a plan for spreading the word on the things that you think everyone in your company should know about. Again, get your manager's permission and seek his or her guidance on how to communicate the information. Many companies have operations meetings periodically or a newsletter that might facilitate your efforts in this area.

Glossary

Approvals: Authorization to proceed with the flow of work. Necessary approvals are identified in the project specifications and local building codes. Allowing time for approvals is a key factor in effectively planning the work.

Bonding: Contractor or subcontractor provided guarantees for the quality of the work (performance bond) and payment of all suppliers and vendors (payment bond).

Cash Flow: The inflows (revenues) and outflows (expenditures) of money on the project. Calculation of cash flows is important to accurately projecting the contractor's borrowing requirements on a project.

Closeout: Completion of final inspections and punch list, and turnover of replacement stock (extra ceiling tile, light fixtures, paint, etc.), as-built drawings, and operation and maintenance material to the owner. Proper closeout is frequently a requirement for retainage release.

Coercive Power: Using threats such as termination or refusal to pay as a technique for motivating an individual to perform. Coercive power loses its effectiveness over time.

Compliance: Conditions of employment that an employer must follow as dictated by corporate policy or governmental regulations. Examples include passing drug tests, OSHA 300 postings, and Right-to-Know laws.

Construction Manager as Agent: Same process as Design-Bid-Build, with the addition of an owner-hired consultant to assist with the management of the project in return for a fee.

Construction Management at Risk: A project delivery system in which the owner, designer and construction manager work together to provide value to the owner. The contractor takes on additional duties in the preconstruction phase in this delivery system, compared to Design-Bid-Build.

Control System: Any method for comparing actual performance (schedule, cost, quality, etc,) to a predetermined standard.

Corporate Overhead: Costs to the company which cannot be allocated to any specific project, such as office rent, property taxes, and salaries for certain types of executive and support personnel. Profits on projects must be sufficient to cover corporate overhead plus some additional amount for company profit.

Corporate Culture: The values of a company that impact the way is business is transacted and relationships with employees are managed. The company's "personality."

Cost Information Cycle: The movement of information regarding costs—from a historical archive into an estimate, then to a budget, then to a report of actual costs, which is then transferred to the historical costs archive.

Design-Build: A contractual arrangement in which the owner enters into an agreement with a single firm for both design and construction services.

Design-Bid-Build Delivery: A project delivery system, sometimes referred to as "traditional delivery," wherein the owner hires an architect/engineer to design the project, then seeks bids, then enters into a second contract with the low bidder for construction.

REFERENCE

Design Risk: The risk that an assembly or system will not perform the intended function because of insufficient or inappropriate design. Design risk is borne by the architect on Design-Bid-Build projects and by the design/builder on Design-Build projects, with CM at Risk varying in allocation of design risk.

Diversification: An approach to business that attempts to spread business risk across a variety of project types, project locations, and project complexities.

Dual Gate System: A means for accommodating both union and non-union workers on a project. It involves setting up one gate for union members and a separate gate for non-union members to enter the project site and where union members can picket.

Expediting: The process of getting all the necessary materials delivered to the jobsite at the appropriate time to prevent a slowdown in work, while at the same time preventing clutter and premature cash expenditures.

Fabrication: The task of assembling building components such as exterior wall spandrels or roof trusses. The decision to field-fabricate versus shop-fabricate (panelize) represents a tradeoff between cost, schedule, and quality.

Financial Risk: The risk that project costs will exceed project revenues, resulting in an unprofitable project.

Idea Management System: A system of communication for sending information from the various craftworker crews back to the project management team. These ideas can be valuable for identifying waste and improving productivity and safety.

Information Management System: A system of communication for sending information from the project management team to the craftworker crews in the field. This information assists in risk management, scope control, and managing change.

Information Planning: The process of identifying an efficient and secure method for gathering, storing, retrieving, and distributing information on a project.

Insurance: A method of risk management that involves paying another firm to take certain defined risks such as worker injuries, injuries to third parties or their property, or equipment accidents.

Leadership Style: The preference of an individual leader, usually determined by the leader's skills and preferences for managing tasks or people. Different followers and situations require different leadership styles.

Legitimate Power: The power to compel and direct employees that comes from an individual's position as supervisor, manager, boss, chief, etc.

Mobilization: The first construction task on most projects, mobilization involves bringing temporary utilities to the site, moving trailers and equipment to the site, and assembling the project team.

Modularization: The fabrication process of assembling building components offsite and delivering them to the job in "modules."

Negotiated General Contract: In this type of agreement between the owner and the contractor for the construction of a specific project, the price is determined as a result of give-and-take on risk allocation and scope of work, as opposed to being determined by competitively low bids.

Panelization: Similar to modularization, panelization involves offsite construction of panels (usually wall or roof panels) which are then shipped to the site for erection into place. Panelization or modularization usually reduce field labor, but may increase field equipment needs.

Personality Style: An individual's preference for using information, making decisions, dealing with people, and organizing aspects of life.

Professional Development: The professional activities undertaken by an individual to improve knowledge and skills for potential career advancement or job development.

Project Agreement: A means for allowing both union and non-union workers on a jobsite through a special agreement for a specific project that supplants local collective bargaining agreements.

Project Life Cycle: The identifiable phases of a project from beginning to end, including feasibility, conception, programming, design, preconstruction, construction, and closeout.

Project Planning: The process of breaking the project down into manageable tasks that can be scheduled, budgeted, delegated or assigned, and explained.

Project Portfolio: The types of projects a company currently has under contract, which may include diversification by including some high-risk projects, some low-risk projects, and some new project types.

Project Scheduling: Assigning a duration to each of the tasks identified in the project plan, and sequencing the tasks in a logical way. Durations are affected by determinations of crew sizes and use of equipment.

Punishment: A source of power that can be used to motivate or compel performance through threats or termination, refusal to pay, etc. Punishment loses its effectiveness if used over the long term.

Purchasing: The process of ensuring that agreements have been reached for the provision of all material, labor, equipment, shipping, etc. required for successful completion of the project. Purchasing requires use of purchase orders, subcontracts, or standing accounts.

Quality Risk: The risk of reducing the value of a project and/or the reputation of the owner, designer, and contractor because of inferior material or workmanship.

Relationship-Oriented Skills: Leadership capabilities in working with team members, including such skills as motivation, negotiation, communication, and assisting team members with professional development goals.

Responsibility Matrix: A method for managing tasks or risks on a project in which the task or source of risk is listed along one side of the table and team members are listed along the other, with checks indicating which team member is responsible for which task.

Retainage: The amount of payment an owner withholds from the contractor to ensure that the contractor continues to perform high-quality work on the project until completion.

Reward Power: The use of rewards such as recognition, awards, money (bonuses), or privileges to motivate individuals.

Risk Management: The probability of an event causing a loss of time, profits, quality, or functionality on a project.

REFERENCE

REFERENCE

Sales Prospecting: The methods companies use to identify upcoming projects for bid or negotiation. Some examples include networking, phone calls, newsletters to repeat clients, and active membership in trade associations.

Safety Risk: The probability of an accident that can result in worker injury, lost time, and financial costs.

Schedule of Payments: The estimate of monthly billings, based on costs and schedule of the work, given to the owner and their financial lender at the beginning of a project in order to project cash flows.

Schedule Risk: The probability of an event (weather, shipment delay, poor productivity) that results in lost time on a project.

Self-performing: A decision by the contractor to perform some of the job tasks with its own labor force (as opposed to subcontracting).

Site Security: The comprehensive approach to preventing theft losses, third-party injuries, trespassing or loss of documentation on a jobsite.

Site Management: The process of maintaining clear traffic routes, arranging for delivery, unloading, and hoisting, and controlling the flow of people on a project.

Site Planning: Locating temporary utilities, job trailers, parking areas, portable toilets, etc., in a way that balances safety and efficiency.

Subcontracting: A decision by the contractor to hire another company to perform some of the tasks on a project (as opposed to self-performing).

Surety: A company that assumes the risk of non-payment or non-performance by the contractor to protect the owner's interests. Sureties issue bonds on projects.

Task-Oriented Skills: Leadership capabilities in supervising the details of a project, such as estimating, scheduling, planning, and executing the work.

Value Engineering: The process of calculating first costs and lifetime costs of different types of systems, construction methods, or products in order to advise the owner of the best value on the project.

Index

A

Agencies, working with 8-4, 8-5
Approvals 5-4, 5-5

B

Bimonthly management meetings 2-9
Blueprint 6-9
Bonding 3-13

C

Cash flow 7-4
Chains of command 2-11
Closeout 5-6
Co-workers, working with 8-6, 8-7
Coercive power 9-7
Compliance issues 10-1–10-3
Construction delivery systems 1-1, 1-2
Construction management at-risk 1-3–1-5
    characteristics of 1-3–1-5
Construction phase tasks 5-1, 5-2
Construction process 3-6, 3-7
Control system 2-6, 2-7
Corporate policies/procedures 10-1–10-24
Cost coding accuracy 7-3
Cost information cycle 7-1, 7-2
Customer satisfaction 3-8

D

Design, as source of risk, ... 3-3
Design-bid-build delivery, ... 1-1
Design-build, ... 1-4, 1-5
Design review meetings 2-10
Design risk 3-3
Designers, working with 8-4
Diversification 10-3
Documentation 2-2–2-7
Dual gate system 8-6

E

Equipment selection 6-4, 6-5
Expediting 5-3, 5-4
Expert power 9-7

F

Fabrication 6-6, 6-7
Finances 7-1–7-6, 10-16, 10-17
    cost coding accuracy 7-3
    cost information cycle 7-1, 7-2
Financial risk 3-2

G

Government agencies, working with
    .... 8-4, 8-5

H

Handling material 6-5, 6-6

I

Idea management system 2-3
Information, project control 2-5–2-7
Information flows 7-2
Information management
    .... 2-1–2-12, 10-10,10-11
Information planning, preconstruction 4-4
Inspectors, working with 8-4, 8-5
Insurance, management 3-12
    as source of risk 3-13, 3-14
Interdependence of project team roles 1-6
Internal stakeholders, working with 8-6, 8-7

K

Kickoff meetings 2-9

L

Labor cost control 3-9
Leader 9-1
Leadership skills 9-5–9-7

REFERENCE

REFERENCE

Leadership style................................... 9-5
Legitimate power................................ 9-7
Location of project 3-5, 3-6

M

Materials management
.....................6-1–6-10, 10-15, 10-16
Mobilization..................................... 5-2
Modular units/panelization, vs. onsite
fabrication 6-6, 6-7
Money, as source of risk.....................3-2, 3-3
Motivation.................................. 9-2–9-4

N

Nature of project 3-6

O

Onsite fabrication, vs. modular units/
panelization................................ 6-6, 6-7
Overhead, corporate 10-5, 10-6
Owners, working with 8-1–8-3

P

Panelization, vs. onsite fabrication 6-6, 6-7
Participant's profile............................ R:5–R:6
Partners in project 8-1–8-8, 10-18, 10-19
owners, working with 8-1–8-3
Pay-when-paid method 7-5
People, understanding
.....................9-1–9-10, 10-19, 10-20
Personality of corporation............... 10-6–10-8
Personality styles 9-8, 9-9
Phase planning, preconstruction,
management................................ 4-1, 4-2
Phase tasks, construction.................... 5-1, 5-2
Policies/procedures, corporate 10-1–10-24
Portfolio 10-3, 10-4
Pre-award conference meeting with
subcontractors 2-8
Preconstruction planning meetings............. 2-8

Professional development.................... 9-8, 9-9
Project cash flow 7-4, 7-5
Project delivery system 1-1–1-8, 10-9, 10-10
Project life cycles 2-1, 2-2
Project organization 3-7
Project planning, preconstruction 4-2, 4-3
Project portfolio........................... 10-3, 10-4
Project S curve 7-4
Project scheduling........................... 4-4, 4-5
Project team 9-1, 9-2
role in risk control........................ 3-1, 3-2
Property losses................................... 3-11
Protection of materials...................... 6-5, 6-6
Protocols, chains of command......... 2-11, 2-12
Punishment 9-3
Purchasing..................................... 5-2, 5-3

Q

Quality 3-3
Quality assurance................................ 3-8
Quality risk.. 3-6

R

Referent power 9-7
Responsibility matrix 2-11
Retainage 7-5, 7-6
Reward power..................................... 9-7
Rewards 9-2–9-4
Risk diversification 10-3, 10-4
Risk management
.....................3-1–3-17, 10-11, 10-12

S

Safety issues 3-4, 3-7, 3-8
Sales prospecting........................... 10-4, 10-5
Salesperson, supervisor as 8-1–8-3
Scheduling of project,
preconstruction........................... 4-4, 4-5
Self-performed work...................... 3-15, 3-16
Site layout 6-1–6-3

Site management 3-16
Site planning, preconstruction 4-3, 4-4
Sources of risk 3-2–3-7
Staffing decisions..................................... 10-4
Storage of materials 6-5, 6-6
Subcontracting 3-14, 6-15
Subcontractors
      in field, working with................... 8-3, 8-4
      pre-award conference meeting with.... 2-8
Submittals... 5-3
Sureties... 3-13

T

Team... 9-5
Technology for managing
     information............................. 2-10, 2-11
Time, as source of risk 3-3

Types of documentation 2-4, 2-5
Types of meetings............................. 2-8–2-10

U

Understanding of people 9-1–9-10
Unions, working with 8-5, 8-6

V

Value engineering 7-2

W

Weekly project meetings 2-9
Work plan 4-1–4-6, 10-12–10-15
Workers compensation losses................... 3-11
Working plan 5-1–5-8

REFERENCE

Participant's Profile

Your name _____

How long have you worked in the construction industry? _____ years

Your company's name _____

What kind of work does your company do? Check any that apply.

❏ building   ❏ heavy   ❏ highway   ❏ M/U   ❏ industrial   ❏ other _____

How long have you been with this company? _____ years

What is your job title or function?_____

How many people do you directly supervise? ___ people

Where do you work?   ❏ jobsite   ❏ home office   ❏ other

What project are you working on now? Project name, location, type of project.

_____

Check the STP courses you have previously taken:

❏ *Construction Supervisor*

❏ *Heavy/Highway Construction Supervisor*

❏ Unit 1: *Leadership and Motivation*

❏ Unit 2: *Oral and Written Communication*

❏ Unit 3: *Problem Solving and Decision Making*

❏ Unit 4: *Contract Documents and Construction Law*

❏ Unit 5: *Planning and Scheduling*

❏ Unit 6: *Understanding and Managing Project Costs*

❏ Unit 7: *Accident Prevention and Loss Control*

❏ Unit 8: *Managing the Project: The Supervisor's Role*

❏ Unit 9: *Productivity Improvement*

❏ Unit 10: *General and Specialty Contractor Dynamics*

Who pays your course fee?   ❏ company   ❏ I do   ❏ other _____

Why did you enroll in this course? Check any that apply.

❏ I've taken other STP courses and I wanted to take this one also

❏ I was asked or told to take this course by_____

❏ The Supervisory Training Program (or this course) was recommended by _____

_____

❏ I want to take all 10 courses so I can get a certificate from AGC

❏ I read or heard about STP (or this course) and it seemed worthwhile

❏ Other _____

REFERENCE WORKSHEETS

MANAGING THE PROJECT—THE SUPERVISOR'S ROLE
PARTICIPANT'S PROFILE — CONT.

What is the thing you like best about your work?

_____
_____
_____
_____

What is the most difficult part of your work?

_____
_____
_____
_____

What are your expectations or goals for the time you spend in this course?

_____
_____
_____
_____

If there is a specific question, topic, situation or problem you want to be sure we talk about sometime during this course, please list or describe it below:

_____
_____
_____
_____

What are your personal activities and interests?

_____
_____
_____
_____

If there is any other information that has a bearing on your participation in this course, please list or describe it below — your career goals, other construction training courses you've taken, special assignments you've had or might have in the future, something else you have on your mind.

_____
_____
_____
_____
_____
_____
_____

Unit 8, Managing the Project: The Supervisor's Role

Pre-Knowledge Survey

This survey is designed to check your knowledge about project management on the construction site. This survey is not graded, and the information in it is for your use only. Answer each question to the best of your ability. Circle the letter next to your choice, or respond as directed in the question.

1. In which of the following delivery systems does the construction owner execute one contract with a single organization for all phases of the project?
   a. Construction Management at-Risk
   b. Traditional low bid
   c. Multiple prime
   d. Design-Build

2. In a cost control system, what is the function of a labor productivity budget?
   a. To set a standard for achievement
   b. To create an accurate field report
   c. To project final costs of the work
   d. To implement corrective action

3. Responsibility for which of the following risk categories is typically assigned to the project supervisor in the field?
   a. Overall project profitability
   b. Safety of the workers
   c. Design function
   d. Financial strength of subcontractors

4. Which of the following does NOT help reduce the risk exposure of contractors?
   a. Insurance
   b. Self-performing
   c. Bonding
   d. Subcontracting

5. Gantt charts, or bar chart schedules, show precedence relationships between work tasks.
   a. True
   b. False

6. What is the first field activity on any construction project?
   a. Expediting
   b. Purchasing
   c. Mobilization
   d. Closeout

7. Which of the following organizations does NOT typically have inspection and approval authority on a construction project?
   a. Government agencies (EPA, OSHA, local building departments)
   b. Testing agency retained by the owner
   c. Designers (architect, engineers)
   d. Subcontractors

8. The decision to prefabricate versus field-assemble represents a tradeoff of cost, schedule and quality factors.
   a. True
   b. False

9. Which of the following should be considered prior to finalizing equipment selections?
   a. Means and methods for construction
   b. Ability of equipment to improve safety of working conditions
   c. Schedule of delivery and availability of onsite storage
   d. All of the above factor into equipment selection

10. Which of the following best represents the cost information cycle in construction companies?
   a. Project budgets→historical records→actual costs→future estimates→back to project budgets
   b. Historical records→future estimates→project budgets→actual costs→back to historical records
   c. Actual costs→future estimates→historical records→project budgets→back to actual costs
   d. Future estimate→actual costs→project budgets→historical records→back to future budgets

11. What is the general shape of the curve for monthly payments on a construction project (as a percent of total project cost)?
   a. U-shaped
   b. C-shaped
   c. S-shaped
   d. M-shaped

12. Which of the following delivery systems creates the most adversarial relationships between project partners on a construction project?
   a. Low-bid award of a general contract
   b. Negotiated award of a general contract
   c. Construction Management at-Risk with a GMP
   d. Design-Build

13. Which of the following represents an option for working with both union and non-union subcontractors on a project?
   a. Project agreement
   b. Dual-gate system
   c. Both a. and b.
   d. There are no options for having union and non-union workers on a jobsite

14. Which of the following uses of power provides the greatest motivation for workers over the long term?
   a. Coercion
   b. Rewards
   c. Punishment
   d. Legitimacy (I'm the boss—do what I say)

15. Managing tasks is the most important aspect of project leadership.
   a. True
   b. False

16. Which of the following will most influence the continuing professional development of your project management skills?
   a. Your willingness to take educational and training programs offered by your company and construction trade associations
   b. Your employer's level of corporate overhead
   c. Your ability to find new business opportunities for your employer
   d. Your employer's project portfolio

Reference Worksheets for In-Class Activities

RWS 1

Ice-breakers

To maximize the benefit of this course, it will be necessary for you to work in teams on in-class exercises allowing you to apply what you have learned in the sessions. You will be able to work more effectively as a team if you get to know other members of your team before working on any of the activities.

Another goal of this class is to get the participants to share their knowledge with each other through in-class discussions of the topics presented. It will be easier to start this discussion if you know the other individuals in the class.

For these reasons, the instructor may begin the first session with some "ice-breakers." There are a number of different ways to get people in the class talking to each other. Use the space below to write down some things you learned about other members of the class.

There are no right or wrong methods for ice-breakers. However, there a few rules you should follow when forming a team:

- **Respect the others in your team**
- **Do not reveal potentially embarrassing facts about a team member**
- **When you are putting a team together, make the team your top priority (no cell phones, no reading while the team is working, etc.)**
- **Speak the truth, hear the truth—be honest about your skills, your abilities, your interests, etc., and listen carefully to others as they do the same**

RWS 2

Sponsor's Guide

The sponsor's guide is intended to help you implement what you have learned in the everyday activities of your company. The instructor will work with you on implementation details using the Sponsor's Guide. In the space below, write the details of your Sponsor's Guide.

Sponsor name: _____

Weekly meeting time: _____

Contact information: _____

_____

_____

There are no perfect choices for a sponsor, and there may be many individuals who would make good sponsors in your firm. When choosing a sponsor, keep in mind that you will need to work closely with this person to complete the Sponsor's Guide and implement what you have learned. Try to choose someone with whom you can meet regularly and talk openly, and someone who can help you transfer what you have learned to others in your organization.

RWS 3

Best Delivery Method

Design-Bid-Build is the dominant delivery method for public-sector construction such as transportation systems, government office buildings, etc.

Construction Management is a popular choice of delivery for school districts and state prisons (among others).

Design-Build is the preferred choice of real estate developers, and is used for transportation projects involving reconstruction of heavily traveled urban corridors.

Discuss among your team some ideas related to the following question:

Why do you think these different types of owners use different types of delivery systems?

Write down your team's answers in the space below.

Public sector	School board	RE developer
Many laws require public agencies to take bids from any qualified contractor **Transportation, water/ wastewater, power, and other similar public-sector projects are very engineering-intensive** **Governments must use tax money to build, and using a low bid method allows for the best use of tax dollars**	**Schedules are critical** **Missing completion and move-in dates can cause huge problems for school districts** **Speed is not quite as important as reliability and control** **Schools are bonded, with strict spending limits, so keeping projects on budget is crucial** **Schedule and budget control create need to move some risk and control to contractor (CM)**	**Speed of construction— Design-Build is faster** **Owner takes less risk in Design-Build, but gives up some control in return** **Real estate development projects are typically not as engineering-intensive as projects like major highways or reconstruction of power plants** **"Time is money" to developers** **For-profit companies like developers think about projects differently from nonprofit organizations like schools or DOTs**

(Answers given are examples only for guidance in completing the assignment.)

RWS 4

Delivery Team Roles and Responsibilities

Review the Sure Fresh documents contained in your STP Unit 8 Participant's Manual. The course instructor will assign members of your team different roles to play during your review of the Sure Fresh project documents.

Team member	Project Role	Experience
	Field Engineer (QC/QA)	**3 years**
	Concrete Foreman	**30 years**
	Carpenter Foreman	**12 years**
	Project Manager	**8 years**
	Safety Director	**6 months**

You are a project team that has to meet the new project supervisor in an hour. You need to tell him or her what your expectations are for supervisory performance. In particular, you have to tell the project supervisor what the expectations are for managing people, tasks, and risk.

The course instructor will also assign some project attributes for you to consider.

Delivery type	Repeat owner?	Market conditions	Other	Other
CM at-Risk	**Yes**	**Lots of work**	**Winter**	**Tight schedule**

What will you tell the new project supervisor when you meet with him/her? Use the Performance Profile on PowerPoint Slide 13 as a guide for thinking about the type of project supervisor you need on the project.

The following represents one possible solution, and should NOT be viewed as the single right answer. Also, if your instructor has given you different roles, different experience levels, and different project attributes, your answer will be different. The solution provided below is offered as an example of the thought process used to determine project roles.

Because this project is using CM at-Risk, the contractor will have much responsibility for oversight and management. However, because there is a lot of other work, and the schedule for this project is tight, people may have a tendency to rush through tasks and push crews pretty hard. The safety director has only six months' experience and may not be comfortable directing crews to carefully check for safety issues. Therefore, the team expects the project supervisor to work very closely with the experienced foremen to ensure safe working conditions.

Also, the fact that this is a repeat client represents an opportunity to strengthen a long-term relationship that is likely to result in future business. The quality of the work will be key in creating a satisfied customer, but the field engineer responsible for quality control and quality assurance is relatively inexperienced. Because this is winter construction, the quality control of concrete flatwork is a little trickier.

Because the concrete foreman has 30 years of experience, he should work pretty closely with the field engineer to help her understand some of the things to look for in winter concrete work.

Because the carpenter foreman, the concrete foreman, and the project manager are all reasonably experienced, and because the project is relatively simple, labor cost control and budget updating should not be as big an issue on this project as it might be with less experienced crew foremen or project managers. Therefore, the project supervisor should focus more attention on safety and quality issues and less on labor cost control. Also, because it is CM at-Risk and the project manager has experience, the project team may add value or decrease cost through design reviews and value engineering. This may generate future business, as this an owner who has shown a willingness to work with the firm in the past.

RWS 5

Design an Information/Idea Management System

Using the diagram on page 2-3 of your Participant's Manual as a guide, complete the following worksheet. In the left column, list the types of information you manage on a project, including design information, planning information, safety information, cost information, etc. Create as many categories as you need to capture all of the different types of information you receive, create, distribute, or archive on a project.

In the next three columns, make a list of where this information comes from, where it needs to go, and where it must be stored. Many types of information must go to more than one member of the project team, so be thorough.

In the last column, list the factors that influence the amount, complexity, and pace of information. This can include factors such as the type of delivery system used, the amount of self-perform work, or the relationship with the owner.

Now draw a diagram of all of the sources of information, receivers of information, and keepers of information. **Don't worry, the diagram should be messy!!** You should have something resembling a giant spider's web when you are through. The objective is to understand the complexity of information management on a construction project.

After you have shared the diagram with others in the class, and have tried to explain to them the types of information flows your diagram represents, discuss some ideas (e.g., filing systems, electronic archives, back-up files, etc.) for tracking and maintaining information on a construction project. You may use the space below to record your team's ideas.

Info type	Info comes from:	Info goes to:	Info stored at:	Factors influencing info
Design	Architect/ engineer	Subcontractors / crew foremen	PM office and job trailer	Delivery system Project type
Budgets	Estimator	Crew foremen	PM office	Self-performed
Schedules	PM and subcontractors	Crew foremen	Office and job trailer	Weather Type of owner
Labor hours	Crew foremen	Payroll office	Accounting	Self-performed
Changes	PM/Owner	Subcontractors/ crew foremen	PM office	Delivery system Project type
Inspections	Gov't. agents	Owner/architect	Jobsite	Project location
Approvals	Testing agency	Owner/ engineer	Jobsite	Project type QA/QC plan
Delivery tickets	Vendors and suppliers	Accounting office	Accounting	Project location Self-performed
Material invoices	Vendors and suppliers	Project manager	Accounting	Local availability
Accident reports	Safety director	General superintendent	Field shop	Project type Project location
Daily activity logs	Field engineer	Project manager	PM office	Delivery system Self-performed

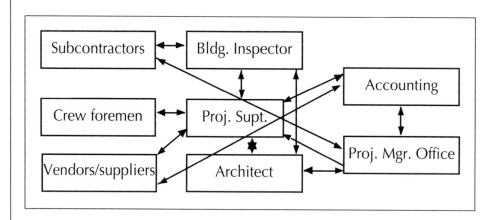

The solution above represents one possible configuration, and should NOT be viewed as the single right answer. Also, if your instructor has given you different project attributes, your answer will be different. The solution provided above is offered as an example of the thought process used to determine the nature and complexity of information systems.

RWS 6

Control Systems

In the first column, list all the factors and processes that must be controlled on a construction project (e.g., cost, quality, risk, etc.). The number of factors that must be controlled is probably larger than you might think at first, so take some time to brainstorm among the team.

In the second column, list the type of information needed in order to "know" whether a process or issue is under control (e.g., concrete strengths, labor productivity).

In the third column, list the type of document that best captures and conveys the required information to the project team members who must be involved in the control function.

Factors to be controlled	Information needed	Documents created
Field labor costs	**Labor hours and quantities**	**Field labor report**
Project schedule	**Tasks and durations**	**Bar chart progress schedule**
Quality of the work	**Material compliance**	**Testing log**
Worker safety	**Injuries and accidents**	**Accident report**

For each of the factors above, discuss where the control standard came from and what type of corrective action you will take if actual performance falls outside the

Factors	Source of standard	Corrective action
Field labor costs	**Estimate**	**Change method/crew size**
Project schedule	**Estimate**	**Change method/crew size**
Quality of the work	**Specifications**	**Change vendors or conditions**
Worker safety	**Insurance carrier**	**Improve conditions**

standard.

The solution above represents one possible configuration, and should NOT be viewed as the single right answer. Also, if your instructor has given you different project attributes, your answer will be different. The solution provided above is offered as an example of the thought process used to determine project risks and controls.

RWS 7

Responsibility Matrix

Review the Sure Fresh documents that came with your Participant's Manual. The course instructor may give you some additional information to consider while you review them.

Each of the control factors and corrective actions listed in Worksheet 6 must be assigned to some member of the project team. Such assignments of responsibility are frequently communicated in a "responsibility matrix."

The course instructor may give you some information regarding the composition of your project team. If not, assign responsibilities to team members that you would normally consider part of every project team (project manager, architect, project supervisor, lead foreman, etc.). In the matrix below, list each of the control factors in the leftmost column, and then list each team member across the top row. Assign each factor to a specific team member by placing an "X" in the box intersecting factor and team member.

Team member → Supervisor ↓ Factor of Control	Project Manager	Project Engineer	Field Director	Safety Director
Field labor cost control	XX			
Overall project cost control		XX		
Quality control			XX	
Safety assurance				XX
Site security				XX
Site management	XX			
Owner relations		XX		
Procurement/scheduling	XX			
Material delivery/ storage			XX	
Design review	XX			
Scope control		XX		

The solution above represents one possible solution, and should NOT be viewed as the single right answer. Also, if your instructor has given you different project roles your answers might be different. The solution above is offered as an example of the thought process used to determine project responsibilities.

RWS 8

Risk Trade-off in Schedule Acceleration

Using the Sure Fresh documents as a context for discussion, complete the following worksheet. Your instructor will give you additional information to consider in your discussions.

In the left column, list the types of issues or processes on the project that will create risk. Some of the risk factors will be common to almost all construction projects, and you may think of some that are specific to the Sure Fresh project or other parameters given to you by your instructor. Create as many issues as you need to capture all of the different types of risk you think you might encounter on the project. Put a check-mark in the category of risk (schedule, cost, safety, design, quality) that you think best describes the issue.

What would happen to the risk issues if the owner of the Sure Fresh project came to you after the contract had been signed (but before the work began) and said he or she needed to take occupancy of the building one month sooner than originally scheduled? Indicate which risk issues would be increased by noting a plus sign (+) next to the checkmark in the category columns. How much do you think you should be paid to assume these additional risks?

Issues	Schedule	Cost	Safety	Design	Quality
Staying on budget		✔+			
Staying on schedule	✔+				
Loss time accidents			✔+		
Weather	✔	✔			✔
Soil conditions		✔		✔	
Material fit					✔
Workmanship					✔+
Inspections				✔	
Water/moisture/ mold				✔	✔

Should be paid actual costs of the extra work plus some additional fee for assuming the additional risk.

The solution above represents one possible configuration, and should NOT be viewed as the single right answer. The solution above is offered as an example of the thought process used to determine project risk.

RWS 9

Risk Allocation in Supplemental Conditions

Review the AGC 200 general conditions contained in your Sure Fresh packet and use the information to complete this worksheet. In each of the sections and/or articles of the supplemental conditions, note what types of risk are assigned to each party on the project team. For instance, note who is responsible for replacing the work-in-place in case of fire or windstorm.

Identify each area of risk described in the supplemental conditions by writing a short descriptor in the first column. Then, put a checkmark in the appropriate column denoting which member of the project team (designer, builder, owner) has responsibility for that risk. The resulting product represents a risk allocation table that project managers and construction executives sometimes use to organize their risk management plans.

Area of Risk	Design-Builder		
	Builder	Designer	Owner
Completion of work (3.1.1)	XX		
Labor hours (3.1.1)	XX		
Unsafe practices (3.1.2)	XX		
Coordination (3.1.2)	XX		
Defects (3.2.4)			XX
Design errors (3.3.2)		XX	XX
Safety (3.11)	XX		
Quality of work (3.7)	XX		
Hazardous material (3.13)			XX
Site conditions (3.16.2)		XX	XX
Site control (3.20)	XX		
Liens and payments (9.2.3)	XX		
Worker's Comp (10.3.1)	XX		
Indemnification/ negligence (10.1)	XX	XX	XX
Loss of work, e.g. wind, hail, etc.(10.4)			XX

Copy each of the areas of risk assigned to the builder in the table above to the left-hand column in the table below. Then, indicate how you will manage that risk. For example, quality of work may best be managed by subcontracting if special tools or technology are required for high-quality craftsmanship. Some types of risk are best managed by insuring against their occurrence.

Area of Risk Allocated to (Design) Builder	Best Method of Managing the Risk
Site control	**Security and supervision**
Workers Compensation	**Insurance**
Liens and payment	**Bonding**
Completion of the work	**Subcontracting**
Quality of the work	**Quality Control plan**

The solution above represents one possible solution, and should NOT be viewed as the single right answer. Also, if your instructor has given you different project roles your answers might be different. The solution above is offered as an example of the thought process used to determine project risks.

RWS 10

Work Breakdown Structure for Sure Fresh Project

A work breakdown structure (WBS) is fundamental to developing a detailed project schedule and project labor cost codes, and to tracking the project's cost, schedule and, therefore, productivity performance. On very large projects involving multiple bridges or buildings, a work breakdown structure would begin with major facilities, such as the different buildings or bridges on the project. The smallest unit would be work packages, such as drywall for the offices in a specific building on the project. For the Sure Fresh project, one would start with the facilities level such as site work/building. The next level would consist of trade-specific activities like "electrical work" and "painting." We would next move to the task level with examples like "power distribution" and "priming," followed by a distinct, identifiable grouping of the task, such as office vs. warehouse, or 2nd floor, 3rd floor, 4th floor, etc. The example below provides a graphic illustration of how to organize a work breakdown structure.

Facilities:	site work	building
		/ \
Trades:		electrical painting
		/ \
Tasks:		priming finish coat
		/ \
Work packages:		offices warehouse

Using the example above as a guide, break down the work of a trade of your choice on the Sure Fresh project (use a separate sheet of paper).

The example above illustrates a partial breakdown of the work for the painting contractor.

Now that you have developed a WBS for the trade work, discuss within your group at what level it would be practical to track the cost. For example, you may choose to separate the work by trade (e.g., carpenters, laborers, tinners) or operation (e.g., clean up, hang doors, trim windows, etc.).

The key point is to track costs at a level of detail that provides the required input to the cost accounting system and meaningful feedback to the estimator. The cost of tracking a particular cost should never exceed the benefit derived from tracking the cost. For example, there would not be any benefit in determining how many drywall screws were put into a specific stud.

Also discuss how you would go about determining schedule durations for each of the work packages for the trade. Options may include experience or quantities multiplied by productivity rates.

Schedule durations are sometimes determined by experience with similar projects; however, a more sophisticated method is based upon multiplying a quantity times a productivity rate. For example, if one carpenter can install eight pre-hung doors in a day and there are 24 doors on the job, hanging doors will take three days (if there is only one carpenter).

The solution above represents one possible configuration, and should NOT be viewed as the single right answer. Also, if your instructor has given you different project attributes, your answer will be different. The solution provided above is offered as an example of the thought process used to determine work breakdown structures.

RWS 11

Preconstruction Plan for Sure Fresh Project

Using the Sure Fresh documents for project scope and background information, complete the following worksheet. Your instructor may give you additional information to consider in your discussions.

WHAT: Describe the overall scope of work in terms of site work and building construction required to construct the project:

The project consists of an office building and two warehouse buildings. There is a small gatehouse by each of two bridges over a small river. There is a stormwater storage pond, employee and visitor parking, a truck waiting area, roads, and dock approaches.

HOW: Discuss the means and methods that will be used to complete the excavation and foundation work:

The excavation for the foundation work will be completed with a large backhoe. Footings will be formed, poured, cured and stripped. Foundation walls will be formed, poured, cured and stripped. The backhoe will be used for backfilling, and the backfill will need to be compacted on the inside of the building.

WHO: Discuss who will do the work (self-perform or subcontract), and how the choice of project delivery system would affect your options:

If the project were Design-Build or negotiated general contractor, we'd subcontract the excavation and self-perform the concrete work. If the work was competitively bid general contractor, we'd estimate the concrete work, but we might have to subcontract the work if a sub had a better price. If we were construction managers, we might not be allowed to do any of the work ourselves.

WHY: Explain why you have chosen this assignment of work:

We prefer to do our own concrete work whenever possible.

WHERE: Discuss where on the project and when you will begin the excavation and foundation work. Also, explain why you have chosen this approach:

We would start with the office building, because this building will take the most time (of the buildings) to complete.

The solution above represents one possible configuration, and should NOT be viewed as the single right answer. Also, if your instructor has given you different project attributes, your answer will be different. The solution provided above is offered as an example of the thought process used for preconstruction planning.

RWS 12

Summary Schedule for Sure Fresh Project

The Sure Fresh project is typical of many building construction projects. Develop three summary schedules based upon the project delivery system chosen for the project:

1. General contracting

2. Design-Build

3. Construction Management

Your summary schedule should have general phases and milestones such as design, procurement, mobilization, construction, substantial completion and closeout. Use a bar chart format to communicate your summary schedule, overlapping bars where appropriate. Use graph paper to make your schedule, with a scale of each square equal to one week.

Which project delivery system has the shortest summary schedule duration?

Design-Build

Why?

With Design-Build, we can start work before the design is completed, and we can self-perform work, so we need not wait for subcontractor quotes before starting.

Which project delivery system has the longest summary schedule duration?

General Contracting

Why?

With general contracting, we need to wait for all of the design and bidding work to be completed prior to starting work.

Discuss within your group how the choice of project delivery system affects the duration of each phase of the project, as well as how effectively these phases can be overlapped.

Design-Build and Construction Management offer advantages over general contracting regarding schedule, in that design and construction can overlap. Overall project duration typically will be shortest with Design-Build, followed by Construction Management, with general contracting having the longest overall duration. The construction phase duration can sometimes be the shortest in general contracting because all design details are known when construction starts and everything can be ordered; however, pre-ordering long-lead items in the other two project delivery methods can negate this apparent advantage.

RWS 13

Identify Team Members for Sure Fresh Project

Using the Sure Fresh documents for project scope and background information as well as your completed Activity 10, complete the following worksheet. Your instructor may give you additional information to consider in your discussions.

Choose two trades involved with considerable work on the project that your employer might be capable of self-performing:

Excavating, concrete

Discuss how the size of the project relative to your employer's overall organization would affect your ability to get the foremen you desire for this project:

We only have one excavating crew, so I will get our one and only excavating foreman; however, we have many concrete crews, but this project is rather simple (although somewhat large), so I'll be getting one of our average foremen.

Assume that your employer is the hard-bid GC for the project and that your employer used subcontractors for the two trades of work you listed above. How much input will you have regarding the subcontractor foremen chosen?

I'll have very little input into the selection of foremen, because we'll be stuck with the low bidders' choice of foremen.

Let's say that your employer is the negotiated GC on a cost-plus basis for the project with a conservatively estimated guaranteed maximum price (GMP). How much input do you have now regarding the selection of foremen?

We can decide what work to get sub bids on, and we can choose to do this work for better schedule control. However, I probably won't get our best foremen, because there is not a lot of cost risk.

Assume you are the CM's project supervisor on a public project and the CM is not allowed to self-perform any work. Do you have much influence as to who the prime foremen will be?

I have virtually no control over who the foremen will be, as the low bidders will select the foremen of their choosing.

The solution above represents one possible configuration, and should NOT be viewed as the single right answer. Also, if your instructor has given you different project attributes, your answer will be different. The solution provided above is offered as an example of the thought process used in putting together project teams.

RWS 14

Analyze General Requirements

The general requirements in the specifications for a project (usually Division 1 on a building project) will address who is responsible for temporary utilities and facilities. Examples include temporary electricity and parking for the workers.

Within your Sure Fresh teams, discuss the types of temporary utilities and facilities on some of your recent projects, and complete the following list:

Temporary Utility or Temporary Facility	Provided by	Usage Paid by
Temporary Power	**Local utility**	**Owner**
Temporary parking for workers	**Owner**	**Contractor (snow removal)**
Temporary water	**Local utility**	**Contractor**
Temporary trailers/offices	**Contractor**	**Contractor**
Storage of owner-provided material	**Contractor**	**Owner**
Mock-up wall system	**Architect/vendor**	**Architect**

The solution above represents one possible configuration, and should NOT be viewed as the single right answer. Also, if your instructor has given you different project attributes, your answer will be different. The solution provided above is offered as an example of the thought process used to analyze general requirements.

RWS 15

Rent or Buy Decision

The first step in analyzing the rent or buy decision for a piece of equipment is to gather data. To gather that data, we must ask questions. The questions will deal with everything from costs to maintenance to insurance. If you have ever looked at leasing a new car instead of buying one, you have thought through some similar questions.

Form a group of three and complete the following lists:

What questions would you ask if you wanted to rent or lease a piece of equipment?

What is the minimum rental period?
What is the rental cost for a day? week? month?
After how many days is it best to rent for a week?
After how many weeks is it best to rent for a month?
Will the rental company deliver and pick up the equipment?
What are the delivery and pick-up charges?
Who is responsible for maintenance?
Who is responsible for damage?
When can we get the equipment?
How long can we have the equipment?
How much money is in the estimate for this equipment?
What kind of production can we expect from the equipment?
Is there any special training required to operate the equipment?
What are the consumables (fuel, material, etc.)?

What questions would you ask if you wanted to buy a piece of equipment?

What is the cost?
Can we pay cash, or do we need to finance? If so, what is the interest rate?
What is the expected lifetime?
What value will the equipment have in the future?
What is the expected production rate?
What are the operating expenses?
Can we do our own maintenance?
What is the warranty period and what does it cover?
What accessories, if any, are included?
What accessories do we need to buy to get it to do what we want it to do?
When can we get it?
What will the delivery cost?
Is there any special training required?
What does it cost to insure?

Your instructor will go group to group to compile the lists of the entire class.

RWS 16

Develop Procurement Schedule for Sure Fresh

While we do not have the luxury of time to develop a full-blown procurement schedule in this session, we can identify the types of materials and equipment that would and would not warrant careful tracking during the expediting task. Review the Sure Fresh drawings and provide up to five examples of each classification of materials and equipment:

Custom-made for this project with a long (say a month or more) lead time:

Wall Panels   **Electric Switchgear**   **HVAC Rooftop Units**

Custom-made for this project with a short (a few weeks) lead time:

Reinforcing Steel   Door Frames

Commodity items that are readily available:

Paint   **Wire**   **Piping**

Commodity items that are sometimes subject to shortage:

Gypsum Board   **Concrete (Portland Cement)**   **Structural Steel**

1. Which long-lead item would be the most disruptive to the overall schedule if its delivery date were delayed one month?

The wall panels

2. If you could change the project delivery system to Design-Build, what design change would you make that could have the largest impact on reducing the schedule duration?

Be flexible with the size of the wall panels so that the precaster with the fastest delivery could be used

3. Besides price, what criteria might you use to select the supplier of the item you named in the first question above?

Delivery date, quality

The solution above represents one possible configuration, and should NOT be viewed as the single right answer. Also, if your instructor has given you different project attributes, your answer will be different. The solution provided above is offered as an example of the thought process used for procurement scheduling.

RWS 17

Site Layout for Sure Fresh Project

The Sure Fresh project site plan is typical of many building construction projects. Using your Sure Fresh site plan, develop a site layout for construction. Your instructor may direct you further as to the location of existing utilities, zoning constraints and other "challenges" to your task.

First, generate a list of all of the temporary facilities, ranging from trailers and lay-down areas to parking and utilities, that you will need in order to safely and efficiently construct the project:

Job Office Trailer	**Equipment and Tools Trailer**
Material Storage Trailer	**Portable Toilets**
Temporary Telephone/Fax	**Temporary Electricity**
Temporary Water	**Temporary Heat**
Worker Parking	**Temporary Bridge**

Using graph paper, sketch out a construction site layout plan for the project. After you have experimented with the graph paper, transfer your "final" plan to the Sure Fresh site plan, taking care to keep the trailers, lay-down areas and parking areas to scale.

Plan should show haul routes, unloading areas, parking, trailers, temporary facilities, etc.

After you have drawn your site plan, your instructor will go around the room asking each group for an item to put onto the master list of temporary facilities. Add to the list until there are no unique items remaining. Use the input from the other groups to add to your list above and rework your plan to incorporate those items that you believe should be included.

Time permitting, your instructor may ask each group to make a brief (two- to three-minute) presentation of its design.

The solution above represents one possible configuration, and should NOT be viewed as the single right answer. Also, if your instructor has given you different project attributes, your answer will be different. The solution provided above is offered as an example of the thought process used to determine effective site planning.

RWS 18

Design the 'Dream' Company Yard

In an ideal world, construction supervisors could focus solely on putting work into place. Making sure that the tools, equipment and things like concrete formwork are ready to go would be someone else's job. However, the supervisor sometimes lands in the position of playing "go-fer," especially on smaller projects. In other cases, the supervisor is busy calling the rental houses in town to find a concrete chainsaw for a unique demolition task. Yet at other times, the supervisor is playing mechanic or trying to find someone who can fix a plate compactor that's lost its "shake."

Wouldn't it be great to have a highly skilled yard person who had the resources and talents to take care of all of these requests with the simple press of a "push-to-talk" button? While some larger companies might have just such a person (or a team of people), most companies are going to have to settle for something less because they simply don't have the economies of scale necessary to "pay" for a fully stocked yard including dedicated mechanics. Therefore, we need to strike a balance between what the supervisor would like to have available in a yard and what the company can afford to have in a yard.

Team with individuals who work for similar companies. This exercise might require working with a different group than your usual Sure Fresh team. Once you have formed a team of three to five, work with your group to design the "dream" yard for the type of work you do.

How would you staff your yard?

If I had a small company, I'd have a part-time yard person available in the morning. If I had a medium-sized company, I'd go to a full-time person. As the company grew, I'd add a mechanic. Regardless of company size, I'd try to make certain that there was enough value-added work to justify the hiring of warehouse staff.

What would you have in your yard? Make a list on a separate sheet of paper.

I'd keep a stock of the items that we use on nearly every project: concrete form panels, edge forms, vibrators, vibratory screeds, insulated blankets, finishing machines, scaffolding and planks, mortar mixers, etc.

What would you plan on always renting? Make a list on a separate sheet of paper.

I'd plan on renting a laser screed, as we don't do that many large floor pours.

How did you determine what to own and what to rent?

I'd decide to own what we used on a regular basis and rent everything else.

How would you handle maintenance?

I'd try to do as much maintenance as possible with our warehouse staff; however, I would outsource the portion of the maintenance that could not be handled by our staff. I wouldn't add another staffer until the cost of outsourcing exceeded the cost of the additional staff position.

For the remaining questions, the following assumptions apply:

1,000 SF of warehouse per $2,000,000 worth of work in place per year
Warehouse costs $40 per SF to construct, including design
For each SF of warehouse, 2 SF are needed for setbacks, parking, landscaping, etc. (43,560 SF to the acre)
1 acre of outside storage per $24,000,000 worth of work in place per year ___
Land costs $50,000 per acre
Annual "rent" is equal to one-tenth of the land and construction cost
Annual property taxes are equal to one-hundredth of the land and construction cost
Annual utilities are equal to $1.25 per SF of warehouse
Each full-time yard person costs $40,000 per year. You will have one yard person until you exceed $40,000,000 in work in place per year, adding another each time you exceed the next multiple of $40,000,000 in volume
Each full-time mechanic costs $70,000 per year. You will add your first mechanic once you reach $40,000,000 in work in place per year, adding another one at $80,000,000, $120,000,000, etc.

Using the assumptions above, the annual cost to build and staff a warehouse at various levels of annual volume would be:

Volume	Annual Cost, $	% of Volume
$20,000,000	$580,973	2.90%
$50,000,000	$1,502,433	3.00%
$100,000,000	$2,964,866	2.96%

How will you account for this cost? (charge to company overhead or charge to projects)

I'd charge the costs for the warehouse to company overhead, except on cost-plus projects, where I'd try to charge projects when practical.

Let's say that your company averages two to three percent profit before income taxes. Relative to the company profit, is the cost of the warehouse and yard significant?

Yes, the cost of the warehouse is significant.

Therefore, is it feasible to have everything you'd ever want in the warehouse and yard, or do you need to work to minimize this cost?

No, I need to be careful about how much warehouse cost I incur.

The solution above represents one possible configuration, and should NOT be viewed as the single right answer. Also, if your instructor has given you different project attributes, your answer will be different. The solution provided above is offered as an example of the issues involved in establishing a company yard.

RWS 19

Compare and Contrast Tilt-up vs. Precast Walls for the Sure Fresh Project

Using the Sure Fresh documents for reference, compare and contrast using tilt-up vs. precast for the wall panels. Your instructor may give you additional information to consider in your discussions.

Which option will require the most field labor? Why?

Tilt-up will require the most field labor, because the panels are cast in the field.

Which option will require the most shop drawing coordination? Why?

Precast would require the most shop drawing coordination, but the tilt-up option would also require a fair amount of coordination with the steel shop drawings. The embeds for connection to the steel must be located in the panels at the proper locations.

Assume that the project is located in International Falls, MN. Which method would be best for this location? Why?

Precast would be the best option because the wall panels could be erected and the building enclosed prior to the placement of slabs.

In addition to cold weather, what other weather phenomenon would prove challenging for tilt-up? Why?

Rain would be a challenge for tilt-up, as the panels are cast outdoors.

Assuming that the weather conditions are cooperative, which method provides you with the most control as project supervisor? Why?

Tilt-up would be the best method in terms of local schedule control, because the work would occur onsite. The project would not be at the mercy of the precast plant's schedule.

The solution above represents one possible configuration, and should NOT be viewed as the single right answer. Also, if your instructor has given you different project attributes, your answer will be different. The solution provided above is offered as an example of the thought process used in contrasting alternative means and methods.

RWS 20

Labor Cost Cycle

Break into your Sure Fresh teams. Identify all of the concrete work (CSI Division 3) that must be performed on the Sure Fresh project. You have been asked by the vice president of operations of your company to develop an estimating template that can be used to perform the initial estimate, relate estimate information to the field in the form of budgets (labor, material, and equipment), track actual costs, and store the actual cost information for use in improving estimate accuracy on future bids.

In the table on the following page, list all the concrete work that needs to be estimated for the Sure Fresh project. Think through the level of detail that is best for keeping track of information through the cost cycle.

Next, describe how you will determine the costs associated with each item of work (vendor quotes, historical costs, "best guess" of the superintendent or yard foreman, equipment lease rate lists, etc.). Discuss among your team the most reliable (least risky) method for estimating costs.

After you have determined where the cost information will come from, define how the information will be communicated to the field in the form of budgets. Some issues to consider are:

- Should the field supervisors receive material, equipment, and labor budgets expressed as dollars?
- Should the field supervisors receive only unit budgets (labor hours, material quantities, equipment lease periods)?
- What are the tradeoffs between giving budgets in dollars vs. units?
- What level of detail will be used for communicating budget information? In other words, how far will work activities be broken down for budget tracking purposes?
- How will the budgets reflect "indirects," such as hoisting, cleanup, and temporary enclosures? In other words, if a carpenter is assisting in the hoisting of formwork, should those hours be charged to hoisting, or to formwork? What are the pros and cons of assigning indirect costs to items of work rather than using separate budgets?

Now that you have set up a system for communicating estimate information to the field, think about how the actual units or costs are going to be communicated back to the office. How are costs going to be tracked? What types of special or unique information should the estimator be aware of if he/she is going to use the Sure Fresh project as a basis for future estimates of similar jobs?

Use the table on the following page to guide development of the cost cycle template.

Work item	Source of cost information	Type of budget to field	Method of tracking actual cost	Special or unique issues affecting cost to be noted on future estimates
Rebar in caissons	Sub quote	Lump sum	Subcontractor billing	Diameter & depth
Pour caissons	Best guess	Hours per caisson	Time cards + delivery tix	Diameter & depth
Form grade beam	Historical cost	Productivity per unit	Time cards	Bad soil
Place rebar	Sub quote	Lump sum	Subcontractor billing	Tonnage
Pour grade bm	Historical cost	Productivity per unit	Time cards + delivery tix	Square footage of wall area
Strip forms	Best guess	Total hours	Time cards	Square footage of wall area
Backfill grade beam	Yard or rental quote	Equipment hours	Equipment rental slips	Bad soil
Bulkhead slab-on-grade	Historical cost	Productivity per unit	Time cards	Lineal feet of bulkhead
Set mesh	Sub quote	Lump sum	Contractor billing	Square footage of floor
Place slab-on-grade	Historical cost	Productivity per unit; equip. rates	Time cards, delivery tix, equipment rental slips	Square footage of floor area
Finish slab-on-grade	Historical cost	Productivity per unit; equip. rates	Time cards; equipment rental slips	Square footage of floor area
Erect pre-cast wall panels	Sub quote	Lump sum (includes hoisting)	Subcontractor billing	No hoisting by general contractor
Bulkhead sidewalks	Historical cost	Productivity per unit	Time cards	Includes stripping
Pour & finish sidewalks	Historical costs	Productivity per unit	Time cards & delivery tickets	Square footage of sidewalk area
Bulkhead patio	Best guess	Total hours	Time cards	Perimeter areas
Pour & finish patio	Best guess	Total hours	Time cards & delivery tickets	One-time set-up will affect productivity
Bridges & abutments	Sub quote	Lump sum	Subcontractor billing	Special work

RWS 21

Ideal Labor Cost Coding System

What would be your ideal cost coding system for use in tracking actual costs on a construction job? What are some of the issues that need to be considered, such as level of detail, use of technology, value of time spent recording data, etc.? How much detail is needed to give the project manager an accurate picture of the costs incurred on the project and make margin projections? At what point does cost detail lose its effectiveness and become just a waste of time? How will mixed trade work units (e.g., concrete slabs) and indirect work (e.g., cleanup) be coded in such a way as to be useful to the project manager and the estimator?

Discuss these items with your team and present a short report to the class. Consider different ways of categorizing the work (e.g., by specification division, by trade, by system, etc.). Use the space below to list your ideas.

How are we going to categorize the work?

The work will be categorized by trade (carpenter, mason, operator, painter, electrician, etc.)

How far are we going to break down records? To what level of detail are we going to record costs?

The costs will be recorded for each building component such as footings, foundations, columns, slabs, spandrels, windows, etc.

How can we track indirect costs such as hoisting and cleanup so that the estimator knows what costs to use for these items on future projects?

We can track indirect items by the hours for each category by general area (cleanup for masonry, hoisting for formwork, etc.). As a backup, we will also keep track of indirect hours as a percentage of total hours for the week.

The solution above represents one possible solution, and should NOT be viewed as the single right answer. Also, if your instructor has given you different project roles your answers might be different. The solution above is offered as an example of the thought process used to determine project cost codes.

RWS 22

Project Cash Flow

Break into your Sure Fresh teams. Your team is to play the role of the concrete subcontractor. Your company will come to the site after the excavation is complete.
It has received a subcontract for all concrete work, including strip footings for the cast-in-place concrete walls, column pad footings, CIP walls, and slab-on-grade. You are responsible for all formwork, material, labor and equipment to complete the concrete on the project.

Plan the sequence of work and then estimate the cash flow based on the following assumptions:

- You start work on the first day of the month, a Monday
- You had to buy $2,000 worth of lumber on the first day, for which you had to pay cash
- Uniform pay rate of $25/hour for all trades and scales and payday is every Friday
- Material invoices are paid 10 working days after delivery
- Ready-Mix is $70/CY for material
- Reinforcing steel is $10/CY for material
- Equipment rental charges are paid every two weeks, on Friday
- Equipment needs are:
    - one ground crane at $1,000/day, plus
    - one concrete pump at $500/day when more than 15 yards are poured

Use the costs and assumptions above to complete the cash flow table on the following page. The asterisks indicate where you should have a cash expense entry using the assumptions above. Your instructor may have different or additional assumptions that change the dates that cash is needed. Work closely with your instructor on this activity.

		Labor hrs	Labor expense	Material units	Material expense	Equip used	Equip expense
Week 1	Mon	40		10 CY	$2,000	1	
	Tue	40		10 CY		1	
	Wed	48		15 CY		1 + 1	
	Thu	48		15 CY		1 + 1	
	Fri	56	$5,800	15 CY		1 + 1	
Week 2	Mon	56		15 CY		1 + 1	
	Tue	48		10 CY		1	
	Wed	48		10 CY		1	
	Thu	40		10 CY		1	
	Fri	40	$5,800	6 CY		1	$12,000
Week 3	Mon	40			$800	1	
	Tue	36			$800	1	
	Wed	36			$1,200	1	
	Thu	32			$1,200	1	
	Fri	24	$4,200		$1,200	1	
Week 4	Mon	24			$1,200	1	
	Tue	24			$800	0	
	Wed	16			$800	0	
	Thu	16			$800	0	
	Fri	8	$2,200		$480	0	$6,000
TOTALS			$18,000		$11,280		$18,000

Total cash on hand required or credit available is $47,280

RWS 23

Sure Fresh Conflict Resolution

The Sure Fresh project is not particularly complicated, but every project is susceptible to conflict. It turns out that your plumbing subcontractor and the plumbing inspector do not get along very well with each other. It can be said that they "have a history." Specifically, the owner of the plumbing subcontractor (who also works with his tools) and the plumbing inspector were partners in business at one time, but had a less-than-amicable separation.

The applicable code for the project is the State Plumbing Code. In the past, the code has been very conservative regarding the adoption of new materials and techniques. Previously, the code required all waste piping, whether above or below grade, to be cast iron. Recently, the code has been revised to permit PVC piping. In the interest of saving money on the project for the owner, the plumbing subcontractor suggested value engineering the waste piping to PVC in lieu of cast iron. The mechanical engineer of record recommended this change to the owner (but did not update the drawings and specifications), and the owner accepted the credit to the contract for this change.

Unfortunately, the plumbing inspector is not aware of the change to the project plans and specifications and is upset when he comes out to do the underground rough-in inspection and sees PVC piping. The inspector is just back from his annual two-week trip to the family cabin and has not read the amendment to the code from the State Plumbing Commission that is sitting in his "in" basket at the office. He immediately "red flags" the project, thinking that the plumber is willfully violating the plumbing code, and threatens to call the sheriff's deputy out to arrest the plumbing subcontractor.

Knowing that your structural steel is set to arrive the next morning, you realize that the inspector's actions are going to delay the progress on the project if the job is shut down. It does not help anything that your plumber has an anger management problem and is ready to go toe-to-toe with the inspector.

Given that the inspector and the subcontractor have this antipathy, how do you go about getting the PVC approved and inspected and getting the project back on track?

I'd keep the plumbing sub out of the discussion at this point. I'd show the inspector the documentation about the engineer's approval and the state code revision, and ask him to re-inspect the work.

Remember that you are caught between two individuals who dislike each other, *and* that you'll need cooperation from both of them after this issue is resolved in order to complete the project successfully.

Discuss proposed solutions among your group for about five minutes. Your instructor will then ask each group for its proposed solution to the conflict.

There will be many different ways of resolving the conflict. Which ones will be the most uncomfortable for the inspector?

The methods involving interaction with the plumbing sub would be least comfortable.

Why might it be a good idea to give the inspector a "way out" even though he is clearly wrong given the amendment to the code?

The inspector must know you handled the situation professionally—you can't have him carrying a grudge.

The solution above represents one possible configuration, and should NOT be viewed as the single right answer. Also, if your instructor has given you different project attributes, your answer will be different. The solution provided above is offered as an example of the thought process used in conflict resolution.

RWS 24

OSHA Visit to Sure Fresh

Although your project is located in a remote area, the site borders on an interstate right-of-way. Several OSHA inspectors happen to travel past your site each week on their way to another metropolitan area that does not have a local OSHA office. Even though you do your best to comply with all the OSHA regulations, you have a momentary lapse of caution when you climb onto a snorkel-style lift to inspect some work done by the outside sheet metal subcontractor.

Since "timing is everything," you manage to pick one of the five times this week that an OSHA inspector is driving by on the interstate to have your lapse of caution. Specifically, you have forgotten to put on a harness and to attach a lanyard to yourself as you zoom up to look at the sheet metal coping that "just doesn't look right." The OSHA inspector sees you on the lift without the proper safety gear and says to herself "that just doesn't look right." She exits at the next opportunity and nine minutes later, she is waiting for you to return to earth from your daring adventure.

After completing your inspection, you turn around to lower yourself to the ground and see the OSHA vehicle next to the trailer. You look closer to the base of the snorkel lift and see that the agent wants to take your picture. You feel uneasy, but you still have not figured out what the interest is in your use of the lift until you lower the boom and begin to climb out. The inspector has caught you "red-handed," and now wants to inspect the entire project.

What do you do first?

First, I would ask the inspector to wait in the trailer until our safety director arrives. Next, I'd step out of the inspector's earshot and call my supervisor and let him know what's happened and ask to get the safety director onsite. I know that my supervisor is eventually going to get a full report from OSHA, so I would not attempt to "spin" the facts.

How do you interact with the inspector, knowing that your momentary lapse of caution is likely to result in a fine to your employer?

I'd try my best to be polite and respectful and to avoid making things worse by angering or upsetting the inspector.

During the whole site inspection, no further violations are noted; however, you know that your lift exercise likely will result in a citation and fine.

Discuss with your small group how to handle the situation. In 10 minutes your instructor will go around the room to solicit your ideas so that the class can develop a strategy for handling the inspection.

The solution above represents one possible configuration, and should NOT be viewed as the single right answer. The answers above are examples for guidance only.

RWS 25

Sure Fresh Jurisdictional Dispute Project

The Sure Fresh project has been designed with precast concrete walls. The precaster is from out of state and always quotes its products erected. The precaster's sub-subcontractor employs only steelworkers and equipment operators. The logic in its home territory is that the precast, albeit concrete, erects most like structural steel with the intense use of a crane and welded and bolted connections. Unfortunately, in the locale of the project, the concrete workers claim the precast erection because the panels are made of concrete. To make matters worse, you are also from out of state and have no idea that a jurisdictional dispute is about to occur on your project.

The precast panels are scheduled to arrive on Tuesday next week. It's Friday, and your concrete paving subcontractor is onsite pouring the loading dock slabs. The concrete paving foreman happens to come into the jobsite trailer while you are on the phone coordinating the move-in of the crane for the precast erection crew for Monday. In the course of the conversation, the concrete paving foreman overhears you talking about the steelworkers coming onto the site first thing Tuesday morning. Before you finish the phone call, the foreman is out of your trailer and sitting in his truck calling his union business agent. However, you are oblivious to any poten-tial issue until an hour later (just 30 minutes prior to quitting time for the weekend) when the business agent for the concrete workers arrives at your jobsite.

As you are from out of town, you do not have any experience with this business agent. All you know is that he is making it very clear that he wants his concrete workers to erect the precast panels and if the steelworkers show up to erect the pre-cast, there will be "trouble." All of a sudden, your dream of spending the weekend fishing begins to evaporate. You know that the project is going to be delayed unless you can figure out a way to solve the problem quickly. And you know that your weekend is going to be ruined either way.

Based upon your experience, the suggestions in the Participant's Manual, and your instructor's comments, how would you proceed?

I would call my supervisor for advice and suggest that he or she get the company owner and/or our AGC chapter involved.

Work with your group to develop possible courses of action to keep the project moving. Your instructor will go around the room after about five minutes to give you the opportunity to share your solution with the class. Again, there are multiple ways to handle the situation, which you must do, as it clearly will not go away on its own.

Because the concrete work is not complete on the project yet, I'd need to formu-late a solution that keeps the concrete workers on the job.

Your instructor might challenge you by throwing out "twists" to the scenario:

1. The project is in a right-to-work state. How does this affect your plan? What if your firm is merit shop? What if your firm is union shop?
2. The project is not in a right-to-work state. How does this affect your plan? What if your firm is merit shop? What if your firm is union shop?

The solution above represents one possible configuration, and should NOT be viewed as the single right answer. Also, if your instructor has given you different project attributes, your answer will be different. The solution provided above is offered as an example of the thought process used in resolving jurisdictional disputes.

RWS 26

Low-cost/No-cost Rewards for Craftworkers

Your instructor will assign you to teams of four and give you a time limit for this activity.

Within the allotted time, come up with as many low-cost or no-cost means of rewarding craftworkers as possible. Feel free to include ideas that you have actually used on some of your previous projects. When you get the "two-minute warning" from your instructor, narrow your list down to the five ideas you think will be most effective. The instructor will direct you to share them with others in the class.

Low-cost/No-cost Reward ideas:

Project stickers for hardhats

Candies, cookies, doughnuts

PM buys breakfast for crews

Employee profiles for company newsletter

Birthday cakes

Point out high-quality work on job site tours with owner, community group

Anniversary buttons for each year of work with the company

Gift certificates to local restaurants

Top Five Ideas:

1. **Hardhat stickers**

2. **PM buys breakfast for one crew every month**

3. **Put employee profiles in company newsletters**

4. **Make sure to point out high-quality work on job site tours**

5. **Friday morning doughnuts**

The solution above represents one possible solution, and should NOT be viewed as the single right answer. Also, if your instructor has given you different project roles your answers might be different. The solution above is offered as an example of ideas for reward and motivation.

RWS 27

Matching Leadership Style to Optimal Project Type

If you had to rate yourself on a 1-to-10 scale on working with tasks (budget, schedule, work, coordination, etc.) and 1-to-10 on working with people (motivating, rewarding, communicating, listening, etc.), how would you score yourself? Place your scores in the following grid and think for a moment about your leadership style.

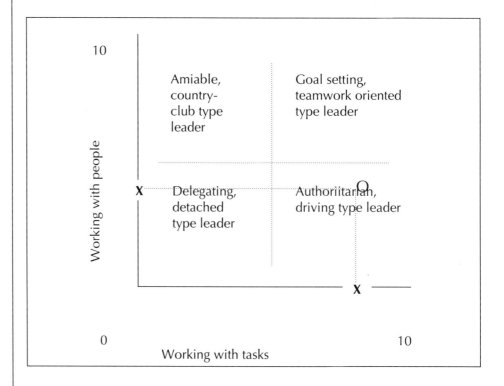

In the space below, list the project characteristics that you think are best suited for your leadership style. Think about issues such as team size, number of people you have to coordinate, complexity of the tasks, schedule flexibility, budget certainty, design completeness, etc.

Tight schedule, small crews, direct reporting to superintendent (not much delegation needed), low-bid, demanding owner, experienced crews

Which areas of leadership do you think you could improve to make yourself a more effective project leader?

Delegation, communication, helping team members develop their skills, working with younger, less experienced workers, listening

The solution above represents one possible solution, and should NOT be viewed as the single right answer. Also, if your instructor has given you different project roles your answers might be different. The solution above is offered as an example of the thought process used in thinking about leadership style and project/team fit.

RWS 28

Personality Interaction Exercise

This in-class activity should be fun and straightforward. Your instructor will assign you a partner for this activity. Spend 15 to 20 minutes having a conversation with your activity partner, but instead of just casually conversing, ask questions and listen to answers with the intent of making some assumptions about your partner's personality.

There are many personality tests available from consultants or online testing sites. These can be valuable in understanding yourself and how you relate to others. However, when placed in a team situation, no one comes up and says, "Hi, I'm Bill, and I am an Introverted, Detail-Oriented, Rational, Logical, Planning Personality." (If only it were that simple!) People usually have to spend time with their team members, make observations, and listen carefully to perceive what type of personality they are dealing with. Remember, the goal is not to categorize the other person for the sake of labeling, but to help you communicate better.

Some of the personality traits can be inferred from casual conversation. Asking questions and then listening carefully to the answers is a good practice for leaders to learn. Some examples follow.

To learn whether someone is extroverted or introverted, ask them what they do after work or in their spare time. If the answer is reading books, tinkering in the workshop, or watching TV, they are most likely an introvert. If the answer is going to the sports bar, dancing, or volunteering in the community, then they may be more extroverted.

To try to determine their preference for detail, ask them to describe a vehicle they drive, or tell you about their favorite vacation. If the answer to the first question is "red," you are talking to an intuitive, big-picture personality. If you get color, make, model, year, size of engine, type of transmission, accessories, and upgrades, you are likely talking to a sensing, detail-oriented person. The same would hold true for asking about the vacation. An intuitive type might say "fishing," whereas a sensing personality would give specific details about where they would fish, for what type of fish, whether they would fly-fish or troll, etc.

For the personality dimension involving thinking types (logical, rational, and objective), vs. feeling types (emotional, aesthetic, and subjective) you can ask how your partner about their job. If they talk about the processes and the tasks, they are probably thinking types. If they talk about the people and the teamwork, they are probably feeling types.

Organizational types (perceiving vs. judging) can be more difficult to guess at from a conversation. Remember that perceiving types appear unorganized, are unconcerned about deadlines, and prefer creativity and flexibility. Judging types are natural planners, with details, tasks and routines to guide their lives. You can ask some questions about their typical day or have them describe a project they worked on to see if the answers fall more into the perceiving or judging category.

Use the space below to write down the questions you will ask as well as the relevant comments from your partner's answers, then circle the personality type you think best describes them. Remember, this is just practice! You wouldn't actually write down answers during a casual conversation with a team member, but good leaders train themselves to pick up on the personality types and preferences of their team members through interactions.

Extrovert/Introvert (Circle partner's most likely type)

Question to ask:

What do you like to do in your free time?

Relevant insights from the answers:

Answer: Read books (probably an Introvert)
Answer: Go to parties or travel (probably an Extrovert)

Sensing/Intuition (Circle partner's most likely type)
Question to ask:

What do you think the coach should have done in the Vikings game last night?

Relevant insights from the answers:

Answer: He should have passed (probably Intuition)
Answer: He should have had the quarterback fake a screen pass and then reverse field on a naked bootleg and throw the ball to the tight end who held for a three count at the line and then ran a crossing route over the middle (probably Sensing)

Thinking/Feeling (Circle partner's most likely type)
Question to ask:

Where do you want to go for lunch?

Relevant insights from the answers:

Answer: Burger King—it's close and I don't have much time (probably Thinking)
Answer: I don't know; where do you think we should go? (probably Feeling)

Judging/Perceiving (Circle partner's most likely type)
Question to ask:

Where are you going on vacation this year?

Relevant insights from the answers:

Answer: I don't know. We'll probably decide the night before we leave and just take off (probably Perceiving)

Answer: We have already bought tickets on a cruise for next winter (probably Judging)

The solution above represents one possible solution, and should NOT be viewed as the single right answer. Also, if your instructor has given you different project roles your answers might be different. The solution above is offered as an example of the thought process used when attempting to understand personality types.

RWS 29

Bouncing Up the Sales Lead

Many companies have a dedicated sales staff, while others have project managers who also sell and bid work. Regardless of how your company handles the sales function, it rarely hurts to have everyone in the company helping with sales. While you don't want your mason tenders leaving in the middle of the day to make sales calls, it wouldn't hurt to have them tell you about their in-law's restaurant that is about to open a second location.

How do you get everyone involved in the sales effort? The first step is probably letting them know that sales leads are welcome. However, you also need to let everyone know that the sales staff cannot physically follow up on all potential leads. How the leads are prioritized will be driven by the corporate culture (see WS 30), the current workload, profit potential, competition, etc.

Work with the same partner that you worked with on the previous activity. Your charge is to develop a system for bouncing up sales leads from the field to the office. Some things to think about include:

- Must leads follow the chain of command (craftworker to foreman to supervisor to office), or do you designate a person in the home office to receive leads?
- Do you provide incentives for providing leads? Or, do you only reward lead providers whose leads result in actual projects? If so, do you calculate the reward based upon project profitability?
  - How do you handle the "reward" aspect if two or more employees submit the same lead?
  - How do you handle the employee who is upset that his or her lead wasn't followed up on aggressively?
  - Do you provide rewards for leads that could have been read about in the paper or heard on the radio or TV?
  - Do you provide rewards for leads for publicly bid projects?
- Do you provide incentives to people in estimating and sales, especially if they do not currently have a performance bonus system in place? (While sales and estimating might be their main job, these employees might want to be rewarded for the leads they generate.)

These are just some of the things to think about in designing your lead generation and incentive program. Using a blank sheet of paper, develop your program. Your instructor will give you approximately 10 to 15 minutes to work on your design. At the end of the work time, your instructor will go around the room and ask you to present your plan.

There are no right or wrong answers to this exercise. The questions above lead the participants to some possible solutions.

RWS 30

Corporate Culture and Project Selection

While there are some companies that will bid everything in sight, most companies have a culture-driven philosophy or strategy that determines what projects they will bid or not bid (or, in the case of negotiated projects, pursue or not pursue). Some of the factors that contribute to the "bid/no bid" determination are the client, size of project, location of project, type of work, competition, risk, volume, etc.

Work with a partner and develop a company profile for your hypothetical construction company. Make sure that you include the following characteristics:

Self-performed trades: **foundation excavation, concrete, masonry, carpentry**

Annual volume: **$40,000,000**   Bonding capacity: **$50,000,000**

Location of home and branch offices, if any: **Chicago, IL, Milwaukee, WI**

Type(s) of work: **commercial, light industrial, institutional**

Current/recent clients: **University of Illinois at Chicago, University of Wisconsin at Milwaukee, International Motors Company, Chicago Public School District, United States Warehousing**

Attitude toward risk: **We'll try anything once, but tend to like projects with lots of work we can do ourselves.**

Other items of note: **We have unionized field employees.**

Your instructor will describe various projects that your firm could pursue. Work with your partner to determine which projects you will "chase" based upon your company's characteristics.

Why did you choose to pursue the projects that you did?

We chose the ones that fit within our bonding capacity and had a lot of concrete and masonry work, since these are our specialties.

Why did you reject the ones that you did?

They were too small, too large, were the wrong type of work or didn't have much concrete and masonry work.

The solution above represents one possible configuration, and should NOT be viewed as the single right answer. Also, if your instructor has given you different project attributes, your answer will be different. The solution provided above is offered as an example of the thought process used in thinking about project selection.

RWS 31

Personal Development Plan

After each session, you have been asked to write down one thing that everyone in your company should know, one thing that your company should include in its project management training program, and one thing that you intend to use on your next project to make it more successful.

At this time, please review your short memos you have developed over the course of STP Unit 8. Focus on the 10 things that you chose to use on your next project. Group together the ones that have related concepts and write a paragraph for each group. Each paragraph should indicate how you can work on or implement the items in the group over the course of the next year. Again, it is important to choose something "achievable" to work on first, so that you have some early success in your personal development plan. After you enjoy some successes, move on to some of your more difficult goals.

While many of your personal development goals may be implemented on your own, you may need your manager's support to implement some of your ideas. Hopefully you have been working with your manager after each of the sessions and already have his or her buy-in for your development plan. If you do not have this consensus developed yet with your manager, it is important to get it prior to implementing any ideas that are contrary to standard company practice. You probably have shared many great ideas with your classmates over the course of the 10 sessions, but no one in the class has the authority to grant you permission to conduct your job in a manner that is inconsistent with company policy.

If you have been working with your supervisor over the course of the 10 sessions, you might want to help him or her develop a plan for "spreading the word" on the things that you think everyone in your company should know about. Again, get your manager's permission and seek his or her guidance on how to communicate the information. Many companies have operations meetings periodically or a newsletter that might facilitate your efforts in this area.

The answers for this activity are provided by each participant based on their individual reflections over the 10 sessions.

Notes

Unit 8, Managing the Project: The Supervisor's Role

Post-Knowledge Survey

This survey is designed to check your knowledge about project management on the construction site. This survey is not graded, and the information in it is for your use only. Answer each question to the best of your ability. Circle the letter next to your choice, or respond as directed in the question.

1. In which of the following delivery systems does the construction owner execute one contract with a single organization for all phases of the project?
    a. Construction Management at-Risk
    b. Traditional low bid
    c. Multiple prime
    d. Design-Build

2. In a cost control system, what is the function of a labor productivity budget?
    a. To set a standard for achievement
    b. To create an accurate field report
    c. To project final costs of the work
    d. To implement corrective action

3. Responsibility for which of the following risk categories is typically assigned to the project supervisor in the field?
    a. Overall project profitability
    b. Safety of the workers
    c. Design function
    d. Financial strength of subcontractors

4. Which of the following does NOT help reduce the risk exposure of contractors?
    a. Insurance
    b. Self-performing
    c. Bonding
    d. Subcontracting

5. Gantt charts, or bar chart schedules, show precedence relationships between work tasks.
    a. True
    b. False

6. What is the first field activity on any construction project?
    a. Expediting
    b. Purchasing
    c. Mobilization
    d. Closeout

7. Which of the following organizations does NOT typically have inspection and approval authority on a construction project?
    a. Government agencies (EPA, OSHA, local building departments)
    b. Testing agency retained by the owner
    c. Designers (architect, engineers)
    d. Subcontractors

8. The decision to prefabricate versus field-assemble represents a tradeoff of cost, schedule and quality factors.
    a. True
    b. False

9. Which of the following should be considered prior to finalizing equipment selections?
   a. Means and methods for construction
   b. Ability of equipment to improve safety of working conditions
   c. Schedule of delivery and availability of onsite storage
   d. All of the above factor into equipment selection

10. Which of the following best represents the cost information cycle in construction companies?
    a. Project budgets→historical records→actual costs→ future estimates→back to project budgets
    b. Historical records→future estimates→project budgets→actual costs→back to historical records
    c. Actual costs→future estimates→historical records→project budgets→back to actual costs
    d. Future estimate→actual costs→project budgets→historical records→back to future budgets

11. What is the general shape of the curve for monthly payments on a construction project (as a percent of total project cost)?
    a. U-shaped
    b. C-shaped
    c. S-shaped
    d. M-shaped

12. Which of the following delivery systems creates the most adversarial relationships between project partners on a construction project?
    a. Low-bid award of a general contract
    b. Negotiated award of a general contract
    c. Construction Management at-Risk with a GMP
    d. Design-Build

13. Which of the following represents an option for working with both union and non-union subcontractors on a project?
    a. Project agreement
    b. Dual-gate system
    c. Both a. and b.
    d. There are no options for having union and non-union workers on a jobsite

14. Which of the following uses of power provides the greatest motivation for workers over the long term?
    a. Coercion
    b. Rewards
    c. Punishment
    d. Legitimacy (I'm the boss—do what I say)

15. Managing tasks is the only important aspect of project leadership.
    a. True
    b. False

16. Which of the following will most influence the continuing professional development of your project management skills?
    a. Your willingness to take educational and training programs offered by your company and construction trade associations
    b. Your employer's level of corporate overhead
    c. Your ability to find new business opportunities for your employer
    d. Your employer's project portfolio

Unit 8, Managing the Project: The Supervisor's Role

Post-Knowledge Survey Answers

This survey is designed to check your knowledge about project management on the construction site. This survey is not graded, and the information in it is for your use only. Answer each question to the best of your ability. Circle the letter next to your choice, or respond as directed in the question.

1. In which of the following delivery systems does the construction owner execute one contract with a single organization for all phases of the project?
    a. Construction Management at-Risk
    b. Traditional low bid
    c. Multiple prime
    d. **Design-Build**

2. In a cost control system, what is the function of a labor productivity budget?
    a. **To set a standard for achievement**
    b. To create an accurate field report
    c. To project final costs of the work
    d. To implement corrective action

3. Responsibility for which of the following risk categories is typically assigned to the project supervisor in the field?
    a. Overall project profitability
    b. **Safety of the workers**
    c. Design function
    d. Financial strength of subcontractors

4. Which of the following does NOT help reduce the risk exposure of contractors?
    a. Insurance
    b. **Self-performing**
    c. Bonding
    d. Subcontracting

5. Gantt charts, or bar chart schedules, show precedence relationships between work tasks.
    a. True
    b. **False**

6. What is the first field activity on any construction project?
    a. Expediting
    b. Purchasing
    c. **Mobilization**
    d. Closeout

7. Which of the following organizations does NOT typically have inspection and approval authority on a construction project?
    a. Government agencies (EPA, OSHA, local building departments)
    b. Testing agency retained by the owner
    c. Designers (architect, engineers)
    d. **Subcontractors**

8. The decision to prefabricate versus field-assemble represents a tradeoff of cost, schedule and quality factors.
    a. **True**
    b. False

9. Which of the following should be considered prior to finalizing equipment selections?
   a. Means and methods for construction
   b. Ability of equipment to improve safety of working conditions
   c. Schedule of delivery and availability of onsite storage
   d. **All of the above factor into equipment selection**

10. Which of the following best represents the cost information cycle in construction companies?
    a. Project budgets→historicalrecords→actual costs→future estimates→back to project budgets
    b. **Historical records→future estimates→project budgets→actual costs→back to historical records**
    c. Actual costs→future estimates→historical records→project budgets→back to actual costs
    d. Future estimate→actual costs→project budgets→historical records→back to future budgets

11. What is the general shape of the curve for monthly payments on a construction project (as a percent of total project cost)?
    a. U-shaped
    b. C-shaped
    c. **S-shaped**
    d. M-shaped

12. Which of the following delivery systems creates the most adversarial relationships between project partners on a construction project?
    a. **Low-bid award of a general contract**
    b. Negotiated award of a general contract
    c. Construction Management at-Risk with a GMP
    d. Design-Build

13. Which of the following represents an option for working with both union and non-union subcontractors on a project?
    a. Project agreement
    b. Dual-gate system
    c. **Both a. and b.**
    d. There are no options for having union and non-union workers on a jobsite

14. Which of the following uses of power provides the greatest motivation for workers over the long term?
    a. Coercion
    b. **Rewards**
    c. Punishment
    d. Legitimacy (I'm the boss—do what I say)

15. Managing tasks is the only important aspect of project leadership.
    a. True
    b. **False**

16. Which of the following will most influence the continuing professional development of your project management skills?
    a. **Your willingness to take educational and training programs offered by your company and construction trade associations**
    b. Your employer's level of corporate overhead
    c. Your ability to find new business opportunities for your employer
    d. Your employer's project portfolio

We don't want to pester you with so many questions that you toss out this whole evaluation form, so **this page is optional**. However, we hope you will provide as much feedback as you can because we base revisions and improvements to *Managing the Project: The Supervisor's Role* on responses from participants and instructors.

Instructions: *For each session*, check any boxes that describe how you feel about *that session*. For example, if you feel that the topics covered in Session 3 on developing the project plan have **some** relevance to your work, you would check the box as shown below. (If **some** is not your answer, just ■ the **some** box and ✓ one of the others.)

	1. Understanding Project Delivery Systems	2. Managing Information	3. Understanding and Managing risk	4. Planning the Work	5. Working the Plan	6. Managing Methods and Materials	7. Understanding Finances	8. Working with Project Partners	9. Understanding People	10. Understanding Corporate Policies
Concepts and skills presented were:										
too complex or difficult										
just about right										
too general or easy										
The amount of time spent on these topics was:										
too much										
about right										
not enough										
The relevance of these topics to my work was:										
much										
some			✔							
little										
none										
The activities in this session were (check all that apply):										
useful										
boring										
confusing										
interesting										
fun										
well designed										
busy work										
The reading material in the Participant's Manual was:										
clearly written										
hard to understand										
about the right amount of information										
too much to read										
needed more explanation										

Please use the back of this page for any additional comments or observations that you feel might be helpful to the developers of the Supervisory Training Program. Thank you.

Thank you for completing the registration and evaluation. Your comments will help us improve future courses and provide higher levels of educational services to our members.

We appreciate your participation in the Supervisory Training Program of the Associated General Contractors of America. We hope you enjoyed *Managing the Project: The Supervisor's Role*, and look forward to seeing you in another STP program in the near future.

Amy Fields, STP Program Director
Associated General Contractors of America

If your instructor is collecting the completed registration and evaluation forms for the class, please give this form to your instructor.

If you are returning the form yourself, please fold so the "Business Reply Mail" address is showing, tape the edges, and drop in the mail.

Name _____

Address _____

City _____ State ____ ZIP _____

Phone (_____) _____

NO POSTAGE
NECESSARY
IF MAILED
IN THE
UNITED STATES

BUSINESS REPLY MAIL
FIRST CLASS MAIL PERMIT NO 1017 ARLINGTON, VA

POSTAGE WILL BE PAID BY ADDRESSEE

Associated General Contractors of America
2300 Wilson Blvd, Suite 400
Arlington, VA 22201

Attn: Director, Supervisory Training Programs

INSTRUCTIONS FOR COMPLETION OF
AGC DOCUMENT NO. 200
STANDARD FORM OF AGREEMENT AND GENERAL CONDITIONS BETWEEN OWNER AND CONTRACTOR
(Where the Contract Price is a Lump Sum)

2000 EDITION

The Standard Form of Agreement and General Conditions Between Owner and Contractor (Where the Contract Price is a Lump Sum), AGC Document No. 200 (AGC 200), is intended to form an integrated agreement and general conditions document between the owner and the contractor performing work on a lump sum basis. Specific areas of focus within AGC 200 include site conditions, Changes in the Work, delays, acceleration, Defective Work, safety, indemnity, insurance, hazardous materials, limits of liability and final acceptance. This document replaces the 1997 edition of AGC 200.

AGC 200, 2000 edition, benefited from an inclusive development process. It was developed with the advice and cooperation of the AGC Private Industry Advisory Council, consisting of design and construction professionals within Fortune 500 companies representing many sectors of the U.S. economy, such as automobile manufacturing, entertainment, banking, insurance, retailing, energy generation and distribution, and health care. PIAC members meet regularly with AGC contractors to discuss construction contracting issues of mutual concern and to participate in the development and revision of AGC standard form contract documents. AGC gratefully acknowledges the contributions of the PIAC owners who participated in this effort to produce the new edition of AGC 200.

AGC 200 is intended to be compatible with other AGC 200 series documents and 600 series subcontracts.

GENERAL INSTRUCTIONS

Standard Form

These instructions are for the information and convenience of the users of AGC 200, 2000 Edition. They are neither part of the Agreement nor a commentary on or interpretation of the standard form. The intent of the parties to a particular agreement controls its meaning and not that of the writers and publishers of the standard form. As a standard form, this Agreement has been designed to establish the relationship of the parties in the standard situation. Recognizing that every project is unique, modifications will be required. See the following recommendations for modifications.

Related AGC Documents

AGC 200, is part of the AGC 200 series of contract documents. Consider also using these AGC documents.

AGC Document No. 205, *Standard Short Form Agreement Between Owner and Contractor (Where the Contract Price is a Lump Sum) Order No. 1872*

AGC Document No. 220, *Construction Contractor's Qualification Statement for Engineered Construction Order No. 176*

AGC Document No. 230, *Standard Form of Agreement and General Conditions Between Owner and Contractor*

(Where the Basis of Payment is the Cost of the Work With An Option for Preconstruction Services) Order No. 1880

AGC Document No. 235, *Standard Short Form Agreement Between Owner and Contractor (Where the Basis of Payment is the Cost of the Work) Order No. 1881*

AGC Document No. 240, *Standard Form of Agreement Between Owner and Architect/Engineer Order No. 1885*

AGC Document No. 250, *Standard Form of Agreement and General Conditions Between Owner and Contractor (Where the Basis of Payment is a Guaranteed Maximum Price with an Option for Preconstruction Services) Order No. 1890*

AGC Document No. 260, *Performance Bond Order No. 1895*

AGC Document No. 261, *Payment Bond Order No. 1896*

Legal and Insurance Counsel

THIS DOCUMENT HAS IMPORTANT LEGAL AND INSURANCE CONSEQUENCES, AND IT IS NOT INTENDED AS A SUBSTITUTE FOR COMPETENT PROFESSIONAL SERVICES AND ADVICE. CONSULTATION WITH AN ATTORNEY AND AN INSURANCE ADVISER IS ENCOURAGED WITH RESPECT TO ITS COMPLETION OR MODIFICATION. FEDERAL, STATE AND LOCAL LAWS AND REGULATIONS MAY VARY WITH RESPECT TO THE APPLICABILITY AND/OR ENFORCEABILITY OF SPECIFIC PROVISIONS IN THIS DOCUMENT.

AGC SPECIFICALLY DISCLAIMS ALL WARRANTIES, EXPRESS OR IMPLIED, INCLUDING ANY WARRANTY OF MERCHANTABILITY OR FITNESS FOR A PARTICULAR PURPOSE. PURCHASERS ASSUME ALL LIABILITY WITH RESPECT TO THE USE OR MODIFICATION OF THIS DOCUMENT, AND AGC SHALL NOT BE LIABLE FOR ANY DIRECT, INDIRECT OR CONSEQUENTIAL DAMAGES RESULTING FROM SUCH USE OR MODIFICATION.

COMPLETING THE AGREEMENT

Completing Blanks
Diamonds (♦) in the margins indicate provisions requiring the parties to fill in blanks with information. The checklist for completion can also be used to ensure important information is not omitted.

Checklist for Completion of AGC 200
The following provisions, identified within the text of the standard form with a diamond (♦), require the parties to insert information in order to complete the Agreement.

Article 1	3.15	6.1.2	10.4.4	Exhibit No. 1
2.3.2	4.6	7.1	10.7.1	
3.4.4	4.7	9.2.1	11.4.2	
3.11.3	5.4	9.2.4	13.9	
3.14.6	6.1.1	10.3.1	14.1	

Modifications
Supplemental conditions, provisions added to the printed agreement, may be adopted by reference. It is always best for supplements to be attached to the agreement. Provisions in the printed document that are not to be included in the agreement may be deleted by striking through the word, sentence or paragraph to be omitted. It is recommended that unwanted provisions not be blocked out so that the deleted materials are illegible. The parties should be clearly aware of the material deleted from the printed standard form.

It is a good practice for both parties to sign and date all modifications and supplements.

Photocopying the Completed Agreement
The purchaser of this printed, copyrighted document may make up to nine (9) photocopies of a completed document, whether signed or unsigned, for distribution to appropriate parties in connection with a specific project. Any other reproduction of this document in any form is strictly prohibited, unless the purchaser has obtained the prior written permission of The Associated General Contractors of America.

OBTAINING ADDITIONAL INFORMATION

To obtain additional information about AGC standard form contract documents and the AGC Contract Documents Program, contact AGC at 333 John Carlyle Street, Suite 200, Alexandria, VA 22314; phone (703) 548-3118; fax (703) 548-3119, or visit AGC's web site at www.agc.org.

ii

AGC DOCUMENT NO. 200 • STANDARD FORM OF AGREEMENT AND GENERAL CONDITIONS BETWEEN OWNER AND CONTRACTOR (Where the Contract Price is a Lump Sum)
© 2000, The Associated General Contractors of America

AGC Document No. 200
SAMPLE ■ DO NOT COPY

THE ASSOCIATED GENERAL CONTRACTORS OF AMERICA

AGC DOCUMENT NO. 200
STANDARD FORM OF AGREEMENT AND GENERAL CONDITIONS BETWEEN OWNER AND CONTRACTOR
(Where the Contract Price is a Lump Sum)

TABLE OF ARTICLES

1. AGREEMENT
2. GENERAL PROVISIONS
3. CONTRACTOR'S RESPONSIBILITIES
4. OWNER'S RESPONSIBILITIES
5. SUBCONTRACTS
6. CONTRACT TIME
7. CONTRACT PRICE
8. CHANGES
9. PAYMENT
10. INDEMNITY, INSURANCE, WAIVERS AND BONDS
11. SUSPENSION, NOTICE TO CURE AND TERMINATION OF THE AGREEMENT
12. DISPUTE RESOLUTION
13. MISCELLANEOUS PROVISIONS
14. CONTRACT DOCUMENTS

This Agreement has important legal and insurance consequences. Consultation with an attorney and insurance consultant is encouraged with respect to its completion or modification. A diamond "♦" indicates where information is to be inserted to complete this Agreement.

AGC Document No. 200
SAMPLE ■ DO NOT COPY

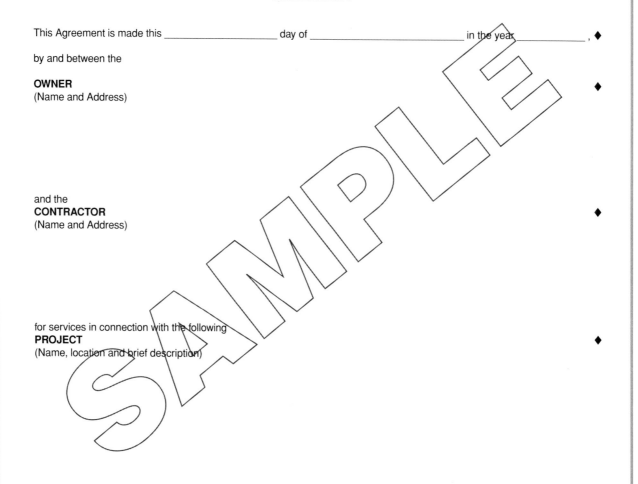

AGC DOCUMENT NO. 200
STANDARD FORM OF AGREEMENT AND GENERAL CONDITIONS
BETWEEN OWNER AND CONTRACTOR
(Where the Contract Price is a Lump Sum)

ARTICLE 1

AGREEMENT

This Agreement is made this _____ day of _____ in the year _____ , ◆

by and between the

OWNER ◆
(Name and Address)

and the
CONTRACTOR ◆
(Name and Address)

for services in connection with the following
PROJECT ◆
(Name, location and brief description)

Notice to the parties shall be given at the above addresses.

2

AGC DOCUMENT NO. 200 • STANDARD FORM OF AGREEMENT AND GENERAL CONDITIONS BETWEEN OWNER AND CONTRACTOR
(Where the Contract Price is a Lump Sum)
© 2000, The Associated General Contractors of America

ARTICLE 2

GENERAL PROVISIONS

2.1 **RELATIONSHIP OF PARTIES** The Owner and the Contractor agree to proceed with the Project on the basis of mutual trust, good faith and fair dealing.

2.1.1 The Contractor shall furnish construction administration and management services and use the Contractor's best efforts to perform the Work in an expeditious manner consistent with the Contract Documents. The Owner and Contractor shall endeavor to promote harmony and cooperation among all Project participants.

2.1.2 The Contractor represents that it is an independent contractor and that in its performance of the Work it shall act as an independent contractor.

2.1.3 Neither Contractor nor any of its agents or employees shall act on behalf of or in the name of Owner except as provided in this Agreement or unless authorized in writing by Owner's Representative.

2.2 **EXTENT OF AGREEMENT** This Agreement is solely for the benefit of the parties, represents the entire and integrated agreement between the parties, and supersedes all prior negotiations, representations or agreements, either written or oral. This Agreement and each and every provision is for the exclusive benefit of the Owner and Contractor and not for the benefit of any third party except to the extent expressly provided in this Agreement.

2.3 **DEFINITIONS**

.1 *Agreement* means this AGC Document No. 200 Standard Form of Agreement and General Conditions Between Owner and Contractor (Where the Contract Price is a Lump Sum), as modified by the parties, and Exhibits and Attachments made part of this Agreement upon its execution.

.2 *Architect/Engineer* means the licensed Architect, Architect/Engineer or Engineer and its consultants, retained by Owner to perform design services for the Project. The Owner's Architect/Engineer for the Project is _____ ◆
_____
_____ .

.3 A *Change Order* is a written order signed by the Owner and the Contractor after execution of this Agreement, indicating changes in the scope of the Work, the Contract Price and/or Contract Time, including substitutions proposed by the Contractor and accepted by the Owner.

.4 The *Contract Documents* consist of this Agreement, the drawings, specifications, addenda issued prior to execution of this Agreement, approved submittals, information furnished by the Owner under Paragraph 4.3, other documents listed in this Agreement and any modifications issued after execution.

.5 The *Contract Price* is the amount indicated in Paragraph 7.1 of this Agreement.

.6 The *Contract Time* is the period between the Date of Commencement and Final Completion. See Article 6.

.7 The *Contractor* is the person or entity identified in Article 1 and includes the Contractor's Representative.

.8 The term *Day* shall mean calendar day unless otherwise specifically defined.

.9 *Fee* means salaries and other mandatory or customary compensation of the Contractor's employees at its principal and branch offices; general and administrative expenses of the Contractor's principal and branch offices other than the field office; and the Contractor's capital expenses, including interest on the Contractor's capital employed for the Work; and profit.

.10 *Final Completion* occurs on the date when the Contractor's obligations under this Agreement are complete and accepted by the Owner and final payment becomes due and payable, as established in Article 6. This date shall be confirmed by a Certificate of Final Completion signed by the Owner and the Contractor.

.11 A *Material Supplier* is a person or entity retained by the Contractor to provide material and/or equipment for the Work.

.12 *Others* means other contractors, material suppliers and persons at the Worksite who are not employed by the Contractor or Subcontractors.

.13 *Owner* is the person or entity identified in Article 1, and includes the Owner's Representative.

.14 The *Project*, as identified in Article 1, is the building, facility and/or other improvements for which the Contractor is to perform Work under this Agreement. It may also include construction by the Owner or Others.

3

.15 The *Schedule of the Work* is the document prepared by the Contractor that specifies the dates on which the Contractor plans to begin and complete various parts of the Work, including dates on which information and approvals are required from the Owner.

.16 A *Subcontractor* is a person or entity retained by the Contractor as an independent contractor to provide the labor, materials, equipment and/or services necessary to complete a specific portion of the Work. The term Subcontractor does not include the Architect/Engineer or Others.

.17 *Substantial Completion of the Work,* or of a designated portion, occurs on the date when the Work is sufficiently complete in accordance with the Contract Documents so that the Owner may occupy or utilize the Project, or a designated portion, for the use for which it is intended. The issuance of a certificate of occupancy is not a prerequisite for Substantial Completion if the certificate of occupancy cannot be obtained due to factors beyond the Contractor's control. This date shall be confirmed by a Certificate of Substantial Completion signed by the Owner and Contractor.

.18 A *Subsubcontractor* is a person or entity who has an agreement with a Subcontractor to perform any portion of the Subcontractor's Work.

.19 *Work* means the construction and services necessary or incidental to fulfill the Contractor's obligations for the Project in conformance with this Agreement and the other Contract Documents. The Work may refer to the whole Project or only a part of the Project if work is also being performed by the Owner or Others.

.1 *Changed Work* means work that is different from the original scope of Work; or work that changes the Contract Price or Contract Time.

.2 *Defective Work* is any portion of the Work that is not in conformance with the Contract Documents, as more fully described in Paragraphs 3.5 and 3.8.

.20 *Worksite* means the geographical area at the location of the Project as identified in Article 1 where the Work is to be performed.

ARTICLE 3

CONTRACTOR'S RESPONSIBILITIES

3.1 GENERAL RESPONSIBILITIES

3.1.1 The Contractor shall provide all labor, materials, equipment and services necessary to complete the Work, all of which shall be provided in full accord with and reasonably inferable from the Contract Documents as being necessary to produce the indicated results.

3.1.2 The Contractor shall be responsible for the supervision and coordination of the Work, including the construction means, methods, techniques, sequences and procedures utilized, unless the Contract Documents give other specific instructions. In such case, the Contractor shall not be liable to the Owner for damages resulting from compliance with such instructions unless the Contractor recognized and failed to timely report to the Owner any error, inconsistency, omission or unsafe practice that it discovered in the specified construction means, methods, techniques, sequences or procedures.

3.1.3 The Contractor shall perform Work only within locations allowed by the Contract Documents, applicable permits and applicable local law.

3.2 COOPERATION WITH WORK OF OWNER AND OTHERS

3.2.1 The Owner may perform work at the Worksite directly or by Others. Any agreements with Others to perform construction or operations related to the Project shall include provisions pertaining to insurance, indemnification, waiver of subrogation, coordination, interference, clean up and safety which are substantively the same as the corresponding provisions of this Agreement.

3.2.2 In the event that the Owner elects to perform work at the Worksite directly or by Others, the Contractor and the Owner shall coordinate the activities of all forces at the Worksite and agree upon fair and reasonable schedules and operational procedures for Worksite activities. The Owner shall require each separate contractor to cooperate with the Contractor and assist with the coordination of activities and the review of construction schedules and operations. The Contract Price and Contract Time shall be equitably adjusted, as mutually agreed by the parties, for changes made necessary by the coordination of construction activities, and the Schedule of the Work shall be revised accordingly. The Contractor, Owner and Others shall adhere to the revised construction schedule until it may subsequently be revised.

4

3.2.3 With regard to the work of the Owner and Others, the Contractor shall (a) proceed with the Work in a manner which does not hinder, delay or interfere with the work of the Owner or Others or cause the work of the Owner or Others to become defective, (b) afford the Owner or Others reasonable access for introduction and storage of their materials and equipment and performance of their activities, and (c) coordinate the Contractor's construction and operations with theirs as required by this Paragraph 3.2.

3.2.4 Before proceeding with any portion of the Work affected by the construction or operations of the Owner or Others, the Contractor shall give the Owner prompt written notification of any defects the Contractor discovers in their work which will prevent the proper execution of the Work. The Contractor's obligations in this Paragraph do not create a responsibility for the work of the Owner or Others, but are for the purpose of facilitating the Work. If the Contractor does not notify the Owner of patent defects interfering with the performance of the Work, the Contractor acknowledges that the work of the Owner or Others is not defective and is acceptable for the proper execution of the Work. Following receipt of written notice from the Contractor of defects, the Owner shall promptly inform the Contractor what action, if any, the Contractor shall take with regard to the defects.

3.3 RESPONSIBILITY FOR PERFORMANCE

3.3.1 In order to facilitate its responsibilities for completion of the Work in accordance with and as reasonably inferable from the Contract Documents, prior to commencing the Work the Contractor shall examine and compare the drawings and specifications with information furnished by the Owner pursuant to Paragraph 4.3, relevant field measurements made by the Contractor and any visible conditions at the Worksite affecting the Work.

3.3.2 If in the course of the performance of the obligations in Subparagraph 3.3.1 the Contractor discovers any errors, omissions or inconsistencies in the Contract Documents, the Contractor shall promptly report them to the Owner. It is recognized, however, that the Contractor is not acting in the capacity of a licensed design professional, and that the Contractor's examination is to facilitate construction and does not create an affirmative responsibility to detect errors, omissions or inconsistencies or to ascertain compliance with applicable laws, building codes or regulations. Following receipt of written notice from the Contractor of defects, the Owner shall promptly inform the Contractor what action, if any, the Contractor shall take with regard to the defects.

3.3.3 The Contractor shall have no liability for errors, omissions or inconsistencies discovered under Subparagraphs 3.3.1 and 3.3.2 unless the Contractor knowingly fails to report a recognized problem to the Owner.

3.3.4 The Contractor may be entitled to additional costs and/or time because of clarifications or instructions arising out of the Contractor's reports described in the three preceding Subparagraphs.

3.4 CONSTRUCTION PERSONNEL AND SUPERVISION

3.4.1 The Contractor shall provide competent supervision for the performance of the Work. Before commencing the Work, Contractor shall notify Owner in writing of the name and qualifications of its proposed superintendent(s) and project manager so Owner may review the individual's qualifications. If, for reasonable cause, the Owner refuses to approve the individual, or withdraws its approval after once giving it, Contractor shall name a different superintendent or project manager for Owner's review. Any disapproved superintendent shall not perform in that capacity thereafter at the Worksite.

3.4.2 The Contractor shall be responsible to the Owner for acts or omissions of parties or entities performing portions of the Work for or on behalf of the Contractor or any of its Subcontractors.

3.4.3 The Contractor shall permit only skilled persons to perform the Work. The Contractor shall enforce safety procedures, strict discipline and good order among persons performing the Work. If the Owner determines that a particular person does not follow safety procedures, or is unfit or unskilled for the assigned work, the Contractor shall immediately reassign the person on receipt of the Owner's written notice to do so.

3.4.4 CONTRACTOR'S REPRESENTATIVE The Contractor's authorized representative is _____ ◆
_____ .
The Contractor's Representative shall possess full authority to receive instructions from the Owner and to act on those instructions. The Contractor shall notify the Owner in writing of a change in the designation of the Contractor's Representative.

3.5 WORKMANSHIP The Work shall be executed in accordance with the Contract Documents in a workmanlike manner. All materials used in the Work shall be furnished in sufficient quantities to facilitate the proper and expeditious execution of the Work and shall be new except such materials as may be expressly provided in the Contract Documents to be otherwise.

3.6 MATERIALS FURNISHED BY THE OWNER OR OTHERS In the event the Work includes installation of materials or equipment furnished by the Owner or Others, it shall be the responsibility of the Contractor to examine the items so provided and thereupon handle, store and install

5

the items, unless otherwise provided in the Contract Documents, with such skill and care as to provide a satisfactory and proper installation. Loss or damage due to acts or omissions of the Contractor shall be the responsibility of the Contractor and may be deducted from any amounts due or to become due the Contractor. Any defects discovered in such materials or equipment shall be reported at once to the Owner. Following receipt of written notice from the Contractor of defects, the Owner shall promptly inform the Contractor what action, if any, the Contractor shall take with regard to the defects.

3.7 TESTS AND INSPECTIONS

3.7.1 The Contractor shall schedule all required tests, approvals and inspections of the Work or portions thereof at appropriate times so as not to delay the progress of the Work or other work related to the Project. The Contractor shall give proper notice to all required parties of such tests, approvals and inspections. If feasible, the Owner and Others may timely observe the tests at the normal place of testing. The Owner shall bear all expenses associated with tests, inspections and approvals required by the Contract Documents, except as provided in Subparagraph 3.7.3, and which, unless otherwise agreed to, shall be conducted by an independent testing laboratory or entity retained by the Owner. Unless otherwise required by the Contract Documents, required certificates of testing, approval or inspection shall be secured by the Contractor and promptly delivered to the Owner.

3.7.2 If the Owner or appropriate authorities determine that tests, inspections or approvals in addition to those required by the Contract Documents will be necessary, the Contractor shall arrange for the procedures and give timely notice to the Owner and Others who may observe the procedures. Costs of the additional tests, inspections or approvals are at the Owner's expense except as provided in Subparagraph 3.7.3.

3.7.3 If the procedures described in Subparagraphs 3.7.1 and 3.7.2 indicate that portions of the Work fail to comply with the Contract Documents, the Contractor shall be responsible for costs of correction and retesting.

3.8 WARRANTY

3.8.1 The Contractor warrants that all materials and equipment shall be new unless otherwise specified, of good quality, in conformance with the Contract Documents, and free from defective workmanship and materials. At the Owner's request, the Contractor shall furnish satisfactory evidence of the quality and type of materials and equipment furnished. The Contractor further warrants that the Work shall be free from material defects not intrinsic in the design or materials required in the Contract Documents. The Con-

tractor's warranty does not include remedies for defects or damages caused by normal wear and tear during normal usage, use for a purpose for which the Project was not intended, improper or insufficient maintenance, modifications performed by the Owner or Others, or abuse. The contractor's warranty pursuant to this Paragraph 3.8 shall commence on the Date of Substantial Completion.

3.8.2 With respect to any portion of Work first performed after Substantial Completion, the Contractor's warranty obligation shall be extended by the period of time between Substantial Completion and the actual performance of the later Work.

3.8.3 The Contractor shall obtain from its Subcontractors and Material Suppliers any special or extended warranties required by the Contract Documents. All such warranties shall be listed in an attached Exhibit to this Agreement. Contractor's liability for such warranties shall be limited to the one-year correction period referred to in Paragraph 3.9. After that period Contractor shall assign them to the Owner and provide reasonable assistance to the Owner in enforcing the obligations of Subcontractors or Material Suppliers.

3.9 CORRECTION OF WORK WITHIN ONE YEAR

3.9.1 If, prior to Substantial Completion and within one year after the date of Substantial Completion of the Work, any Defective Work is found, the Owner shall promptly notify the Contractor in writing. Unless the Owner provides written acceptance of the condition, the Contractor shall promptly correct the Defective Work at its own cost and time and bear the expense of additional services required for correction of any Defective Work for which it is responsible. If within the one-year correction period the Owner discovers and does not promptly notify the Contractor or give the Contractor an opportunity to test and/or correct Defective Work as reasonably requested by the Contractor, the Owner waives the Contractor's obligation to correct that Defective Work as well as the Owner's right to claim a breach of the warranty with respect to that Defective Work.

3.9.2 With respect to any portion of Work first performed after Substantial Completion, the one-year correction period shall be extended by the period of time between Substantial Completion and the actual performance of the later Work. Correction periods shall not be extended by corrective work performed by the Contractor.

3.9.3 If the Contractor fails to correct Defective Work within a reasonable time after receipt of written notice from the Owner prior to final payment, the Owner may correct it in accordance with the Owner's right to carry out the Work in Paragraph 11.2. In such case, an appropriate Change Order shall be issued deducting the cost of correcting such deficiencies from payments then or thereafter due the Con-

6

tractor. If payments then or thereafter due Contractor are not sufficient to cover such amounts, the Contractor shall pay the difference to the Owner.

3.9.4 If after the one-year correction period but before the applicable limitation period the Owner discovers any Defective Work, the Owner shall, unless the Defective Work requires emergency correction, promptly notify the Contractor. If the Contractor elects to correct the Work, it shall provide written notice of such intent within fourteen (14) days of its receipt of notice from the Owner. The Contractor shall complete the correction of Work within a mutually agreed time frame. If the Contractor does not elect to correct the Work, the Owner may have the Work corrected by itself or Others and charge the Contractor for the reasonable cost of the correction. Owner shall provide Contractor with an accounting of correction costs it incurs.

3.9.5 If the Contractor's correction or removal of Defective Work causes damage to or destroys other completed or partially completed construction, the Contractor shall be responsible for the cost of correcting the destroyed or damaged construction.

3.9.6 The one-year period for correction of Defective Work does not constitute a limitation period with respect to the enforcement of the Contractor's other obligations under the Contract Documents.

3.9.7 Prior to final payment, at the Owner's option and with the Contractor's agreement, the Owner may elect to accept Defective Work rather than require its removal and correction. In such case the Contract Price shall be equitably adjusted.

3.10   CORRECTION OF COVERED WORK

3.10.1 On request of the Owner, Work that has been covered without a requirement that it be inspected prior to being covered may be uncovered for the Owner's inspection. The Owner shall pay for the costs of uncovering and replacement if the Work proves to be in conformance with the Contract Documents, or if the defective condition was caused by the Owner or Others. If the uncovered Work proves to be defective, the Contractor shall pay the costs of uncovering and replacement.

3.10.2 If contrary to specific requirements in the Contract Documents or contrary to a specific request from the Owner, a portion of the Work is covered, the Owner, by written request, may require the Contractor to uncover the Work for the Owner's observation. In this circumstance the Work shall be replaced at the Contractor's expense and with no adjustment to the Contract Time.

3.11   SAFETY OF PERSONS AND PROPERTY

3.11.1   SAFETY PRECAUTIONS AND PROGRAMS The Contractor shall have overall responsibility for safety precautions and programs in the performance of the Work. While this Paragraph 3.11 establishes the responsibility for safety between the Owner and Contractor, it does not relieve Subcontractors of their responsibility for the safety of persons or property in the performance of their work, nor for compliance with the provisions of applicable laws and regulations.

3.11.2 The Contractor shall seek to avoid injury, loss or damage to persons or property by taking reasonable steps to protect:

> **.1**   its employees and other persons at the Worksite;

> **.2**   materials and equipment stored at on-site or off-site locations for use in the Work; and

> **.3**   property located at the site and adjacent to Work areas, whether or not the property is part of the Work.

3.11.3   CONTRACTOR'S SAFETY REPRESENTATIVE The Contractor's Worksite Safety Representative is _____ ◆

_____

who shall act as the Contractor's authorized safety representative with a duty to prevent accidents in accordance with Subparagraph 3.11.2. If no individual is identified in this Paragraph 3.11, the authorized safety representative shall be the Contractor's Representative. The Contractor shall report immediately in writing to the Owner all recordable accidents and injuries occurring at the Worksite. When the Contractor is required to file an accident report with a public authority, the Contractor shall furnish a copy of the report to the Owner.

3.11.4 The Contractor shall provide the Owner with copies of all notices required of the Contractor by law or regulation. The Contractor's safety program shall comply with the requirements of governmental and quasi-governmental authorities having jurisdiction.

3.11.5 Damage or loss not insured under property insurance which may arise from the Work, to the extent of the negligence attributed to acts or omissions of the Contractor, or anyone for whose acts the Contractor may be liable, shall be promptly remedied by the Contractor.

3.11.6 If the Owner deems any part of the Work or Worksite unsafe, the Owner, without assuming responsibility for the Contractor's safety program, may require the Contractor to stop performance of the Work or take corrective meas-

7

AGC DOCUMENT NO. 200 • STANDARD FORM OF AGREEMENT AND GENERAL CONDITIONS BETWEEN OWNER AND CONTRACTOR
(Where the Contract Price is a Lump Sum)
© 2000, The Associated General Contractors of America

ures satisfactory to the Owner, or both. If the Contractor does not adopt corrective measures, the Owner may perform them and deduct their cost from the Contract Price. The Contractor agrees to make no claim for damages, for an increase in the Contract Price or for a change in the Contract Time based on the Contractor's compliance with the Owner's reasonable request.

3.12 EMERGENCIES

3.12.1 In an emergency, the Contractor shall act in a reasonable manner to prevent personal injury or property damage. Any change in the Contract Price and/or Contract Time resulting from the actions of the Contractor in an emergency situation shall be determined as provided in Article 8.

3.13 HAZARDOUS MATERIALS

3.13.1 A Hazardous Material is any substance or material identified now or in the future as hazardous under any federal, state or local law or regulation, or any other substance or material that may be considered hazardous or otherwise subject to statutory or regulatory requirement governing handling, disposal and/or cleanup. The Contractor shall not be obligated to commence or continue work until any Hazardous Material discovered at the Worksite has been removed, rendered or determined to be harmless by the Owner as certified by an independent testing laboratory and approved by the appropriate government agency.

3.13.2 If after the commencement of the Work Hazardous Material is discovered at the Worksite, the Contractor shall be entitled to immediately stop Work in the affected area. The Contractor shall report the condition to the Owner, the Architect/Engineer, and, if required, the government agency with jurisdiction.

3.13.3 The Contractor shall not be required to perform any Work relating to or in the area of Hazardous Material without written mutual agreement.

3.13.4 The Owner shall be responsible for retaining an independent testing laboratory to determine the nature of the material encountered and whether the material requires corrective measures and/or remedial action. Such measures shall be the sole responsibility of the Owner, and shall be performed in a manner minimizing any adverse effects upon the Work. The Contractor shall resume Work in the area affected by any Hazardous Material only upon written agreement between the parties after the Hazardous Material has been removed or rendered harmless and only after approval, if necessary, of the governmental agency with jurisdiction.

3.13.5 If the Contractor incurs additional costs and/or is delayed due to the presence or remediation of Hazardous

Material, the Contractor shall be entitled to an equitable adjustment in the Contract Price and/or the Contract Time.

3.13.6 To the extent not caused by the negligent acts or omissions of the Contractor, its Subcontractors and Sub-subcontractors, and the agents, officers, directors and employees of each of them, the Owner shall defend, indemnify and hold harmless the Contractor, its Subcontractors and Subsubcontractors, and the agents, officers, directors and employees of each of them, from and against any and all direct claims, damages, losses, costs and expenses, including but not limited to attorney's fees, costs and expenses incurred in connection with any dispute resolution process, arising out of or relating to the performance of the Work in any area affected by Hazardous Material. To the fullest extent permitted by law, such indemnification shall apply regardless of the fault, negligence, breach of warranty or contract, or strict liability of the Owner.

3.13.7 MATERIALS BROUGHT TO THE WORKSITE

3.13.7.1 Material Safety Data (MSD) sheets as required by law and pertaining to materials or substances used or consumed in the performance of the Work, whether obtained by the Contractor, Subcontractors, the Owner or Others, shall be maintained at the Worksite by the Contractor and made available to the Owner, Subcontractors and Others.

3.13.7.2 The Contractor shall be responsible for the proper delivery, handling, application, storage, removal and disposal of all materials and substances brought to the Worksite by the Contractor in accordance with the Contract Documents and used or consumed in the performance of the Work.

3.13.7.3 To the extent not caused by the negligent acts or omissions of the Owner, its agents, officers, directors and employees, the Contractor shall defend, indemnify and hold harmless the Owner, its agents, officers, directors and employees, from and against any and all direct claims, damages, losses, costs and expenses, including but not limited to attorney's fees, costs and expenses incurred in connection with any dispute resolution procedure, arising out of or relating to the delivery, handling, application, storage, removal and disposal of all materials and substances brought to the Worksite by the Contractor in accordance with the Contract Documents. To the fullest extent permitted by law, such indemnification shall apply regardless of the fault, negligence, breach of warranty or contract, or strict liability of the Contractor.

3.13.8 The terms of this Paragraph 3.13 shall survive the completion of the Work and/or any termination of this Agreement.

8

3.14 SUBMITTALS

3.14.1 The Contractor shall submit to the Owner, and, if directed, to its Architect/Engineer, for review and approval all shop drawings, samples, product data and similar submittals required by the Contract Documents. The Contractor shall be responsible to the Owner for the accuracy and conformity of its submittals to the Contract Documents. The Contractor shall prepare and deliver its submittals to the Owner in a manner consistent with the Schedule of the Work and in such time and sequence so as not to delay the performance of the Work or the work of the Owner and Others. When the Contractor delivers its submittals to the Owner, the Contractor shall identify in writing for each submittal all changes, deviations or substitutions from the requirements of the Contract Documents. The review and approval of any Contractor submittal shall not be deemed to authorize changes, deviations or substitutions from the requirements of the Contact Documents unless express written approval is obtained from the Owner specifically authorizing such deviation, substitution or change. Further, the Owner shall not make any change, deviation or substitution through the submittal process without specifically identifying and authorizing such deviation to the Contractor. In the event that the Contract Documents do not contain submittal requirements pertaining to the Work, the Contractor agrees upon request to submit in a timely fashion to the Owner for review and approval any shop drawings, samples, product data, manufacturers' literature or similar submittals as may reasonably be required by the Owner.

3.14.2 The Owner shall be responsible for review and approval of submittals with reasonable promptness to avoid causing delay.

3.14.3 The Contractor shall perform all Work strictly in accordance with approved submittals. Approval of shop drawings is not authorization to Contractor to perform Changed Work, unless the procedures of Article 8 are followed. Approval does not relieve the Contractor from responsibility for Defective Work resulting from errors or omissions of any kind on the approved Shop Drawings.

3.14.4 Record copies of the following, incorporating field changes and selections made during construction, shall be maintained at the Project site and available to the Owner upon request: drawings, specifications, addenda, Change Order and other modifications, and required submittals including product data, samples and shop drawings.

3.14.5 No substitutions shall be made in the Work unless permitted in the Contract Documents and then only after the Contractor obtains approvals required under the Contract Documents for substitutions.

3.14.6 The Contractor shall prepare and submit to the Owner

(Check one only)

_____ final marked up as-built drawings, ◆
or
_____ updated electronic data ◆
or
_____ such documentation as defined by the ◆
parties by attachment to this Agreement,

in general documenting how the various elements of the Work were actually constructed or installed.

3.15 PROFESSIONAL SERVICES

3.15 **PROFESSIONAL SERVICES** The Owner, through its Architect/Engineer, shall provide all professional services required for the completion of the Work, except the following: ◆

_____

_____

_____. The Contractor shall not be required to provide professional services which constitute the practice of architecture or engineering unless the Contractor needs to provide such services in order to carry out its responsibilities for construction means, methods, techniques, sequences and procedures, or unless such services are specifically called for by the Contract Documents. If professional services are required of the Contractor, the Owner shall indicate all performance and design criteria to be satisfied. The Contractor shall not be responsible for the adequacy of such performance and design criteria. The Contractor shall obtain professional services and any design certifications required from licensed design professionals. All drawings, specifications, calculations, certifications and submittals prepared by such design professionals shall bear the signature and seal of such design professionals and the Owner and the Architect/Engineer shall be entitled to rely upon the adequacy, accuracy and completeness of such design services. The Contractor shall not be required to provide such services in violation of existing laws, rules and regulations in the jurisdiction where the Project is located.

3.16 WORKSITE CONDITIONS

3.16.1 **WORKSITE VISIT** The Contractor acknowledges that it has visited, or has had the opportunity to visit, the Worksite to visually inspect the general and local conditions which could affect the Work.

3.16.2 **CONCEALED OR UNKNOWN SITE CONDITIONS** If the conditions at the Worksite are (a) subsurface or other physical conditions which are materially different from those indicated in the Contract Documents, or (b) unusual or unknown physical conditions which are materially different from conditions ordinarily encountered and generally recognized as inherent in Work provided for in the Contract Documents, the Contractor shall stop Work and give

AGC DOCUMENT NO. 200 • STANDARD FORM OF AGREEMENT AND GENERAL CONDITIONS BETWEEN OWNER AND CONTRACTOR
(Where the Contract Price is a Lump Sum)
© 2000, The Associated General Contractors of America

AGC Document No. 200
SAMPLE ■ DO NOT COPY

immediate written notice of the condition to the Owner and the Architect/Engineer. The Contractor shall not be required to perform any work relating to the unknown condition without the written mutual agreement of the parties. Any change in the Contract Price and/or the Contract Time as a result of the unknown condition shall be determined as provided in this Article. The Contractor shall provide the Owner with written notice of any claim as a result of unknown conditions within the time period set forth in Paragraph 8.4.

3.17   PERMITS AND TAXES

3.17.1   Contractor shall give public authorities all notices required by law and, except for permits and fees which are the responsibility of the Owner pursuant to Paragraph 4.4, shall obtain and pay for all necessary permits, licenses and renewals pertaining to the Work. Contractor shall provide to Owner copies of all notices, permits, licenses and renewals required under this Agreement.

3.17.2   Contractor shall pay all applicable taxes legally enacted when bids are received or negotiations concluded for the Work provided by the Contractor.

3.17.3   The Contract Price and/or Contract Time shall be equitably adjusted by Change Order for additional costs resulting from any changes in laws, ordinances, rules and regulations enacted after the date of this Agreement, including increased taxes.

3.17.4   If in accordance with the Owner's direction, the Contractor claims an exemption for taxes, the Owner shall defend, indemnify and hold the Contractor harmless from any liability, penalty, interest, fine, tax assessment, attorneys fees or other expense or cost incurred by the Contractor as a result of any such action.

3.18   CUTTING, FITTING AND PATCHING

3.18.1   The Contractor shall perform cutting, fitting and patching necessary to coordinate the various parts of the Work and to prepare its Work for the work of the Owner or Others.

3.18.2   Cutting, patching or altering the work of the Owner or Others shall be done with the prior written approval of the Owner. Such approval shall not be unreasonably withheld.

3.19   CLEANING UP

3.19.1   The Contractor shall regularly remove debris and waste materials at the Worksite resulting from the Work. Prior to discontinuing Work in an area, the Contractor shall clean the area and remove all rubbish and its construction equipment, tools, machinery, waste and surplus materials. The Contractor shall minimize and confine dust and debris resulting from construction activities. At the completion of the

Work, the Contractor shall remove from the Worksite all construction equipment, tools, surplus materials, waste materials and debris.

3.19.2   If the Contractor fails to commence compliance with cleanup duties within forty-eight (48) hours after written notification from the Owner of non-compliance, the Owner may implement appropriate cleanup measures without further notice and the cost shall be deducted from any amounts due or to become due the Contractor.

3.20   ACCESS TO WORK   The Contractor shall facilitate the access of the Owner, Architect/Engineer and Others to Work in progress.

3.21   CONFIDENTIALITY   The Contractor shall treat as confidential and not disclose to third persons, except Subcontractors, Subsubcontractors and Material Suppliers as is necessary for the performance of the Work, or use for its own benefit, any of the Owner's confidential information, know-how, discoveries, production methods and the like that may be disclosed to the Contractor or which the Contractor may acquire in connection with the Work. The Owner shall treat as confidential information all of the Contractor's estimating systems and historical and parameter cost data that may be disclosed to the Owner in connection with the performance of this Agreement.

ARTICLE 4

OWNER'S RESPONSIBILITIES

4.1   INFORMATION AND SERVICES   Any information or services to be provided by the Owner shall be provided in a timely manner so as not to delay the Work.

4.2   FINANCIAL INFORMATION   Prior to commencement of the Work and thereafter at the written request of the Contractor, the Owner shall provide the Contractor with evidence of Project financing. Evidence of such financing shall be a condition precedent to the Contractor's commencing or continuing the Work. The Contractor shall be notified prior to any material change in Project financing.

4.3   WORKSITE INFORMATION   Except to the extent that the Contractor knows of any inaccuracy, the Contractor is entitled to rely on Worksite information furnished by the Owner pursuant to this Paragraph 4.3. To the extent the Owner has obtained, or is required elsewhere in the Contract Documents to obtain, the following Worksite information, the Owner shall provide at the Owner's expense and with reasonable promptness:

.1   information describing the physical characteristics of the site, including surveys, site evaluations, legal descriptions, data or drawings depicting

10

existing conditions, subsurface conditions and environmental studies, reports and investigations;

.2 tests, inspections and other reports dealing with environmental matters, Hazardous Material and other existing conditions, including structural, mechanical and chemical tests, required by the Contract Documents or by law; and

.3 any other information or services requested in writing by the Contractor which are relevant to the Contractor's performance of the Work and under the Owner's control.

The information required by Paragraph 4.3 shall be provided in reasonable detail. Legal descriptions shall include easements, title restrictions, boundaries, and zoning restrictions. Worksite descriptions shall include existing buildings and other construction and all other pertinent site conditions. Adjacent property descriptions shall include structures, streets, sidewalks, alleys, and other features relevant to the Work. Utility details shall include available services, lines at the Worksite and adjacent thereto and connection points. The information shall include public and private information, subsurface information, grades, contours, and elevations, drainage data, exact locations and dimensions, and benchmarks that can be used by the Contractor in laying out the Work.

4.4 BUILDING PERMIT, FEES AND APPROVALS Except for those permits and fees related to the Work which are the responsibility of the Contractor pursuant to Subparagraph 3.17.1, the Owner shall secure and pay for all other permits, approvals, easements, assessments and fees required for the development, construction, use or occupancy of permanent structures or for permanent changes in existing facilities, including the building permit.

4.5 MECHANICS AND CONSTRUCTION LIEN INFORMATION Within seven (7) days after receiving the Contractor's written request, the Owner shall provide the Contractor with the information necessary to give notice of or enforce mechanics lien rights and, where applicable, stop notices. This information shall include the Owner's interest in the real property on which the Project is located and the record legal title.

4.6 CONTRACT DOCUMENTS Unless otherwise specified, Owner shall provide _____ (_____) copies ◆ of the Contract Documents to the Contractor without cost.

4.7 OWNER'S REPRESENTATIVE The Owner's authorized representative is _____ ◆
_____ .

The representative shall be fully acquainted with the Project, and shall have authority to bind the Owner in all matters requiring the Owner's approval, authorization or written notice. If the Owner changes its representative or the representative's authority as listed above, the Owner shall immediately notify the Contractor in writing.

4.8 OWNER'S CUTTING AND PATCHING Cutting, patching or altering the Work by the Owner or Others shall be done with the prior written approval of the Contractor, which approval shall not be unreasonably withheld.

4.9 OWNER'S RIGHT TO CLEAN UP In case of a dispute between the Contractor and Others with regard to respective responsibilities for cleaning up at the Worksite, the Owner may implement appropriate cleanup measures and allocate the cost among those responsible.

4.10 COST OF CORRECTING DAMAGED OR DESTROYED WORK With regard to damage or loss attributable to the acts or omissions of the Owner or Others and not to the Contractor, the Owner may either (a) promptly remedy the damage or loss or (b) accept the damage or loss. If the Contractor incurs additional costs and/or is delayed due to such loss or damage, the Contractor shall be entitled to an equitable adjustment in the Contract Price and/or Contract Time.

ARTICLE 5

SUBCONTRACTS

5.1 SUBCONTRACTORS The Work not performed by the Contractor with its own forces shall be performed by Subcontractors.

5.2 AWARD OF SUBCONTRACTS AND OTHER CONTRACTS FOR PORTIONS OF THE WORK

5.2.1 As soon after the award of this Agreement as possible, the Contractor shall provide the Owner and if directed, the Architect/Engineer with a written list of the proposed subcontractors and significant material suppliers. If the Owner has a reasonable objection to any proposed subcontractor or material supplier, the Owner shall notify the Contractor in writing. Failure to promptly object shall constitute acceptance.

5.2.2 If the Owner has reasonably and promptly objected as provided in Subparagraph 5.2.1, the Contractor shall not contract with the proposed subcontractor or material supplier, and the Contractor shall propose another acceptable to the Owner. To the extent the substitution results in an increase or decrease in the Contract Price and/or Contract Time, an appropriate Change Order shall be issued as provided in Article 8.

11

**AGC Document No. 200
SAMPLE ■ DO NOT COPY**

5.3 BINDING OF SUBCONTRACTORS AND MATE-RIAL SUPPLIERS The Contractor agrees to bind every Subcontractor and Material Supplier (and require every Subcontractor to so bind its subcontractors and material suppliers) to all the provisions of this Agreement and the Contract Documents as they apply to the Subcontractor's and Material Supplier's portions of the Work.

5.4 LABOR RELATIONS (Insert here any conditions, obligations or requirements relative to labor relations and their effect on the Project. Legal counsel is recommended.) ♦

5.5 CONTINGENT ASSIGNMENT OF SUBCONTRACTS

5.5.1 If this Agreement is terminated, each subcontract agreement shall be assigned by the Contractor to the Owner, subject to the prior rights of any surety, provided that:

    .1 this Agreement is terminated by the Owner pursuant to Paragraphs 11.3 or 11.4; and

    .2 the Owner accepts such assignment after termination by notifying the Subcontractor and Contractor in writing.

5.5.2 If the Owner accepts such an assignment, and the Work has been suspended for more than thirty (30) consecutive days, following termination, if appropriate, the Subcontractor's compensation shall be equitably adjusted as a result of the suspension.

ARTICLE 6

CONTRACT TIME

6.1 PERFORMANCE OF THE WORK

6.1.1 DATE OF COMMENCEMENT The Date of Commencement is the date of this Agreement as first written in Article 1 unless otherwise set forth below: (Insert here any special provisions concerning notices to proceed and the Date of Commencement.)   ♦

6.1.2 TIME Substantial Completion of the Work shall be achieved in _____ (_____) days from the Date ♦ of Commencement. Unless otherwise specified in the Certificate of Substantial Completion, the Contractor shall achieve Final Completion within _____ (_____) ♦ days after the date of Substantial Completion, subject to adjustments as provided for in the Contract Documents.

6.1.3 Time limits stated above are of the essence of this Agreement.

6.1.4 Unless instructed by the Owner in writing, the Contractor shall not knowingly commence the Work before the effective date of insurance that is required to be provided by the Contractor and Owner.

6.2 SCHEDULE OF THE WORK

6.2.1 Before submitting the first application for payment, the Contractor shall submit to the Owner, and if directed, its Architect/Engineer, a Schedule of the Work that shall show the dates on which the Contractor plans to commence and complete various parts of the Work, including dates on which information and approvals are required from the Owner. On the Owner's written approval of the Schedule of the Work, the Contractor shall comply with it unless directed by the Owner to do otherwise. The Contractor shall update the Schedule of the Work on a monthly basis or at appropriate intervals as required by the conditions of the Work and the Project.

6.2.2 The Owner may determine the sequence in which the Work shall be performed, provided it does not unreasonably interfere with the Schedule of the Work. The Owner may require the Contractor to make reasonable changes in the sequence at any time during the performance of the Work in order to facilitate the performance of work by the Owner or Others. To the extent such changes increase Contractor's time and costs the Contract Price and Contract Time shall be equitably adjusted.

6.3 DELAYS AND EXTENSIONS OF TIME

6.3.1 If the Contractor is delayed at any time in the commencement or progress of the Work by any cause beyond the control of the Contractor, the Contractor shall be entitled to an equitable extension of the Contract Time. In addition, if the Contractor incurs additional costs as a result of such delay, the Contractor shall be entitled to an equitable adjustment in the Contract Price subject to Paragraph 10.2. Examples of causes beyond the control of the Contractor include, but are not limited to, the following: acts or omissions of the Owner, the Architect/Engineer or Others; changes in the Work or the sequencing of the Work ordered by the Owner, or arising from decisions of the Owner that impact the time of performance of the Work; labor disputes not involving the Contractor; fire; encountering Hazardous

12

AGC Document No. 200
SAMPLE ■ DO NOT COPY

Materials; adverse weather conditions not reasonably anticipated; concealed or unknown conditions; delay authorized by the Owner pending dispute resolution and suspension by the Owner under Paragraph 11.1. The Contractor shall process any requests for equitable or extensions of Contract Time and/or equitable adjustment in the Contract Price in accordance with the provisions of Article 8.

6.3.2 To the extent a delay in the progress of the Work is caused by adverse weather conditions not reasonably anticipated, fire, unusual transportation delays, general labor disputes impacting the Project but not specifically related to the Worksite, governmental agencies, or unavoidable accidents or circumstances, the Contractor shall only be entitled to its actual costs without fee and an extension of the Date of Substantial Completion and/or the Date of Final Completion.

6.3.3 NOTICE OF DELAYS In the event delays to the Work are encountered for any reason, the Contractor shall provide prompt written notice to the Owner of the cause of such delays after Contractor first recognizes the delay. The Owner and Contractor agree to undertake reasonable steps to mitigate the effect of such delays.

6.4 NOTICE OF DELAY CLAIMS If the Contractor requests an equitable extension of Contract Time and/or an equitable adjustment in Contract Price as a result of a delay described in Subparagraph 6.3.1, the Contractor shall give the Owner written notice of the claim in accordance with Paragraph 8.4. If the Contractor causes delay in the completion of the Work, the Owner shall be entitled to recover its additional costs subject to Paragraph 10.2. The Owner shall process any such claim against the Contractor in accordance with Article 8.

ARTICLE 7

CONTRACT PRICE

7.1 LUMP SUM As full compensation for performance by the Contractor of the Work in conformance with the Contract Documents, the Owner shall pay the Contractor the lump sum price of _____ Dollars ◆ ($_____)). The lump sum price is hereinafter ◆ referred to as the Contract Price, which shall be subject to increase or decrease as provided in Article 8.

7.2 ALLOWANCES

7.2.1 All allowances stated in the Contract Documents shall be included in the Contract Price. While the Owner may direct the amounts of, and particular material suppliers or subcontractors for, specific allowance items, if the Contractor reasonably objects to a material supplier or subcontractor, it shall not be required to contract with them. The Owner

shall select allowance items in a timely manner so as not to delay the Work.

7.2.2 Allowances shall include the costs of materials, supplies and equipment delivered to the Worksite, less applicable trade discounts and including requisite taxes, unloading and handling at the Worksite, and labor and installation, unless specifically stated otherwise. The Contractor's overhead and profit for the allowances shall be included in the Contract Price, but not in the allowances. The Contract Price shall be adjusted by Change Order to reflect the actual costs when they are greater than or less than the allowances.

ARTICLE 8

CHANGES

Changes in the Work that are within the general scope of this Agreement shall be accomplished, without invalidating this Agreement, by Change Order, and Interim Directed Change.

8.1 CHANGE ORDER

8.1.1 The Contractor may request and/or the Owner may order changes in the Work or the timing or sequencing of the Work that impacts the Contract Price or the Contract Time. All such changes in the Work that affect Contract Time or Contract Price shall be formalized in a Change Order. Any such requests for a change in the Contract Price and/or the Contract Time shall be processed in accordance with this Article 8.

8.1.2 The Owner and the Contractor shall negotiate in good faith an appropriate adjustment to the Contract Price and/or the Contract Time and shall conclude these negotiations as expeditiously as possible. Acceptance of the Change Order and any adjustment in the Contract Price and/or Contract Time shall not be unreasonably withheld.

8.2 INTERIM DIRECTED CHANGE

8.2.1 The Owner may issue a written Interim Directed Change directing a change in the Work prior to reaching agreement with the Contractor on the adjustment, if any, in the Contract Price and/or the Contract Time.

8.2.2 The Owner and the Contractor shall negotiate expeditiously and in good faith for appropriate adjustments, as applicable, to the Contract Price and/or the Contract Time arising out of Interim Directed Change. As the Changed Work is performed, the Contractor shall submit its costs for such work with its application for payment beginning with the next application for payment within thirty (30) days of the issuance of the Interim Directed Change. If there is a dispute

13

as to the cost to the Owner, the Owner shall pay the Contractor fifty percent (50%) of its estimated cost to perform the work. In such event, the parties reserve their rights as to the disputed amount, subject to the requirements of Article 12.

8.2.3 When the Owner and the Contractor agree upon the adjustment in the Contract Price and/or the Contract Time, for a change in the Work directed by an Interim Directed Change, such agreement shall be the subject of a Change Order. The Change Order shall include all outstanding Interim Directed Changes issued since the last Change Order.

8.3   DETERMINATION OF COST

8.3.1 An increase or decrease in the Contract Price and/or the Contract Time resulting from a change in the Work shall be determined by one or more of the following methods:

.1   unit prices set forth in this Agreement or as subsequently agreed;

.2   a mutually accepted, itemized lump sum;

.3   costs calculated on a basis agreed upon by the Owner and Contractor plus a Fee (either a lump sum or a Fee based on a percentage of cost) to which they agree; or

.4   if an increase or decrease cannot be agreed to as set forth in Clauses .1 through .3 above, and the Owner issues an Interim Directed Change, the cost of the change in the Work shall be determined by the reasonable actual expense and savings of the performance of the Work resulting from the change. If there is a net increase in the Contract Price, the Contractor's Fee shall be adjusted accordingly. In case of a net decrease in the Contract Price, the Contractor's Fee shall not be adjusted unless ten percent (10%) or more of the Project is deleted. The Contractor shall maintain a documented, itemized accounting evidencing the expenses and savings.

8.3.2 If unit prices are set forth in the Contract Documents or are subsequently agreed to by the parties, but the character or quantity of such unit items as originally contemplated is so different in a proposed Change Order that the original unit prices will cause substantial inequity to the Owner or the Contractor, such unit prices shall be equitably adjusted.

8.3.3 If the Owner and the Contractor disagree as to whether work required by the Owner is within the scope of the Work, the Contractor shall furnish the Owner with an esti-

mate of the costs to perform the disputed work in accordance with the Owner's interpretations. If the Owner issues a written order for the Contractor to proceed, the Contractor shall perform the disputed work and the Owner shall pay the Contractor fifty percent (50%) of its estimated cost to perform the work. In such event, both parties reserve their rights as to whether the work was within the scope of the Work, subject to the requirements of Article 12. The Owner's payment does not prejudice its right to be reimbursed should it be determined that the disputed work was within the scope of Work. The Contractor's receipt of payment for the disputed work does not prejudice its right to receive full payment for the disputed work should it be determined that the disputed work is not within the scope of the Work.

8.4   CLAIMS FOR ADDITIONAL COST OR TIME
Except as provided in Subparagraph 6.3.2 and Paragraph 6.4 for any claim for an increase in the Contract Price and/or the Contract Time, the Contractor shall give the Owner written notice of the claim within fourteen (14) days after the occurrence giving rise to the claim or within fourteen (14) days after the Contractor first recognizes the condition giving rise to the claim, whichever is later. Except in an emergency, notice shall be given before proceeding with the Work. Any change in the Contract Price and/or the Contract Time resulting from such claim shall be authorized by Change Order.

ARTICLE 9

PAYMENT

9.1   SCHEDULE OF VALUES Within twenty-one (21) days from the date of execution of this Agreement, the Contractor shall prepare and submit to the Owner, and if directed, the Architect/Engineer, a schedule of values apportioned to the various divisions or phases of the Work. Each line item contained in the schedule of values shall be assigned a value such that the total of all items shall equal the Contract Price.

9.2   PROGRESS PAYMENTS

9.2.1   APPLICATIONS The Contractor shall submit to the Owner, and if directed, its Architect/Engineer, a monthly application for payment no later than the _____ day ◆ of the calendar month for the preceding thirty (30) Days. Contractor's applications for payment shall be itemized and supported by the Contractor's schedule of values and any other substantiating data as required by this Agreement. Payment applications shall include payment requests on account of properly authorized Change Orders or Interim Directed Change. The Owner shall pay the amount otherwise due on any payment application, no later than twenty (20) days after the Contractor has submitted a complete and

14

accurate payment application. The Owner may deduct from any progress payment amounts as may be retained pursuant to Subparagraph 9.2.4.

9.2.2   STORED MATERIALS AND EQUIPMENT If approved by the Owner, applications for payment may include materials and equipment not yet incorporated into the Work but delivered to and suitably stored on-site or off-site including applicable insurance, storage and transportation costs to the Worksite. Approval of payment applications for stored materials and equipment stored off-site shall be conditioned on submission by the Contractor of bills of sale and proof of applicable insurance, or such other procedures satisfactory to the Owner to establish the proper valuation of the stored materials and equipment, the Owner's title to such materials and equipment, and to otherwise protect the Owner's interests therein, including transportation to the site.

9.2.3   LIEN WAIVERS AND LIENS

9.2.3.1 PARTIAL LIEN WAIVERS AND AFFIDAVITS If required by the Owner, as a prerequisite for payment, the Contractor shall provide partial lien and claim waivers in the amount of the application for payment and affidavits from its Subcontractors, and Material Suppliers for the completed Work. Such waivers shall be conditional upon payment. In no event shall the Contractor be required to sign an unconditional waiver of lien or claim, either partial or final, prior to receiving payment or in an amount in excess of what it has been paid.

9.2.3.2 RESPONSIBILITY FOR LIENS If Owner has made payments in the time required by this Article 9, the Contractor shall, within thirty (30) days after filing, cause the removal of any liens filed against the premises or public improvement fund by any party or parties performing labor or services or supplying materials in connection with the Work. If the Contractor fails to take such action on a lien, the Owner may cause the lien to be removed at the Contractor's expense, including bond costs and reasonable attorney's fees. This Clause shall not apply if there is a dispute pursuant to Article 12 relating to the subject matter of the lien.

9.2.4   RETAINAGE From each progress payment made prior to Substantial Completion the Owner may retain _____ ◆ _____ percent (_____) of the ◆ amount otherwise due after deduction of any amounts as provided in Paragraph 9.3. If the Owner chooses to use this retainage provision:

> .1   once each early finishing Subcontractor has completed its work and that work has been accepted by the Owner, the Owner may release final retention on that portion of the Work;

> .2   after the Work is fifty percent (50%) complete, the Owner shall withhold no additional

retainage and shall pay the Contractor the full amount of what is due on account of progress payments;

> .3   the Owner may, in its sole discretion, reduce the amount to be retained at any time.

In lieu of retainage, the Contractor may furnish securities, acceptable to the Owner, to be held by the Owner. The interest on such securities shall accrue to the Contractor.

9.3   ADJUSTMENT OF CONTRACTOR'S PAYMENT APPLICATION The Owner may adjust or reject a payment application or nullify a previously approved payment application, in whole or in part, as may reasonably be necessary to protect the Owner from loss or damage based upon the following, to the extent that the Contractor is responsible therefor under this Agreement:

> .1   the Contractor's repeated failure to perform the Work as required by the Contract Documents;

> .2   loss or damage for which the Owner may be liable arising out of or relating to this Agreement and caused by the Contractor to the Owner or to Others;

> .3   the Contractor's failure to properly pay Subcontractors and Material Suppliers following receipt of such payment from the Owner;

> .4   Defective Work not corrected in a timely fashion;

> .5   reasonable evidence of delay in performance of the Work such that the Work will not be completed within the Contract Time, and

> .6   reasonable evidence demonstrating that the unpaid balance of the Contract Price is insufficient to fund the cost to complete the Work.

The Owner shall give written notice to the Contractor at the time of disapproving or nullifying an application for payment of the specific reasons therefor. When the above reasons for disapproving or nullifying an application for payment are removed, payment shall be made for the amounts previously withheld.

9.4   ACCEPTANCE OF WORK Neither the Owner's payment of progress payments nor its partial or full use or occupancy of the Project constitutes acceptance of Work not complying with the Contract Documents.

9.5   PAYMENT DELAY If for any reason not the fault of the Contractor the Contractor does not receive a progress payment from the Owner within seven (7) days after the time

15

such payment is due, as defined in Subparagraph 9.2.1, then the Contractor, upon giving seven (7) days' written notice to the Owner, and without prejudice to and in addition to any other legal remedies, may stop Work until payment of the full amount owing to the Contractor has been received, including interest from the date payment was due in accordance with Paragraph 9.9. The Contract Price and Contract Time shall be equitably adjusted by a Change Order for reasonable cost and delay resulting from shutdown, delay and start-up.

9.6 SUBSTANTIAL COMPLETION

9.6.1 The Contractor shall notify the Owner and, if directed, its Architect/Engineer when it considers Substantial Completion of the Work or a designated portion to have been achieved. The Owner, with the assistance of its Architect/Engineer, shall promptly conduct an inspection to determine whether the Work or designated portion can be occupied or utilized for its intended use by the Owner without excessive interference in completing any remaining unfinished Work by the Contractor. If the Owner determines that the Work or designated portion has not reached Substantial Completion, the Owner shall promptly compile a list of items to be completed or corrected so the Owner may occupy or utilize the Work or designated portion for its intended use. The Contractor shall promptly complete all items on the list.

9.6.2 When Substantial Completion of the Work or a designated portion is achieved, the Contractor shall prepare a Certificate of Substantial Completion that shall establish the date of Substantial Completion, and the respective responsibilities of the Owner and Contractor for interim items such as security, maintenance, utilities, insurance and damage to the Work, and insurance. The certificate shall also list the items to be completed or corrected, and establish the time for their completion or correction. The Certificate of Substantial Completion shall be submitted by the Contractor to the Owner for written acceptance of responsibilities assigned in the Certificate.

9.6.3 Unless otherwise provided in the Certificate of Substantial Completion, warranties required by the Contract Documents shall commence on the date of Substantial Completion of the Work or a designated portion.

9.6.4 Upon acceptance by the Owner of the Certificate of Substantial Completion, the Owner shall pay to the Contractor the remaining retainage held by the Owner for the Work described in the Certificate of Substantial Completion less a sum equal to two hundred percent (200%) of the estimated cost of completing or correcting remaining items on that part of the Work, as agreed to by the Owner and Contractor as necessary to achieve final completion. Uncompleted items shall be completed by the Contractor in a mutually agreed upon time frame. The Owner shall pay the

Contractor monthly the amount retained for unfinished items as each item is completed.

9.7 PARTIAL OCCUPANCY OR USE

9.7.1 The Owner may occupy or use completed or partially completed portions of the Work when (a) the portion of the Work is designated in a Certificate of Substantial Completion, (b) appropriate insurer(s) consent to the occupancy or use, and (c) appropriate public authorities authorize the occupancy or use. Such partial occupancy or use shall constitute Substantial Completion of that portion of the Work.

9.8 FINAL COMPLETION AND FINAL PAYMENT

9.8.1 Upon notification from the Contractor that the Work is complete and ready for final inspection and acceptance, the Owner with the assistance of its Architect/Engineer shall promptly conduct an inspection to determine if the Work has been completed and is acceptable under the Contract Documents.

9.8.2 When Final Completion has been achieved, the Contractor shall prepare for the Owner's acceptance a final application for payment stating that to the best of the Contractor's knowledge, and based on the Owner's inspections, the Work has reached Final Completion in accordance with the Contract Documents.

9.8.3 Final payment of the balance of the Contract Price shall be made to the Contractor within twenty (20) days after the Contractor has submitted a complete and accurate application for final payment, including submissions required under Subparagraph 9.8.4, and a Certificate of Final Completion has been executed by the Owner and the Contractor.

9.8.4 Final payment shall be due on the Contractor's submission of the following to the Owner:

.1 an affidavit declaring any indebtedness connected with the Work, e.g. payrolls or invoices for materials or equipment, to have been paid, satisfied or to be paid with the proceeds of final payment, so as not to encumber the Owner's property;

.2 as-built drawings, manuals, copies of warranties and all other close-out documents required by the Contract Documents;

.3 release of any liens, conditioned on final payment being received;

.4 consent of any surety; and

.5 any outstanding known and unreported accidents or injuries experienced by the Contractor or its Subcontractors at the Worksite.

16

9.8.5 If, after Substantial Completion of the Work, the Final Completion of a portion of the Work is materially delayed through no fault of the Contractor, the Owner shall pay the balance due for portion(s) of the Work fully completed and accepted. If the remaining contract balance for Work not fully completed and accepted is less than the retained amount prior to payment, the Contractor shall submit to the Owner, and, if directed, the Architect/Engineer, the written consent of any surety to payment of the balance due for portions of the Work that are fully completed and accepted. Such payment shall not constitute a waiver of claims, but otherwise shall be governed by these final payment provisions.

9.8.6 Claims not reserved in writing with the making of final payment shall be waived except for claims relating to liens or similar encumbrances, warranties, Defective Work and latent defects.

9.8.7 ACCEPTANCE OF FINAL PAYMENT Unless the Contractor provides written identification of unsettled claims with an application for final payment, acceptance of final payment constitutes a waiver of such claims.

9.9 LATE PAYMENT Payments due but unpaid shall bear interest from the date payment is due at the prime rate prevailing at the place of the Project.

ARTICLE 10

INDEMNITY, INSURANCE, WAIVERS AND BONDS

10.1 INDEMNITY

10.1.1 To the fullest extent permitted by law, the Contractor shall defend, indemnify and hold the Owner, the Owner's officers, directors, members, consultants, agents and employees, the Architect/Engineer and Others harmless from all claims for bodily injury and property damage, other than to the Work itself and other property insured under Subparagraph 10.3.4, that may arise from the performance of the Work, but only to the extent of the negligent acts or omissions of the Contractor, Subcontractors or anyone employed directly or indirectly by any of them or by anyone for whose acts any of them may be liable. The Contractor shall not be required to defend, indemnify or hold harmless the Owner, the Architect/Engineer or Others for any negligent acts, omissions of the Owner, the Architect/Engineer or Others.

10.1.2 To the fullest extent permitted by law, the Owner shall defend, indemnify and hold harmless the Contractor, its officers, directors, members, consultants, agents, and employees, Subcontractors or anyone employed directly or indirectly by any of them or anyone for whose acts any of them may be liable from all claims for bodily injury and property damage, other than property insured under Subparagraph 10.4.1, that may arise from the performance of work by Owner, Architect/Engineer or Others, to the extent of the negligence attributed to such acts or omissions by Owner, Architect/Engineer or Others.

10.2 MUTUAL WAIVER OF CONSEQUENTIAL DAMAGES The Owner and the Contractor agree to waive all claims against each other for any consequential damages that may arise out of or relate to this Agreement. The Owner agrees to waive damages including but not limited to the Owner's loss of use of the Project, any rental expenses incurred, loss of income, profit or financing related to the Project, as well as the loss of business, loss of financing, principal office overhead and expenses, loss of profits not related to this Project, or loss of reputation. The Contractor agrees to waive damages including but not limited to loss of business, loss of financing, principal office overhead and expenses, loss of profits not related to this Project, loss of bonding capacity or loss of reputation. This Paragraph 10.2 shall not be construed to preclude contractual provisions for liquidated damages when such provisions relate to direct damages only. The provisions of this Paragraph shall also apply to the termination of this Agreement and shall survive such termination.

10.3 INSURANCE

10.3.1 Prior to the start of the Work, the Contractor shall procure and maintain in force Workers Compensation Insurance, Employers' Liability Insurance, Business Automobile Liability Insurance, and Commercial General Liability Insurance (CGL). The CGL policy shall include coverage for liability arising from premises, operations, independent contractors, products-completed operations, personal injury and advertising injury, contractual liability, and broad form property damage. The primary CGL coverage shall also name the Owner as an additional insured for liability arising out of the Work. If requested, the Contractor shall provide the Owner with certificates of the insurance coverages required.

The Contractor's Employers' Liability, Business Automobile Liability, and Commercial General Liability policies, as required in this Subparagraph 10.3.1, shall be written with at least the following limits of liability :

   .1   Employers' Liability Insurance

     a. $_____ ◆
         Bodily Injury by Accident
         Each Accident

     b. $_____ ◆
         Bodily Injury by Disease
         Policy Limit

17

c. $_____   ◆
     Bodily Injury by Disease
     Each Employee

.2   Business Automobile Liability Insurance

     a. $_____   ◆
          Each Accident

.3   Commercial General Liability Insurance   ◆

     a. $_____   ◆
          Each Occurrence

     b. $_____   ◆
          General Aggregate

     c. $_____   ◆
          Products/Completed
          Operations Aggregate

     d. $_____   ◆
          Personal and Advertising
          Injury Limit

10.3.2 Employers' Liability, Business Automobile Liability and Commercial General Liability coverages required under Subparagraph 10.3.1 may be arranged under a single policy for the full limits required or by a combination of underlying policies with the balance provided by Excess and/or Umbrella Liability policies.

10.3.3 The Contractor shall maintain in effect all insurance coverage required under Subparagraph 10.3.1 at the Contractor's sole expense with insurance companies lawfully authorized to do business in the jurisdiction in which the Project is located. If the Contractor fails to obtain or maintain any insurance coverage required under this Agreement, the Owner may purchase such coverage and charge the expense to the Contractor, or terminate this Agreement.

The policies of insurance required under Subparagraph 10.3.1 shall contain a provision that the coverages afforded under the policies shall not be cancelled or allowed to expire until at least thirty (30) days' prior written notice has been given to the Owner. The Contractor shall maintain completed operations liability insurance for one year after acceptance of the Work, Substantial Completion of the Project, or to the time required by the Contract Documents, whichever is longer. Prior to commencement of the Work, Contractor shall furnish the Owner with certificates evidencing the required coverages.

10.4   PROPERTY INSURANCE

10.4.1 Before the start of Work, the Owner shall obtain and maintain Builder's Risk or all risk upon the entire Project for the full cost of replacement at the time of loss. This insurance shall also name the Contractor, Subcontractors, Sub-subcontractors, Material Suppliers and Architect/Engineer as named insureds. This insurance shall be written as a builder's risk "all risk" or equivalent form to cover all risks of physical loss except those specifically excluded by the policy, and shall insure at least against the perils of fire, lightning, explosion, windstorm, and hail, smoke, aircraft (except aircraft, including helicopter, operated by or on behalf of Contractor) and vehicles, riot and civil commotion, theft, vandalism, malicious mischief, debris removal, flood, earthquake, earth movement, water damage, wind, testing if applicable, collapse however caused, and damage resulting from defective design, workmanship or material. The Owner shall be solely responsible for any deductible amounts or coinsurance penalties. This policy shall provide for a waiver of subrogation in favor of the Contractor, Subcontractors, Subsubcontractors, Material Suppliers and Architect/Engineer. This insurance shall remain in effect until final payment has been made or until no person or entity other than the Owner has an insurable interest in the property to be covered by this insurance, whichever is sooner. Partial occupancy or use of the Work shall not commence until the Owner has secured the consent of the insurance company or companies providing the coverage required in this Subparagraph 10.4.1. Prior to commencement of the Work, the Owner shall provide a copy of the property policy or policies obtained in compliance with this Subparagraph 10.4.1.

10.4.2 If the Owner does not intend to purchase the property insurance required by this Agreement, including all of the coverages and deductibles described herein, the Owner shall give written notice to the Contractor before the Work is commenced. The Contractor may then provide insurance to protect its interests and the interests of the Subcontractors and Subsubcontractors, including the coverage of deductibles. The cost of this insurance shall be charged to the Owner in a Change Order. The Owner shall be responsible for all of Contractor's costs reasonably attributed to the Owner's failure or neglect in purchasing or maintaining the coverage described above.

10.4.3 Owner and Contractor waive all rights against each other and their respective employees, agents, contractors, subcontractors and subsubcontractors for damages caused by risks covered by the property insurance except such rights as they may have to the proceeds of the insurance and such rights as the Contractor may have for the failure of the Owner to obtain and maintain property insurance in compliance with Subparagraph 10.4.1.

18

10.4.4 To the extent of the limits of Contractor's Commercial General Liability Insurance specified in Subparagraph 10.3.1 or _____ Dollars ($_____) ◆ whichever is more, the Contractor shall indemnify and hold harmless the Owner against any and all liability, claims, demands, damages, losses and expenses, including attorney's fees, in connection with or arising out of any damage or alleged damage to any of Owner's existing adjacent property that may arise from the performance of the Work, to the extent of the negligent acts or omissions of the Contractor, Subcontractor or anyone employed directly or indirectly by any of them or by anyone for whose acts any of them may be liable.

10.5   OWNER'S INSURANCE

10.5.1 BUSINESS INCOME INSURANCE The Owner may procure and maintain insurance against loss of use of the Owner's property caused by fire or other casualty loss.

10.5.2 OWNER'S LIABILITY INSURANCE The Owner shall obtain and maintain its own liability insurance for protection against claims arising out of the performance of this Agreement, including without limitation, loss of use and claims, losses and expenses arising out of the Owner's errors or omissions.

10.6   ROYALTIES, PATENTS AND COPYRIGHTS The Contractor shall pay all royalties and license fees which may be due on the inclusion of any patented or copyrighted materials, methods or systems selected by the Contractor and incorporated in the Work. The Contractor shall defend, indemnify and hold the Owner harmless from all suits or claims for infringement of any patent rights or copyrights arising out of such selection. The Owner agrees to defend, indemnify and hold the Contractor harmless from any suits or claims of infringement of any patent rights or copyrights arising out of any patented or copyrighted materials, methods or systems specified by the Owner and Architect/Engineer.

10.7   BONDS

10.7.1 Performance and Payment Bonds
(Check one only)

◆

are _____ / are not _____

required of the Contractor. Such bonds shall be issued by a surety licensed in the state of the location of the Project and must be acceptable to the Owner. The penal sum of the Payment Bond shall equal the penal sum of the Performance Bond.

ARTICLE 11

SUSPENSION, NOTICE TO CURE AND TERMINATION OF THE AGREEMENT

11.1   SUSPENSION BY OWNER FOR CONVENIENCE

11.1.1 OWNER SUSPENSION Should the Owner order the Contractor in writing to suspend, delay, or interrupt the performance of the Work for such period of time as may be determined to be appropriate for the convenience of the Owner and not due to any act or omission of the Contractor or any person or entity for whose acts or omissions the Contractor may be liable, then the Contractor shall immediately suspend, delay or interrupt that portion of the Work as ordered by the Owner. The Contract Price and the Contract Time shall be equitably adjusted by Change Order for the cost and delay resulting from any such suspension.

11.1.2 Any action taken by the Owner that is permitted by any other provision of the Contract Documents and that results in a suspension of part or all of the Work does not constitute a suspension of Work under this Paragraph 11.1.

11.2   NOTICE TO CURE A DEFAULT If the Contractor persistently refuses or fails to supply enough properly skilled workers, proper materials, and/or equipment, to maintain the approved Schedule of the Work in accordance with Article 6, or fails to make prompt payment to its workers, Subcontractors or Material Suppliers, disregards laws, ordinances, rules, regulations or orders of any public authority having jurisdiction, or is otherwise guilty of a material breach of a provision of this Agreement, the Contractor may be deemed in default. If the Contractor fails within seven (7) working days after written notification to commence and continue satisfactory correction of such default with diligence and promptness, then the Owner without prejudice to any other rights or remedies may:

    .1   supply workers and materials, equipment and other facilities as the Owner deems necessary for the satisfactory correction of the default, and charge the cost to the Contractor, who shall be liable for the payment of same including reasonable overhead, profit and attorneys' fees;

    .2   contract with Others to perform such part of the Work as the Owner determines shall provide the most expeditious correction of the default, and charge the cost to the Contractor;

    .3   withhold payment due the Contractor in accordance with Paragraph 9.3; and

    .4   in the event of an emergency affecting the safety of persons or property, immediately commence and continue satisfactory correction of such

19

AGC DOCUMENT NO. 200 • STANDARD FORM OF AGREEMENT AND GENERAL CONDITIONS BETWEEN OWNER AND CONTRACTOR
(Where the Contract Price is a Lump Sum)
© 2000, The Associated General Contractors of America

AGC Document No. 200
SAMPLE ■ DO NOT COPY

default as provided in Subparagraphs 11.2.1 and 11.2.2 without first giving written notice to the Contractor, but shall give prompt written notice of such action to the Contractor following commencement of the action.

11.3 OWNER'S RIGHT TO TERMINATE FOR DEFAULT

11.3.1 TERMINATION BY OWNER FOR DEFAULT If, within seven (7) days of receipt of a notice to cure pursuant to Paragraph 11.2, the Contractor fails to commence and satisfactorily continue correction of the default set forth in the notice to cure, the Owner may notify the Contractor that it intends to terminate this Agreement for default absent appropriate corrective action within fourteen additional days. After the expiration of the additional fourteen (14) day period, the Owner may terminate this Agreement by written notice absent appropriate corrective action. Termination for default is in addition to any other remedies available to Owner under Paragraph 11.2. If the Owner's cost arising out of the Contractor's failure to cure, including the cost of completing the Work and reasonable attorneys' fees, exceeds the unpaid Contract Price, the Contractor shall be liable to the Owner for such excess costs. If the Owner's costs are less than the unpaid Contract Price, the Owner shall pay the difference to the Contractor. In the event the Owner exercises its rights under this Paragraph 11.3, upon the request of the Contractor the Owner shall furnish to the Contractor a detailed accounting of the cost incurred by the Owner.

11.3.2 USE OF CONTRACTOR'S MATERIALS, SUPPLIES AND EQUIPMENT If the Owner or Others perform work under this Paragraph 11.3, the Owner shall have the right to take and use any materials, supplies and equipment belonging to the Contractor and located at the Worksite for the purpose of completing any remaining Work. Immediately upon completion of the Work, any remaining materials, supplies or equipment not consumed or incorporated in the Work shall be returned to the Contractor in substantially the same condition as when they were taken, reasonable wear and tear excepted.

11.3.3 If the Contractor files a petition under the Bankruptcy Code, this Agreement shall terminate if the Contractor or the Contractor's trustee rejects the Agreement or, if there has been a default, the Contractor is unable to give adequate assurance that the Contractor will perform as required by this Agreement or otherwise is unable to comply with the requirements for assuming this Agreement under the applicable provisions of the Bankruptcy Code.

11.4 TERMINATION BY OWNER FOR CONVENIENCE

11.4.1 Upon written notice to the Contractor, the Owner may, without cause, terminate this Agreement. The Con-

tractor shall immediately stop the Work, follow the Owner's instructions regarding shutdown and termination procedures, and strive to minimize any further costs.

11.4.2 If the Owner terminates this Agreement pursuant to this Paragraph 11.4, the Contractor shall be paid for the Work performed to date and any proven loss, cost or expense in connection with the Work, including all demobilization costs and a premium as set forth below: (Insert here the amount agreed to by the parties.) ◆

11.4.3 If the Owner terminates this Agreement pursuant to Paragraphs 11.3 or 11.4, the Contractor shall:

    .1   execute and deliver to the Owner all papers and take all action required to assign, transfer and vest in the Owner the rights of the Contractor to all materials, supplies and equipment for which payment has or will be made in accordance with the Contract Documents and all subcontracts, orders and commitments which have been made in accordance with the Contract Documents;

    .2   exert reasonable effort to reduce to a minimum the Owner's liability for subcontracts, orders and commitments that have not been fulfilled at the time of the termination;

    .3   cancel any subcontracts, orders and commitments as the Owner directs; and

    .4   sell at prices approved by the Owner any materials, supplies and equipment as the Owner directs, with all proceeds paid or credited to the Owner.

11.5 CONTRACTOR'S RIGHT TO TERMINATE

11.5.1 Upon seven (7) days' written notice to the Owner, the Contractor may terminate this Agreement if the Work has been stopped for a thirty (30) day period through no fault of the Contractor for any of the following reasons:

    .1   under court order or order of other governmental authorities having jurisdiction;

    .2   as a result of the declaration of a national emergency or other governmental act during which, through no act or fault of the Contractor, materials are not available; or

    .3   suspension by Owner for convenience pursuant to Paragraph 11.1

20

11.5.2 In addition, upon seven (7) days' written notice to the Owner, the Contractor may terminate the Agreement if the Owner:

> **.1** fails to furnish reasonable evidence that sufficient funds are available and committed for Paragraph 4.2, or

> **.2** assigns this Agreement over the Contractor's reasonable objection, or

> **.3** fails to pay the Contractor in accordance with this Agreement and the Contractor has complied with the notice provisions of Paragraph 9.5, or

> **.4** otherwise materially breaches this Agreement.

11.5.3 Upon termination by the Contractor in accordance with Paragraph 11.5, the Contractor shall be entitled to recover from the Owner payment for all Work executed and for any proven loss, cost or expense in connection with the Work, including all demobilization costs plus reasonable overhead and profit on Work not performed.

11.6 OBLIGATIONS ARISING BEFORE TERMINATION Even after termination pursuant to Article 11, the provisions of this Agreement still apply to any Work performed, payments made, events occurring, costs charged or incurred or obligations arising before the termination date.

ARTICLE 12

DISPUTE RESOLUTION

12.1 WORK CONTINUANCE AND PAYMENT Unless otherwise agreed in writing, the Contractor shall continue the Work and maintain the Schedule of the Work during any dispute resolution proceedings. If the Contractor continues to perform, the Owner shall continue to make payments in accordance with this Agreement.

12.2 INITIAL DISPUTE RESOLUTION If a dispute arises out of or relates to this Agreement or its breach, the parties shall endeavor to settle the dispute first through direct discussions between the parties' representatives, who shall have the authority to settle the dispute. If the parties' representatives are not able to promptly settle the dispute, the senior executives of the parties, who shall have the authority to settle the dispute, shall meet within twenty-one (21) days after the dispute first arises. If the dispute is not settled within seven (7) days from the referral of the dispute to the senior executives, the parties shall submit the dispute to mediation in accordance with Paragraph 12.3.

12.3 MEDIATION If the dispute cannot be settled pursuant to Paragraph 12.2, the parties shall endeavor to settle the dispute by mediation under the current Construction Industry Mediation Rules of the American Arbitration Association before recourse to any other dispute resolution procedures. Once one party files a request for mediation with the other party and with the American Arbitration Association, the parties agree to conclude such mediation within sixty (60) days of filing of the request. Either party may terminate the mediation at any time after the first session, but the decision to terminate shall be delivered in person by the party's representative to the other party's representative and the mediator.

12.4 DISPUTE RESOLUTION MENU If the dispute cannot be settled by mediation within sixty (60) days, the parties shall submit the dispute to any dispute resolution procedures selected in Exhibit No. 1.

12.5 MULTIPARTY PROCEEDING All parties necessary to resolve a claim shall be parties to the same dispute resolution proceeding. Appropriate provisions shall be included in all other contracts relating to the Work to provide for the consolidation of such dispute resolution procedures.

12.6 COST OF DISPUTE RESOLUTION The prevailing party in any dispute arising out of or relating to this Agreement or its breach that is resolved by a binding dispute resolution procedures selected in Exhibit No.1 shall be entitled to recover from the other party reasonable attorneys' fees, costs and expenses incurred by the prevailing party in connection with such dispute resolution process.

12.7 LIEN RIGHTS Nothing in this Article 12 shall limit any rights or remedies not expressly waived by the Contractor that the Contractor may have under lien laws.

ARTICLE 13

MISCELLANEOUS PROVISIONS

13.1 ASSIGNMENT Neither the Owner nor the Contractor shall assign their interest in this Agreement without the written consent of the other except as to the assignment of proceeds. The terms and conditions of this Agreement shall be binding upon both parties, their partners, successors, assigns and legal representatives. Neither party to this Agreement shall assign the Agreement as a whole without written consent of the other except that the Owner may assign the Agreement to a wholly owned subsidiary of Owner when Owner has fully indemnified Contractor or to an institutional lender providing construction financing for the Project as long as the assignment is no less favorable to the Contractor than this Agreement. In the event of such assignment, the Contractor shall execute any consents reasonably

21

AGC DOCUMENT NO. 200 · STANDARD FORM OF AGREEMENT AND GENERAL CONDITIONS BETWEEN OWNER AND CONTRACTOR
(Where the Contract Price is a Lump Sum)
© 2000, The Associated General Contractors of America

AGC Document No. 200
SAMPLE ■ DO NOT COPY

Participant's Manual ■ STP ■ Unit 8

required. In such event, the wholly-owned subsidiary or lender shall assume the Owner's rights and obligations under the Contract Documents. If either party attempts to make such an assignment, that party shall nevertheless remain legally responsible for all obligations under this Agreement, unless otherwise agreed by the other party.

13.2   GOVERNING LAW This Agreement shall be governed by the law in effect at the location of the Project.

13.3   SEVERABILITY The partial or complete invalidity of any one or more provisions of this Agreement shall not affect the validity or continuing force and effect of any other provision.

13.4   NO WAIVER OF PERFORMANCE The failure of either party to insist, in any one or more instances, on the performance of any of the terms, covenants or conditions of this Agreement, or to exercise any of its rights, shall not be construed as a waiver or relinquishment of such term, covenant, condition or right with respect to further performance or any other term, covenant, condition or right.

13.5   TITLES AND GROUPINGS The titles given to the articles of this Agreement are for ease of reference only and shall not be relied upon or cited for any other purpose. The grouping of the articles in this Agreement and of the Owner's specifications under the various headings is solely for the purpose of convenient organization and in no event shall the grouping of provisions, the use of paragraphs or the use of headings be construed to limit or alter the meaning of any provisions.

13.6   JOINT DRAFTING The parties expressly agree that this Agreement was jointly drafted, and that both had opportunity to negotiate its terms and to obtain the assistance of counsel in reviewing its terms prior to execution. Therefore, this Agreement shall be construed neither against nor in favor of either party, but shall be construed in a neutral manner.

13.7   RIGHTS AND REMEDIES The parties' rights, liabilities, responsibilities and remedies with respect to this Agreement, whether in contract, tort, negligence or otherwise, shall be exclusively those expressly set forth in this Agreement.

13.8   PRECEDENCE In case of any inconsistency, conflict or ambiguity among the Contract Documents, the documents shall govern in the following order: (a) Change Orders and written amendments to this Agreement; (b) this Agreement; (c) subject to Subparagraph 14.2.2 the drawings, specifications and addenda issued prior to the execution of this Agreement; (d) approved submittals; (e) information furnished by the Owner pursuant to Paragraph 4.3; (f) other documents listed in this Agreement. Among all

the Contract Documents, the term or provision that is most specific or includes the latest date shall control. Information identified in one Contract Document and not identified in another shall not be considered to be a conflict or inconsistency.

13.9   OTHER PROVISIONS
(Insert here other provisions, if any, that pertain to this Agreement) ◆

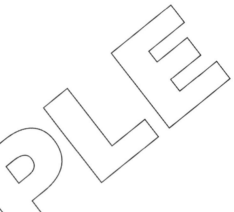

ARTICLE 14

CONTRACT DOCUMENTS

14.1   The Contract Documents in existence at the time of execution of this Agreement are as follows: ◆

22

AGC DOCUMENT NO. 200 • STANDARD FORM OF AGREEMENT AND GENERAL CONDITIONS BETWEEN OWNER AND CONTRACTOR
(Where the Contract Price is a Lump Sum)
© 2000, The Associated General Contractors of America

AGC Document No. 200
SAMPLE ■ DO NOT COPY

Participant's Manual ■ **STP** ■ Unit 8

14.2 INTERPRETATION OF CONTRACT DOCUMENTS

14.2.1 The drawings and specifications are complementary. If Work is shown only on one but not on the other, the Contractor shall perform the Work as though fully described on both consistent with the Contract Documents and reasonably inferable from them as being necessary to produce the indicated results.

14.2.2 In case of conflicts between the drawings and specifications, the specifications shall govern. In any case of omissions or errors in figures, drawings or specifications, the Contractor shall immediately submit the matter to the Owner for clarification. The Owner's clarifications are final and binding on all parties, subject to an equitable adjustment in Contract Time or Price pursuant to Articles 6 and 7 or dispute resolution in accordance with Article 12.

14.2.3 Where figures are given, they shall be preferred to scaled dimensions.

14.2.4 Any terms that have well-known technical or trade meanings, unless otherwise specifically defined in this Agreement, shall be interpreted in accordance with their well-known meanings.

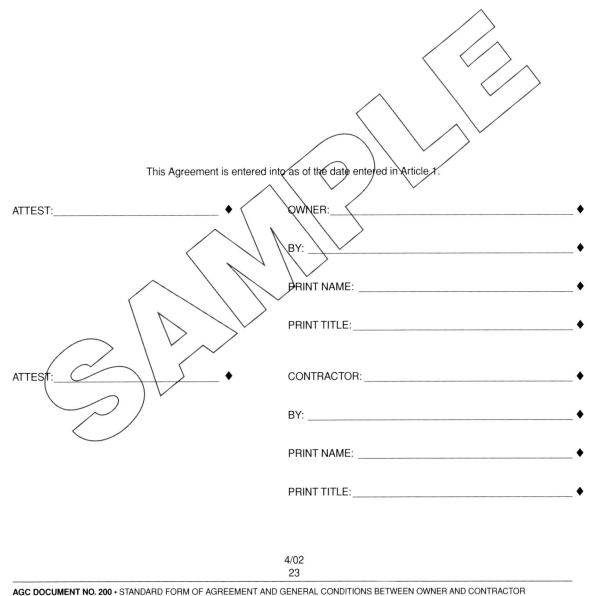

This Agreement is entered into as of the date entered in Article 1.

ATTEST:_____ ◆   OWNER:_____ ◆

BY:_____ ◆

PRINT NAME:_____ ◆

PRINT TITLE:_____ ◆

ATTEST:_____ ◆   CONTRACTOR:_____ ◆

BY:_____ ◆

PRINT NAME:_____ ◆

PRINT TITLE:_____ ◆

4/02
23

AGC DOCUMENT NO. 200 • STANDARD FORM OF AGREEMENT AND GENERAL CONDITIONS BETWEEN OWNER AND CONTRACTOR
(Where the Contract Price is a Lump Sum)
© 2000, The Associated General Contractors of America

AGC DOCUMENT NO. 200
STANDARD FORM OF AGREEMENT AND GENERAL CONDITIONS BETWEEN OWNER AND CONTRACTOR
(Where the Contract Price is a Lump Sum)

DISPUTE RESOLUTION MENU

Pursuant to Paragraph 12.4, if neither direct discussions nor mediation successfully resolve the dispute, the Owner and the Contractor agree the following shall be used to resolve the dispute.

(Check the appropriate selection(s). These procedures can be used singularly or progressively as agreed to by the parties.)

_____ **Dispute Review Board** The Dispute Review Board shall be composed of one member selected by the Owner, one ◆ selected by the Contractor, and a third member selected by the Owner and Contractor selected members. This Board shall be selected prior to commencement of construction, shall meet periodically, and shall make advisory decisions which may be introduced into evidence at any subsequent dispute resolution process. If a Dispute Review Board is selected, it is understood its review shall precede mediation.

_____ **Advisory Arbitration** Advisory Arbitration shall be pursuant to the current Construction Industry Rules of the Amer- ◆ ican Arbitration Association, except that the award shall not be binding on the parties.

_____ **Mini Trial** Each party, in the presence of senior executives, shall submit its position to a mutually selected individ- ◆ ual who shall make a non-binding recommendation to the parties. Such advisory decision may be introduced into evidence at any subsequent dispute resolution process.

_____ **Binding Arbitration** Binding Arbitration shall be pursuant to the current Construction Industry Arbitration Rules of ◆ the American Arbitration Association unless the parties mutually agree otherwise. A written demand for arbitration shall be filed with the American Arbitration Association and the other party within a reasonable time after the dispute or claim has arisen, but in no event after the applicable statute of limitations for a legal or equitable proceeding would have run. The location of the arbitration proceedings shall be at the office of the American Arbitration Association nearest the Worksite, unless the parties agree otherwise. The arbitration award shall be final. Notwithstanding Para- graph 13.2, this agreement to arbitrate shall be governed by the Federal Arbitration Act and judgment upon the award may be confirmed in any court having jurisdiction.

_____ **Litigation** Action may be filed in the appropriate state or federal court located in the jurisdiction in which the Project ◆ is located.

4/02

AGC Document No. 200
SAMPLE ■ DO NOT COPY

AGC 200

Article 1 AGREEMENT
The date of the Agreement and identification of the parties and the Project are essential information to be accurately inserted in this Article.

Article 2 GENERAL PROVISIONS
The relationship of the parties, the extent of the Agreement, and the definitions of key terms, such as Contract Documents, Final Completion, and Work, are described in this Article.

Article 3 CONTRACTOR'S RESPONSIBILITIES
This Article describes the Contractor's general responsibilities for labor, materials, supervision, coordination and construction means and methods; and then provides for cooperation when work is performed by the Owner or Others as defined in Article 2.

3.3 Responsibilities for review of the Contract Documents and reporting errors or inconsistencies discovered are detailed.

3.5-.6 Responsibilities for workmanship and materials furnished by the Owner or Others are described.

3.7 The responsibilities and costs for testing and inspection are set forth here.

3.8-.10 The Contractor's warranty and obligations to correct Work are detailed.

3.11 As between the Owner and Contractor, provisions for safety precautions and programs are detailed.

3.13 Procedures for handling Hazardous Materials are detailed. Hazardous Materials provisions acknowledge that the Owner is responsible for conditions at the site. The Contractor may immediately stop Work in the affected area and is not required to perform Work related to or in the area of Hazardous Materials.

3.14 Procedures for review and approval of shop drawings, samples, product data and other submittals are detailed in this Paragraph. The Owner is responsible for the review and approval of submittals.

3.15 The Owner, through its Architect/Engineer, provides all professional services, unless they are required to carry out the Contractor's responsibilities for construction means and methods.

3.16 Responsibilities for unknown site conditions are described in this Paragraph.

3.17 Responsibilities for permits and taxes are allocated in this Paragraph. Paragraph 4.4 is referenced differentiating the Owner's responsibilities for building permits and approvals, including developers' fees.

3.19 This Paragraph describes the Contractor's responsibilities to keep the Worksite clean.

3.21 This is a general statement about the Contractor's responsibility for keeping certain Owner information in confidence.

Article 4 OWNER'S RESPONSIBILITIES
4.1-.3 and 4.5 The Owner's responsibilities include providing information and services in a timely manner, including financial information, site information, and information necessary to give notice of or to enforce mechanics lien rights.

4.4 Building permits, fees, and approvals that are not the responsibility of the Contractor as described in Paragraph 3.17, are to be secured and paid by the Owner.

4.6-.7 The Owner provides the Contractor with a reasonable number of sets of the Contract Documents and designates its representative with regard to the Project.

4.10 Establishes the Owner's responsibilities regarding damage or loss caused by the Owner or Others.

Article 5 SUBCONTRACTS
5.2-.3 These provisions govern the award of subcontracts as well as the binding of Subcontractors and materials suppliers to the Contract Documents as they apply to their work.

5.4-.5 There is a note to insert any obligations relative to labor relations affecting the project, and a provision for the contingent assignment of subcontracts if the Agreement is terminated.

Article 6 CONTRACT TIME
6.1.1 Provisions concerning notices to proceed and the Date of Commencement are inserted in this Subparagraph.

6.1.2 The number of days from commencement to Substantial Completion is to be filled in a blank at this subparagraph, as well as the number of days within which the Contractor will achieve Final Completion of the Work.

6.2 This provision allows the Owner to determine the sequences of construction within the approved construction schedule.

6.3.1 Delays justifying an equitable extension of the Contract Time and/or equitable adjustment in Contract Price are defined here.

6.3.3 The parties agree to take reasonable steps to mitigate the effects of delays in this Subparagraph.

6.4 Provision is made for notice of delay claims in this Paragraph.

Article 7 CONTRACT PRICE
7.1 The Contract Price is to be inserted here.

7.3 Allowances are defined.

Article 8 CHANGES
8.1 Procedures for Change Orders are detailed.

8.2 Procedures for Interim Directed Changes are detailed.

8.3 Provisions for determining the cost of a change are described.

8.3.2 This provision governs equitable adjustment when unit prices are indicated in the Contract Documents.

8.4 This Paragraph addresses claims for an increase in Contract Price and or in Contract Time.

iii

AGC DOCUMENT NO. 200 • STANDARD FORM OF AGREEMENT AND GENERAL CONDITIONS BETWEEN OWNER AND CONTRACTOR
(Where the Contract Price is a Lump Sum)
© 2000, The Associated General Contractors of America

Article 9 PAYMENT
9.1.1   The Contractor prepares a Schedule of Values apportioning the various divisions or phases of the Work, the total of which equals the Contract Price.

9.2   Progress payment applications are described, including the treatment of stored materials and equipment, partial lien waivers and affidavits, and retainage.

9.2.4   Retainage, if any, is to be inserted here.

9.3   Under specified circumstances, the owner may adjust or reject the Contractor's payment application.

9.5   Procedures for payment delays not the fault of the Contractor are described in this Paragraph.

9.6   Substantial Completion procedures are detailed.

9.7   This provision details the conditions for partial occupancy or use of a portion of the Work.

9.8   The conditions for final payment are detailed.

Article 10 INDEMNITY, INSURANCE and WAIVERS
10.1   The Contractor indemnifies the Owner, Architect/Engineer, and Others as defined in this Agreement, and the Owner causes other contractors to indemnify the Contractor. Contractual indemnification is governed by state law and the states differ as to the types of indemnification agreements they will enforce. Consultation with legal and insurance counsel with knowledge of the jurisdiction is recommended.

10.2   The Contractor and Owner mutually waive claims for consequential damages arising out of the Agreement.

10.3   Insurance provided by the Contractor includes workers' compensation, employer's liability, business automobile liability and commercial general liability insurance. Blanks allow the parties to agree to specific policy limits.

10.4   This provision requires the Owner to obtain property insurance on the entire project.

10.7   The parties are to indicate if performance and payment bonds are required.

Article 11 TERMINATION OF THE AGREEMENT, SUSPENSION AND NOTICE TO CURE
11.1   The consequences of suspension by the Owner for convenience are outlined.

11.2   The Owner's rights in a situation where the Contractor has failed to cure a default within the requisite period of time are outlined in this Paragraph.

11.3   The parties' respective rights when the Owner exercises its right to terminate the Agreement for cause are detailed.

11.4   The Owner has the right to terminate the Agreement for convenience.

11.5   The Contractor has the right to terminate the Agreement for specified reasons.

Article 12 DISPUTE RESOLUTION
Partnering

AGC advocates dispute avoidance through the use of Partnering. While it is not recommended that Partnering be a contractual requirement, experience commends its use to establish working relationships among the parties through a mutually developed, formal strategy of commitment and communication. See Partnering: Concept for Success Booklet, Order No. 2900 (Associated Gen. Contractors of Am. (AGC of Am.), ed. 1991); Partnering: Changing Attitudes in Construction, Order No. 2902 (AGC of Am., ed. 1995); Partnering: A Concept for Success Video, Order No. 2901 (AGC of Am., ed. 1992); and Job Site Partnering Video, Order No. 2907, (AGC of Am., ed. 1999).

12.1   The Contractor is expected to continue performance of the Work and the Owner is expected to continue payment for Work performed during dispute resolution proceedings.

12.2   The parties are encouraged to settle their disputes first through direct discussions. If these discussions are not successful, the parties must attempt mediation as a condition precedent to any other form of binding dispute resolution procedure (Paragraph 12.3). Any disputes not resolved by mediation are to be decided by the dispute resolution procedure selected in Exhibit No. 1, a menu of dispute first resolution methods to which a dispute may be submitted. These provisions can be utilized singularly or progressively.

12.5   This Paragraph provides for the consolidation of dispute resolution procedures in all contracts relating to the Work.

12.6   The prevailing party is entitled to recover attorneys' fees when using the procedures selected in Exhibit No. 1.

Article 13 MISCELLANEOUS PROVISIONS
These general provisions govern:

13.1   Assignment of this Agreement by either party.

13.2   Governing law.

13.3   Severability.

13.4   No waiver of performance.

13.5   Organization of the Agreement form.

13.6   Construction of the Agreement as a jointly drafted document.

13.7   Rights and remedies of the parties.

13.8   Precedence of this Agreement and other Contract Documents.

13.9   Other provisions specific to the Project may be added at this paragraph.

Article 14 CONTRACT DOCUMENTS
14.1   The Contract Documents in existence at the time of execution of the Agreement are listed here.

14.2   This provision governs the interpretation of Contract Documents.

AGC DOCUMENT NO. 200 • STANDARD FORM OF AGREEMENT AND GENERAL CONDITIONS BETWEEN OWNER AND CONTRACTOR
(Where the Contract Price is a Lump Sum)
© 2000, The Associated General Contractors of America

HBP

Instructions for Filling Out and Submitting the
Application for a Supervisory Training Program (STP) Completion Certificate

Who Can Obtain This Special Recognition from AGC?

AGC provides a special certificate of recognition to persons who complete **all ten courses** of the Supervisory Training Program.

The two overview courses for construction supervisors, *Construction Supervisor* and *Heavy/Highway Construction Supervisor* **are not counted** among the ten courses needed to qualify for this recognition certificate. Each overview course has its own certificate.

Who Can Fill Out and Submit This Application?

Normally, this application will be filled out and submitted by the organization which sponsored the STP courses taken by the participant who wishes to be recognized. If this is not possible, this application may be filled out and submitted by the participant.

Where Should the Completed Application Be Sent?

Mail or fax the completed application to: Director, Supervisory Training Programs
AGC of America
2300 Wilson Blvd., Suite 400
Arlington, VA 22201
Fax: (703) 837-5405

What Is the Deadline for Submitting This Application?

To allow adequate leadtime for processing, submit this application at *least 30 days before you want the certificate(s) in your hands.* Applications are processed in the order in which they are received.

What Are the Special Instructions for Filling Out the Application Form?

Section ❶: Fill in each blank, including the Social Security number and birthdate blanks. These two items have been used in the STP database to make sure that course completion data submitted at various times (or by various sponsors) have been credited to the correct participant.

Sections ❷ and ❸: Fill in each blank as appropriate. If you are submitting this application as an individual participant, list your name, address, etc. in Sections 2 and 3.

Section ❹: Fill in as much of this information as possible; it will enable your application to be processed more efficiently and quickly. This information is used to verify your course completions against the STP database.

Application for a Supervisory Training Program (STP) Completion Certificate

❶ This application is for the following STP participant who has completed all ten courses

Name		SS # (last 4 numbers)	
Address		Phone	Birthdate
City		State	Zip

❷ This application is submitted by the following STP class sponsor, organization or person

Name		Organization Name	
Address		Phone	Fax
City		State	Zip

❸ Send the certificate to the following person at this address

Name		Organization Name	
Address		Phone	Fax
City		State	Zip

❹ Course Title	Date Completed	Name of Sponsor	Location
Unit 1: Leadership and Motivation			
Unit 2: Oral and Written Communication			
Unit 3: Problem Solving and Decision Making			
Unit 4: Contract Documents and Construction Law			
Unit 5: Planning and Scheduling			
Unit 6: Understanding and Managing Project Costs			
Unit 7: Accident Prevention and Loss Control			
Unit 8: Managing the Project			
Unit 9: Productivity Improvement			
Unit 10: General and Specialty Contractor Dynamics			

For AGC use only
App received by: ❑ Director, STP _____
App received by: ❑ Database recordkeeper _____
Participant Database Record # _____

TO ALLOW ADEQUATE LEADTIME FOR PROCESSING, SUBMIT THIS APPLICATION AT LEAST **30 DAYS** BEFORE YOU WANT THE CERTIFICATE IN YOUR HANDS.

288